SCREW
BUSINESS AS USUAL

SCREW
BUSINESS AS USUAL

Richard Branson

4 6 8 10 9 7 5 3

First published in the UK in 2011 by Virgin Books, an imprint of Ebury Publishing
A Random House Group Company

www.randomhouse.co.uk

Addresses for companies within The Random House Group can be found at
www.randomhouse.co.uk/offices.htm

The Random House Group Limited Reg. No. 954009

A CIP catalogue record for this book is available from the British Library

ISBN: 9780753539798

The Random House Group Limited supports The Forest Stewardship
Council (FSC®), the leading international forest certification organisation.
Our books carrying the FSC label are printed on FSC® certified paper.
FSC is the only forest certification scheme endorsed by the leading environmental
organisations, including Greenpeace. Our paper procurement policy can be found at
www.randomhouse.co.uk/environment

Designed by carrdesignstudio.com
Printed and bound in England by Clays Ltd, St Ives plc
To buy books by your favourite authors and register for offers visit
www.randomhouse.co.uk

This book is dedicated to my children, Holly and Sam, and their children who will hopefully see that we did the right thing and made sure that we screwed business as usual to protect this beautiful world we live in to ensure that everyone in our global village has the chance to live the wonderful life they deserve.

Just by buying this book you've already made a difference as 100 per cent of my royalties are going to our not for profit foundation, Virgin Unite, to support entrepreneurial initiatives on the front lines.

Thanks for helping to spread the word and join us in screwing business as usual.

To get involved, join in at:

Web
virginunite.com/screwbusinessasusual

Twitter
@virginunite #sbau

Facebook
Facebook.com/VirginUnite

CONTENTS

Preface

On the night of 22nd August 2011, this book was complete. I had written the last words to the Epilogue. Hurricane Irene – at that point still only a tropical storm – was raging, but we have lived through many big storms, so it was life as normal.

After a big family party in our beautiful home on Necker Island with our guests, Kate Winslet and her party, we all retired to bed. My mother, Eve and my daughter Holly and my nephews and nieces were sleeping in the great house, and even though there was room for twenty people, it was full, so with my wife Joan and son Sam we battled the storm and saw the island illuminated by great flashes of lightning and headed a short distance up the hill.

I admit it: I had drunk a lot of wine, so I was a bit confused when I heard explosions and Sam shouting, 'Fire! Fire! At the great house,' and then he was running like a deer, leaping barefoot through thick cactus plants to reach the great house. To my horror, the orange glow of a massive fire was reflected off the rain, flames were sweeping hundreds of feet into the night sky, urged on by the high winds. Naked, as I was, I raced out after Sam and ran straight into a cactus bush. It hurt, but I barely felt it.

Through the fire and the smoke, people emerged. Kate Winslet, carrying my mother down the stairs, followed by Kate's two children, and Holly, all sooty-faced with her cousins. One by one, my family and guests emerged into the wind and the rain. What began as a complete nightmare turned into utter relief as we realised everyone was safe.

The lightning we had seen the night before had been the cause of the fire when it struck the Balinese roof. Sam was in tears, hugging everyone. For minutes we both thought we had lost our family and the relief of finding them sooty, but safe, overwhelmed him. Holly called the manager – who was in another part of the island. The Bransons are renowned for their practical jokes and at first he didn't believe her. (The last words our manager had said to our deputy manager on leaving the island the day before had been, 'Don't burn the house down'.) When he came, instantly he and the staff swung into action, fighting the flames, so they wouldn't spread further through the undergrowth.

The rest of us huddled together in my outhouse watching the 90mph winds fan the massive flames that completely ignored the torrential rain. It's at moments like these one realises how unimportant 'stuff' is. All our family and friends had survived. They had lost all their possessions and were standing in their underwear and bare feet. That house repre-sented so many years of memories for me and my family. The children had grown up there, Joan and I had welcomed friends; we had had some amazing times. I could almost see my father, Ted, who had died recently, leaning back in one of the comfortable rattan chairs in the great room, sipping wine and laughing at a joke. Everything was still so fresh in all our minds and yet no fire can take away the memories or the wonderful projects that have been conceived there.

'Come on,' I rallied everyone the next morning. 'Let's have breakfast and we can talk about the new house we'll build.' We all pitched in with ideas for the new house that, like a phoenix, would rise from the ashes of the old one. It would be more innovative, more beautiful, even more inspiring. We would have many more memorable times and some great parties. Joan and I had married on Necker and Holly and her lucky (!) fiancé, Fred Andrews, would also be married on this magical island in December on the exact spot we had – even if it had to be on the ashes of the old house.

I hope new generations of our family will come to know and love a new great house as much as we have. The future is still ours to hold and share.

Richard Branson
September 2011

Foreword

Over the last few decades as I've started up one exciting business after another, I have often thought that life and work
could not get any better. In writing this book, however,
I've come to realise that we've really been on a dummy run,
preparing ourselves for the greatest challenge and opportunity of our lifetime. We've a chance to take a shot at really
working together to turn upside down the way we approach
the challenges we are facing in the world and to look at them
in a brand new, entrepreneurial way. Never has there been
a more exciting time for all of us to explore this next great
frontier where the boundaries between work and higher
purpose are merging into one, where doing good really *is*
good for business. In this book I'll share some great stories
about people who are already leading the way. We've learned
a great deal from some of these pioneers as the Virgin Group
continues on its journey to transform itself into a force for
good for people and for the planet. I'll also share some of our
own Virgin Group stories and, I hope, help you learn from
some of the many successes and (yes we do have them at
Virgin too) the occasional failure we've had along the way.

First and foremost, I have written this book for the new wave of emerging entrepreneurs as well as for existing business people who are transforming their organisations, at the same time as trying to develop a business and to make a living, trying to do more to help people and to help the planet. It reflects a vibrant and very marked sea change from the way business always used to be done, when financial profit was the only driving force. Today, people aren't afraid to say, *Screw business as usual!* – and show they mean it.

The other day I was speaking to James Kydd, a former marketing director of Virgin Media in the UK, and he was talking about how this new attitude is wired into the next generation. 'Today you've got an emerging generation of young people who have a perspective that's different from the one that politicians and many industry leaders have,' James said. 'They have a more balanced view. Just making money, in order simply to give it away, is out of date. There's a massive generational shift occurring that will blur the distinction between doing good and doing business.' I couldn't agree more. I constantly meet a growing army of entrepreneurs around the world, and when they ask me if I have one single message which will help them, I tell them it's this: doing good can help improve your prospects, your profits and your business; and it can change the world. Fabio Barbosa, the Chairman of the Board of Directors and former CEO of Santander Brasil, recently summed it up beautifully in an interview with *Upsides* magazine: 'It is becoming more and more clear that there is no incompatibility between doing business in an ethical and transparent manner and achieving good financial results. This "false dilemma" needs to be eliminated from business talk. Our social and environmental risk analysis at Santander has shown that, in the long run, companies with adequate environmental policies, well-defined labour relations and a balanced relationship with the community end up achieving more consistent financial results and establishing a more attractive brand name. It is in the company's own interest to adopt corporate governance policies in line with the development of the country.'

It's amazing how I keep coming across the same message, from bustling global cities, small towns in rural England, to the townships of South Africa and to small villages in India, to G8 climate conferences, to new medical centres, to schools. And the message is the same everywhere: we must change the way we do business. In the townships enthusiastic young people are grabbing opportunity by the scruff of the neck to develop their own businesses as a way out of poverty; women in small villages are funding new opportunities with loans as tiny as $15 from microfinance organisations; entrepreneurs in emerging markets are creating enterprises that respond to issues such as lack of sanitation and electricity; successful businesses such as cleaning care company 'method' are emerging and existing giants such as GE have made millions by reinventing their product offerings – at the same time as protecting the planet. Now I am sorry if this is going to smack of the ultimate in name-dropping, but this is a subject that is also discussed at Buckingham Palace. (This reminds me of a lovely joke Archbishop Desmond Tutu once told me: 'People keep accusing me of name-dropping. Only last week I was at Buckingham Palace and the Queen said to me, "Arch, you're name-dropping again."') Anyway, I was recently fortunate enough to be invited to dine there with a cross section of guests to meet Barack Obama and what was it that the Queen and the President of the United States were talking about so animatedly? They were discussing climate change and foreign policy challenges in Afghanistan, Pakistan and Libya, as well as the best ways to address declining living standards and to rebuild post-crash economies.

It's no mere coincidence that so many people are talking about the same thing, and, more interestingly, driving the change. They are doing so because, in our newly intercon-nected world, no one can any longer ignore the issues we are facing. The best bit is that people are finally starting to realise that it's not about throwing charity at issues – it's about working in partnership with people on the front lines to turn those issues into opportunities. Change is happening.

People often associate me with challenges, with trying to break records and occasionally my neck by sailing the Atlantic or flying a balloon in a jet stream at two hundred miles an hour, or going into space with Virgin Galactic. But this book isn't just about fun and adventure and exceeding one's wildest dreams (although, of course, there will be some of that!). It's a different kind of business book. It's about revolution. My message is a simple one: business as usual isn't working. In fact, it's 'business as usual' that's wrecking our planet. Resources are being used up; the air, the sea, the land – are all heavily polluted. The poor are getting poorer. Many are dying of starvation or because they can't afford a dollar a day for life-saving medicine. We have to fix it – and fast. Even people who say they don't believe in climate change, or who simply don't care about pollution, poverty and war – out of sight for them is out of mind – admit that people everywhere are mucking up things.

Despite this, I wake up in the morning feeling positive. I feel positive because I have a great belief that we – ordinary people everywhere – not only want to do the right thing, but we *will* do the right thing. We will fix things, not just because we have no choice, but because this life and this world are all we have. As former Costa Rican President José María Figueres, my esteemed colleague in the Carbon War Room, says, 'There is no Planet B.'

All my life I have thrived on challenges; they're what drive me, whether in business or at play. Writing this book has been a huge challenge because I feel it's very important to get this message across. The message is stark and simple: things have to change.

In this book I will discuss why things have to change – what they must change *from*, what they must change *to*. So far, business, or capitalism, for the most part, has been a means of making money for the directors of a company and its share-holders, rarely about doing good. The means by which that money has been made have not been as important as the end result – the damage that might be inflicted on humanity and the environment. We must work hard to change that.

People are also becoming more aware of unfairness. It's not OK that nearly half the world's population lives on less than $2 a day and that two out of three of these people have no access to clean drinking water. This imbalance is not just isolated to the poorer nations of the world; in wealthy countries like the US more than two million teenagers live on the streets. We're all aware of these statistics; luckily we now live in a new world where one of the great benefits of technology is that people are now directly connected to those suffering as a result of this unfairness and are no longer prepared to accept that it's OK. Those of us who have been fortunate enough to acquire wealth must play a role in looking at how we use these means to make the world a far better place. It's not about martyrdom, it's about balance and compassion and figuring out how we can build new ways to live together, as a truly global village, that allow everyone to prosper. I'm not talking about an uprising, or armed conflict in a Marxist sense – I'm talking about the power of the ordinary, everyday person to become entrepreneurs and change-makers to set up their own businesses, to seek their own fortune and be in control of their own lives, to say – *screw business as usual, we can do it!* We can turn things upside down and make a huge difference.

Throughout the book, the power of communications tools, from mobile phones to the internet, shows how ordinary people can speak out now, where before they didn't have the means to allow them to do so; now, if they don't like something about the way a business is run they'll say so. As they did in the Arab Spring revolutions of early 2011, they'll join protests, they'll blog and tweet. No governments or businesses will be able to hide behind secrecy and jargon any longer. Ordinary people control their brands and their destinies.

Ordinary people have enormous power – let them unleash it. In this book I want to get a particular message over: learn what you can do and – as NIKE would say – just do it.

I know it can be done because, in my way, I did it myself. I was a fledgling entrepreneur when I was nine years old, and while my efforts were more miss than hit, with the occasional dose of 'tough love' my wonderful family encouraged me and believed in me; by the time I was fifteen I was well on the path to making my own way in life with my very first enterprise, a magazine for students.

When things don't work they have to be fixed. In this book I go on to say that if business helped to break it then business must play a role in fixing it. But relax, prophesying doom and gloom is simply not my style. Instead I will attempt to describe how I think business can help fix things and create a more prosperous world for everyone. I happen to believe in business because I believe that business can be a force for good. By that I mean *doing good is good for business*.

Let me elaborate on the meaning of that statement. In a nutshell, I mean that by doing good – doing the right thing – businesses will prosper. Doing the right thing can be profitable, as will be made clear by some of the stories about people and organisations that are already doing it. It's the core message of this book. I often say, 'Have fun and the money will come.' I still believe that, but now I am saying, '*Do good*, have fun and the money will come.'

Each chapter in this book will show examples of how all kinds of businesses, from commercial enterprises to those run by social entrepreneurs, can grow and thrive by doing the right thing – no matter what size they are.

A wise professor of economics once said, 'Bet on people doing good things.' I believe he was spot-on. People inherently want to do the right thing. It's what makes us human.

The words 'doing good' mean many different things for different people. In this book 'doing good' means not damaging the environment, not just *not* polluting but undoing the pollution of the last couple of centuries since the Industrial Revolution. Restoring harmony with nature. But it is not all about doing less harm; our task is also to improve the lives of people and the planet through business. It means helping those less fortunate to build a way of earning a living so that they can live the life of dignity they – that all human beings – deserve. It's a basic, absolutely essential right of every human being to be given the means to earn a living, to keep one's self and family in food and shelter with one's medical needs being met. It means reinventing how we live in the world to create a far more balanced, healthy and peaceful place. I believe that the revolutionary new form of Capitalism 24902 (don't worry I will explain it later) described in this book will operate in such a socially responsible way that it will give poor people economic freedom and that new opportunities for entrepreneurship will arise.

Even as a child I had a strong sense of social responsibility and this has grown over the years so that today I spend as much time on using my entrepreneurial skills to help solve issues as on running the business. Virgin has a foundation, Virgin Unite, and we do a huge amount of work looking at new entrepreneurial approaches to issues. You'll hear from some of the wonderful partners Unite works with throughout this book.

Describing my philanthropic methods somebody recently said: 'Oh, Richard, well yes he does do things differently.' I would like to think that they meant that I don't donate cash willy-nilly, without questioning who is getting their hands on it and what they're using it for. I run Virgin Unite just as I would any other business, making sure that our investments have the best possible social and environmental return. I also feel strongly that it's not all about money – in fact often the money is the least important bit. It's about people using their skills and figuring out ways to use the assets of their businesses to drive not only profits but a better world. Writing a cheque might impact hundreds of people's lives; mobilising your whole business to drive change can impact millions of lives, and give a whole new life purpose to all the people who work in your company. It is this philosophy that is brought to life in this book through the stories of individuals who are taking a radically different path towards a new frontier for business, doing the right thing by people and by our planet and effecting change for the good.

As I write these words for this book here on my home of Necker Island, I sometimes wonder if I'm dreaming. At times my life does seem unreal; I'm sure I'll wake up one day. Earlier this year I had a quite amazing week, one in which I experienced, quite literally, the depths and heights of this planet and of adventure and excitement. I am truly blessed and amazed at my good fortune. We launched the first Virgin submarine at the start of the week – it is designed to descend to the depths of the ocean – and by the end of the same week there I was flying in a Virgin America plane over San Francisco's Golden Gate Bridge in tandem with Virgin Galactic's two spaceships.

Oh, and in the same week we also bought Pluto. No, not the cartoon dog, I actually mean the dwarf planet Pluto. On 1 April 2011 I called a press conference and, with a remarkably straight face, made this announcement: 'Virgin has expanded into many territories over the years, but we have never had our own planet before. This could pave the way for a new age in space tourism.' It took a few moments for the penny to drop!

The plane I flew into Virgin America's new LEED Certified sustainable terminal at San Francisco's International Airport was emblazoned with the tongue-in-cheek bumper sticker 'My Other Ride is a Spaceship'. Many Virgin Galactic and Virgin America people had joined me on the flight, along with a group of young people from KIPP, Knowledge is Power Programme, which runs excellent public charter schools for low-income children, and students from Student Launch, our partners linked with the Spaceport in New Mexico, who were being mentored by Virgin America pilots and engineers. Both the young people and our staff have learned a tremendous amount from each other. Another group which joined us on the flight was some future astronauts who have worked with the teams from Virgin Galactic and Virgin Unite to start a not-for-profit initiative called Galactic Unite. On that one day alone they raised over $385,000 to support young people from low-income families and give them the chance to help encourage careers in maths, science, engineering and technology – including mentoring programmes with Virgin America engineers and pilots. All of our aviation businesses have also teamed up to focus on how we can minimise our carbon output, from innovative new approaches to weight reduction on the plane through to investing in new types of biofuels (more on this later). To me, this is a wonderful example of how this new Capitalism 24902 can work: driving change into the core of our businesses and partnering with our community and great front-line organisations to make change happen in everything we do.

I hope you will be as inspired as I've been while gathering the stories for this book. Each of us really can drive change and change is important, now more than ever. We would also love to hear from you about your own stories, as well as others who have inspired you. We've set up web, Twitter and Facebook discussion spaces that you'll see mentioned at the end of each chapter. At the end of the book you will also find some great ways to get involved in helping radically change the way you view your business.

One word of warning however. Until you read the book and can explain its subject matter, you might want to think twice about leaving something entitled *Screw Business as Usual* lying around on your desk!

Happy reading ...

1

Capitalism 24902

'I think fifteen years ago people started talking about corporate
social responsibility and it was thin. It was a marketing strategy
or something that the chairman said we had to do and people
didn't buy it. This time round to me it feels like it's come from
the grassroots up. It's come from the fact that everyone who
works in business is also a citizen. We read the newspapers, we
watch the news, we go and watch *An Inconvenient Truth*, we are
aware of what's happening in the world. How can you then go
about your day job and not care?' – Richard Reed, Innocent Drinks

I have always loved the question, 'How old would you be if
you didn't know how old you are?' My answer to that would
be 'in my twenties', although with her signature Glaswegian
honesty, my lovely wife Joan would almost certainly add,
'No, Richard, you just act like you're in your twenties which
is not the same thing.' Well, believe it or not I am in my
twenties, it's just a question of the multiple that must be
applied.

Contrary to many people of my age, however, I make a point
of enjoying my birthdays and always attempt to do something

to make them memorable. This year was no different. (You're barking mad, says Joan, as I fly across the Pacific in a flimsy balloon, or hike in the Arctic Circle with a team of dogs.)

So there I was, one blustery day in August 2010, hoping nobody would notice that I was hobbling as I advanced with tender, bare feet, clutching my surf board, across a sharp shingle beach on the south coast of England. With my daughter, Holly, my son, Sam, my teenage nephew, Ivo, and other friends and family members – twelve in all – we were ready to kite-surf across the English Channel. The plan was to get a world record, and the man from *The Guinness Book of Records* was on hand to observe our attempt.

As dangerous enterprises go, kite-surfing a mere twenty-four miles from England to France didn't seem too difficult, particularly given my past apparently reckless efforts to kill myself. (Joan was determined not to be there while she became a widow during some of my more outlandish enterprises over the years. Usually she'd just take herself off home.) The weather was windy but the sun was shining when we waded into the choppy grey sea off Dungeness. I was looking forward to the challenge. Kite-surfing is my favourite sport. Nothing beats that glorious sense of freedom and the adrenalin rush you get as you skim across waves, powered by a beautiful kite soaring overhead. I would have preferred breaking the record in the azure seas of the Caribbean but to paraphrase the late Evel Knievel a challenge has to be risky, to be fun – doesn't it?

There was a force 6 gale blowing which was strong enough to give us a chance of getting the record. But, ten miles into our journey, that had turned into a force 7 or 8 and the small chase boats had to turn back. Although I believed the kiters could have made it without the chase boats, I felt it unwise to take nephews, nieces and kids across the busiest shipping lane in the world and we returned to land for the day. The next day the weather was worse, so while we waited for it to break we did a little sight-seeing around the ancient town of Rye where we were staying, with its cobbled streets, secret tunnels and the ghosts of smugglers.

The previous day we had provided refreshments on the beach at Dungeness for our family and friends and the local lifeboat crew. Shopping at Jempson's, a small grocery store in Peasmarsh near Rye, I'd been interested to see that they had a section labelled 'Local Heroes'. This displayed good locally grown and locally produced food, from seasonable vegetables, soft summer fruits, hand-picked on surrounding farms, to home-baked cakes, and cheeses, sausages, pickles and jams and English wines. They sold organic and they sold Fair Trade. What's more, the prices were impressively modest, compared with city prices or those of the big chain stores. This family-run grocery business, I learned, bought direct from a distribution cooperative, from south coast farmers and other small suppliers and, without high trans-port costs, passed their saving on to the customer. Everyone gained. The store gained customer loyalty and the customers got fresh, wholesome produce at a decent price. I also learned that the company supported a handful of small charities, sponsored and selected by the staff.

In this rural market town I'd come across a good example of how business should be run in a responsible way that gives back to the community and does its best not to harm the planet. This growing sense of change is bubbling up around us. I considered our recent adventures on the beach. Many of us had been wearing warm water-ski clothing made by Finisterre, a small company based in Cornwall on the far west coast of England. Finisterre's gear is ecologically and sustainably made from pure wool and the company is run along lines that reflect a social awareness. So in just a couple of days I had come across two classic models of successful companies that were doing well while doing good.

This is exactly what I am hoping to promote in this book: to find out why we need to change the way we do business, and how that might best be done. I have always tried to be socially aware and have always felt strongly that everyone should have the same chance to thrive in life, which is probably why all my businesses have always focused on giving everyone a 'fair go', as they say in Australia. After starting *Student* magazine while I was still at school, I went on to open a student advisory centre where young people could walk in off the street and get information to help with problems such as venereal disease, psychiatric problems, pregnancy issues and birth control. That centre evolved to provide free mental health support and it still exists in London, on Portobello Road, where it has provided a service for more than forty years. During the height of the HIV/AIDS crisis in 1987 we also set up Mates, a company that produced condoms to be sold at a low price. Profits were ploughed back into building awareness about HIV/AIDS. We even got the BBC to run their first ever advertisements, a cheeky play on that nerve-wracking moment when a young man goes to buy condoms and is mortified at having to ask for them from the girl behind the counter. This is still one of my favourite campaigns as it really helped to build awareness, and was a good reminder for all of us that humour can often be a far better way to change behaviour than just trying to scare the hell out of people. If Martin Luther King's famous quote, 'I have a dream' had been 'I have a nightmare' it would never have been so successful.

As Virgin expanded, so did our ideas for treating the people who worked for us well, and for considering the environment. We've always had at our core a focus on our people and making sure that they are empowered to make decisions and feel part of a company that stands for something beyond making money. I've always believed that by taking care of people in my companies the rest will take care of itself. This can be something simple like allowing people to job share or giving them the chance to run their own show. This has worked for us and has also built a pretty special group of people around the world who are not only passionate about Virgin, but also about making a difference in the world. The great thing is that many entrepreneurial enterprises and businesses all over the world are now doing this instinctively and people everywhere are realising that they truly can make a difference every day, no matter how small the scale. In fact, a good socially aware business doesn't have to be big to make an impact – it just has to have the right people in place. There are many small-scale businesses around the world – from the townships of Johannesburg, to the villages of India, to rural cheesemakers in France, to organic vineyards in Australia, to llama knitwear cooperatives in Ecuador – that are all changing the way business is done for the better. There are also some large multinational corporations that are starting to radically transform themselves to be a force for good. The people in all these organisations – large and small – have the combined power of a hurricane to effect change. It should no longer be just about typical 'corporate social responsibility' (or that horrible acronym CSR) where the 'responsibility' bit is usually the realm of a small team buried in a basement office – now it should be about every single person in a business taking responsibility to make a difference in everything they do, at work and in their personal lives.

The great thing is that, with technology, we've also become far more aware not just of what is happening in our own neighbourhood, but of what is happening on the other side of the world. This technology has also smashed through the top-down approach and shifted the power to the people. I've had the pleasure of working with Pam Omidyar who, along with her husband Pierre, the founder of eBay, joined us in providing initial funding and support for a project you will hear about later on called The Elders. A couple of years ago I was travelling in Morocco with Pam and Pierre, and Pierre's words about this new paradigm shift stuck with me.

He said: 'Long-term sustainable change happens if people discover their own power. The key is moving the centre of gravity in the decision-making, moving it closer to people in the community, in the field, and so forth – and away from a centrally directed, top-down approach. For the first time in human history, technology is enabling people to really maintain those rich connections with much larger numbers of people than ever before.'

There are names for this new approach to business – from Capitalism 2.0 to philanthrocapitalism. None of them has yet captured the essence or the enormity and potential of this exciting new shift we need to make. At a recent Virgin Unite event we had a bit of a brainstorming session and, after a drink or two and much debating, came up with the name that we now use to describe this new type of business: Capitalism 24902. OK it may sound a little bit like *Beverly Hills 90210* but I assure you it is anything but. So, what on earth does that mean? Well, we started talking about how the name had to capture the new level of responsibility that each of us had for others in the global village and how this needed to be a movement that went beyond a handful of businesses or one country. When someone mentioned that the circumference of the earth is 24,902 miles, Capitalism 24902 was born! Very simple really, it does what it says on the tin – that every single business person has the responsibility for taking care of the people and planet that make up our global village, all 24,902 circumferential miles of it. For a long time I have been convinced that this is the way forward if the planet as we know it, and life as we know it, is to survive. I'm not just talking about the disaster facing people and the planet because of climate change; I'm addressing one of the underlying reasons why the climate is changing and a significant threat to humanity – our rapid depletion of our natural resources. In the next couple of decades we could soon end up without oil, minerals, water or fish. Sadly, we are, as I write, already seeing the worst drought in sixty years in eastern Africa, causing monumental suffering in countries like Somalia. Unless we move to Capitalism 24902 rapidly, we are certain to see more wars on a wider scale as people fight over land, food, water and fuel.

This book has been seven years in the making. It's the story of my seven-year journey towards realising that, while business has been a great vehicle for growth in the world, neither Virgin nor many other businesses have been doing anywhere near enough to stop the downward spiral we all find ourselves in; and that in many cases, as demonstrated by the recent financial crises in the world, we have actually been causing that spiral to turn ever faster. We are all part of the problem: we waste, we squander and, to put it bluntly, we screw up. Natural resources are being exhausted faster than they can be replenished. In fact, not to put too fine a point on it, many natural resources – such as oil, forests and minerals – can never be replenished. Once they're gone, they're gone. Capitalism as we know it, which essentially started around the time of the Industrial Revolution, has certainly created economic growth in the world and brought many wonderful benefits to people, but all this has come at a cost that is not reflected on the balance sheet. The focus on profit being king has caused significant negative, unintended consequences. For over a century and a half cheap labour, damaged lives, a destroyed planet and polluted seas were all irrelevant when set against the need for profit. But this is changing.

This is why a new kind of capitalism has slowly been gathering force in the last ten or twenty years. In the 1930s a back-to-the-land movement started; in the sixties and seventies, there was peace, love and brown rice and flower power. A modern green movement started in the eighties and early nineties, originating in Germany and Scandinavia, but it never grew sufficiently. Those movements focused on trying to fix pollution while turning to recycling and organic food as a healthy alternative. Lots of local little green cooperatives and organic smallholdings sprung into being. But few people allowed such developments to change their behaviour or stopped to ask, 'How will we survive when we run out of everything?' It's only fairly recently that we've realised that on a geographical scale minerals and other natural resources are being depleted alarmingly quickly. Many scientists believe that in some areas this will happen *in our lifetime.*

James Lovelock is one of those scientists. He is someone who has for years been brave enough to stand up and warn us about the dangerous path we are on. I was having lunch at James's home one day with my friend and colleague Will Whitehorn and he was saying that rather than thinking about how we can continue to live on our 'host', the earth, we are rapidly killing it, which will eventually lead to our own demise. James's view is: 'A billion could live off the earth; six billion living as we do is far too many, and you run out of planet in no time.'

To understand why this depletion is taking place so rapidly, take a simple item that many people would probably struggle without – a laptop computer. The average laptop weighs about ten pounds, but it took more than ten pounds of raw materials to make. In fact, if you count everything processed and distilled into those ten pounds, your laptop weighs not ten pounds, not a hundred pounds, but a staggering *40,000 pounds*. It contains minerals extracted from mines, using incredible quantities of fuel, itself the product of drilling and mining. Year after year, our laptops become lighter and more powerful – but the ways raw materials are extracted and refined and brought together to make a product aren't much cleaner or more sophisticated today than they were forty years ago. This is changing.

William A McDonough has been a pioneer in working out how we reinvent the way we make things based on learning from our natural systems. I really clicked with his view that it's not about doom and gloom and stopping growth; rather, it is about making different things in a much smarter way by listening to and learning from Mother Nature. I was lucky enough to have him as a guest on Necker for one of our initial Carbon War Room gatherings. He gave an inspiring talk and opened with these words: 'Imagine a world in which all the things we make, use and consume provide nutrition for nature and industry – a world in which growth is good and human activity generates a delightful, restorative ecological footprint.' All the guests sat mesmerised for the next hour as Bill took us through some work he was doing to show that urban architecture can combine the beauty of natural systems to make it far more effective, efficient and aesthetically beautiful, with zero impact on the environment. He showed us buildings that were alive with amazing vertical and roof farms, harvesting the sun for energy, fresh air and flowering plants everywhere. His strong belief is that the issue we've faced since the Industrial Revolution is one of design and that we have the opportunity to change this by learning from Mother Nature and her three billion years of research. I'll share some stories about a few companies that are following this path later in the book.

Seven years ago, when my journey began, I thought I was doing reasonably well as an entrepreneur and as a caring human being. My business life was running smoothly and my personal life was very happy. I believe firmly in delegation and good people were running each of Virgin's three hundred companies worldwide. These managers were so competent that on average it often took me just a few minutes each week on the phone, checking in with them. They could reach me at any time if there was a problem. I always try to see everyone during the course of a year. But, essentially, things were running so smoothly that on the whole I felt very comfortable spending more time on my beloved Necker.

But something was missing. As I grew older it seemed that I wasn't making a big enough difference, particularly given my own incredible good fortune. I went from feeling content that things were going well in my life and in business, and satisfied that in many ways I was contributing to society, to realising that I hadn't even begun to scratch the surface of what needed to be done to help ensure the survival of the planet and life as we know it. I was also very aware that there was too much poverty in the world. Despite great affluence in some parts of the planet, in other parts people were still suffering and dying of famine and diseases such as malaria and HIV/AIDS. I had always wanted Virgin to be a strong role model of social entrepreneurship, but now I knew we would have to do more than lip service to help drive change and get everyone across all of our businesses to be part of that change.

Many good and very bright individuals are working hard, and have been doing so for some time, not only to warn people and governments that we can't continue to deplete the world's resources as if they are everlasting, but that we have to do something about it. But now *everyone* needs to add their voice and energy to stop the perfect storm building up ahead of us. All our combined voices and all our energy are needed if we're to make a real difference. And I have come to realise that this effort is actually good for business. It makes people and businesses better off. The good news is, businesses that are taking this path are also starting to see the rewards, clearly demonstrated by some of the tracking being done by the global business tracking company FTSE: 'Companies that consistently manage and measure their responsible business activities outperformed their FTSE 350 peers on total shareholder return in seven out of the last eight years.'

One of the people who helped crystallise the level of urgency and the scale of change that needs to happen was my good friend Peter Gabriel. Peter and I go back a long way, to when he was the front man in the band Genesis. Virgin signed Genesis in 1983, a couple of years before – with great sadness – I sold the label to EMI in order to raise capital for my fledgling airline. I'm pleased to say Peter and I remained friends. But during the years when I was working hard to develop Virgin as a worldwide company, Peter was marching to a different drumbeat. He became heavily involved with the peace movement. He was an early supporter of Amnesty International and pioneered and performed in all twenty-eight of their Human Rights Concerts. In 1986, he performed his hauntingly powerful song 'Biko' on the Amnesty *Conspiracy of Hope* tour. Steve Biko was a student leader who'd been involved with the Black Consciousness Movement (BCM). He'd coined the phrase 'black is beautiful' and ultimately gave his life to help stop the horrors of apartheid.

The song had – and still has – a huge impact, not least on Peter himself. He has called it a calling card, showing his willingness to be heavily involved in strong social issues. It led to his involvement with World Music. It was the concept of World Music that revived a long-held conviction in him that if the world could be seen as a global village people would connect more. But he always said that he still didn't fully appreciate what a social entrepreneur was until about ten years ago – and, to be honest, neither did I. In the lyrics of 'Biko' were the words *'business as usual'*, a phrase that came to have deeper resonance for me.

My mother, Eve, has always believed passionately in giving people a chance in life. When we first started our foundation, Virgin Unite, she was on a plane within days to kick-start an initiative in the High Atlas Mountains in Morocco to help young girls create their own grassroots businesses. When I was growing up, while I didn't necessarily agree with the concept, she was firmly of the philosophy that happy and healthy children were the ones who were kept busy running errands and helping neighbours. In those days, just after the Second World War, helping the neighbours or the community wasn't considered charity; it was normal behaviour. Charity did play a large part in everyone's life and those without were helped by those with, but more often than not it wasn't just a matter of dishing out money – our family wasn't well off and pocket money was in short supply – it was performing a service. We happened to live in a small, close-knit village in Surrey where everyone knew everyone else's business. My sisters were expected to help in the house, but if someone needed firewood chopped, a dog walked or a garden weeded, I was duly dispatched to perform that task. If I finished a job sooner than expected, I was sent off again to do something else. Lounging around in bed – even, in my case, with a badly damaged leg in plaster after a sports accident at school – was just not on.

My first conscious act of charity was when I took off my clothes and gave them to a tramp. It happened to be in busy Oxford Street in the middle of London when with my mother and sister we were all walking along trying to flog armfuls of the very first issue of *Student* magazine. I didn't have a change of clothes handy, so I spent the rest of the day walking along a busy city pavement, wrapped in a scratchy blanket.

Mum shook her head despairingly, hiding a smile. 'Oh dear, Ricky, what will you think of next? You're not supposed to give your clothes away' – while Dad chuckled, 'Poor old tramp! All he wanted was some loose change and he got a set of infested clothes from you!'

At the time, I'd left Stowe when I was sixteen to start *Student* magazine (more on that later) and I and my friend and co-publisher, Jonny Holland-Gems were living in his parents' scruffy basement just off Oxford Street, practically starving, and I well remember each time my mother dropped in with a 'Red Cross' picnic hamper, she'd say, 'Have you washed recently?' Meanwhile, upstairs, Jonny's incredibly arty parents were entertaining the coolest people in London from most of the staff of *Private Eye* to the Garrick Club, many of whom wrote articles or granted us interviews. I'd never lived in London before, never dreamed any of this would be possible. For me, a shy only-just ex-schoolboy, it was mind-blowing.

Yes, it was 1967 – the Summer of Love – and Jonny and I were suddenly part of the glorious fun-filled Swinging Sixties. Unbelievably, *Student* opened doors we'd never imagined would open to us. Mick Jagger welcomed us into his home in Cheyne Walk – and I went weak at the knees when I saw Marianne Faithfull lounging in the living room, though she did very quickly vanish upstairs under our drooling gazes. We interviewed John Lennon and started by spouting some nonsense about TS Eliot and *The Waste Land* being like *A Day in the Life* to impress him, and he said with his flat Liverpool twang, 'I don't know about that. Not very hip on me culture, you know.' But as well as interviewing icons, there were some incredible, iconic moments in the furore against the Vietnam War. I marched side by side through Central London with Tariq Ali and Vanessa Redgrave (both of whom gave us good interviews) to protest the war outside the American Embassy; and campaigned with as much fervour to raise money for starving orphans in Biafra, which was really when the terrible plight of famine victims and wars were becoming more widely known to the public. *Student* magazine was developing a very high profile in a very short space of time. It was making waves. I was having huge amounts of fun, but my future as a campaigner for the less well-off and against unjustness was also being forged, right there in the streets of London in the magical flower power years and the fiery sixties when times were indeed a-changing.

Years later, as Virgin expanded and we started to see healthy profits, I wanted to find a mechanism by which we could use everything we had as a group of businesses to make positive change happen. I didn't want just to throw money at it; I wanted to offer targeted help and entrepreneurial thinking where it would be most effective, and I spent some time thinking about how this could be set up. At around about that time I met Jean Oelwang.

After university, Jean spent a few years helping to build a mobile phone company in the United States. Her job was increasingly high-pressured and exciting, but she felt something was lacking. She had always wanted to explore how to get the business and social sectors working together to help improve the lives of people who were not even being given a chance for a better life. Her solution to her frustration was to join VISTA, a little known organisation rather like a sort of domestic Peace Corps. She signed up for a year to work in a walk-in and live-in shelter, called Neon Street, for homeless young people who lived on the streets in Chicago.

It was a big wake-up call for Jean to discover that in the US almost two million young people experience homelessness every year. She hadn't realised that there were so many homeless youths living on the streets of America. None of the youngsters chose that way of life but they had no option. It was a big shock, too, to learn that some of those children fending for themselves were as young as twelve. Most of them had escaped from gangs or from horrifying situations at home. Most of them were being abused at home, either sexually or physically, or their parents were into drugs. Now Jean had a new frustration: to shift the way that government, businesses and society worked together driving change. The current system simply wasn't effective. In fact, Jean felt the welfare system in the US was actually promoting the problem.

She returned to business and started helping to set up mobile phone companies in different countries around the world, from Bulgaria, to Colombia, to South Africa, and throughout Asia. In each country she watched as the mobile phone companies grew rapidly and became successful, yet when she dug deeper, everywhere she went she saw the same social issues, of poverty, homelessness and lack of opportunities for people to make their own living. Eventually, she arrived in Australia; it was then that her path crossed with Virgin's. We decided to set up a mobile phone company in Australia and tracked her down, telephoned her out of the blue and offered her a job.

Before long she had once again reached the point at which she wanted to get involved with an organisation that drove change – but her ideal job, a mix of the social and business sectors, didn't exist. She discussed this with Gordon McCullum, who was on her board. What she didn't know was that I had reached exactly the same place myself in my philosophical journey. I wanted to find a way that Virgin could help drive dramatic change to make the world a better place and to help people. I decided to establish a foundation so that everyone working together within the Virgin Group could pull together, but at that point I had no real idea of what shape it would take or how it would operate for maximum effectiveness. One thing I didn't want was a philanthropic organisation that was run on the standard charity sector lines, where money was just handed out. There had to be a new way of doing things. I discussed it with the managers across the group, looking for ideas. One of the people I mentioned this to just happened to be Gordon McCullum. He told Jean she needed to write a plan and send it to me.

When Jean's plan landed in my hands I was immediately excited. Our thinking was fully aligned; we were as one in realising that there was a huge opportunity to take all the incredible entrepreneurial energy across the Virgin Group to make positive change happen in the world.

I telephoned Jean and said: 'Hello, it's Richard Branson. We're on. Come to London and let's do this.' What I didn't know until much later was that as soon as she put the phone down she danced around the room. She had found her dream job.

When Jean arrived in London we had plenty of long conversations about how we could turn typical corporate philanthropy upside down, moving away from solely the 'golden cheque' philosophy to becoming a true partner for front-line organisations and leveraging absolutely everything we possessed in order to drive change. We wanted every single person in the Virgin family to feel part of this community of change and to realise that every day, in everything they did they could be thinking about what was right for people and for the planet. We also knew we wanted to do what Virgin does best and go out and find the gaps, issues that no one else would touch, so that we could work with partners to come up with entrepreneurial solutions.

As I have mentioned, I try to spend time with each of the Virgin companies during the course of a year. Jean shadowed me, and she also met up with everyone on her own over the next six months and spent loads of time talking to charities. Everyone was consulted. They were told that this foundation was for them, as a means of connecting with each other and then for them to link up with people across the planet in all areas, people who needed help not just to survive but to achieve their potential. We didn't tell them how we thought it ought to be shaped – but we asked them what *they* wanted to see and what *they* wanted from us. Everyone took it to their hearts. The name and logo, Virgin Unite, were even created by staff members. We then pulled the plan together and Virgin Unite was launched in 2004 at our annual company summer party at my home outside Oxford.

I explained that we wanted to do something radically different. Virgin Unite would not be just another 'charity', but it would become an integral part of Virgin Group philosophy and at the core of everything we did as a group. Over the course of some weeks, we received good feedback from the thousands of people who work for Virgin companies and the hundreds of front-line organisations we met with in order to truly launch Unite. They wanted Unite to be an engine that connects people and entrepreneurial ideas to make change happen. This, then, was the beginning of the journey for many of the initiatives we will touch on in this book, and a whole new way of doing business for the Virgin Group. We recognise that this is likely a 'never-ending journey' and we are learning a great deal en route from many of the incredible people and organisations profiled in this book.

One thing I noticed about Jean and myself was that there was a bit of a philosophical collision. I have already stated I am not a believer in just handing out cheques; you should run charity like a business driving change. That is, I believe that most people, even the poorest and most deprived, don't just want to be told what's good for them; they want to be involved in helping to make their own lives better. Also, no matter how well-meaning you may be, you can't always know what works best in other countries – local people know that best. Of course, Jean agrees with that but her passion had always been to find ways of bringing together businesses, governments and the social sector. She believes that Virgin's businesses should themselves drive change. This philosophical collision actually proved very effective because it had a push–pull result whereby we ended up with something entirely new that mobilised our businesses and everything we have across the Group to make a difference. Being in the airline business we don't have the vast funding that some of the newer technology start-ups have, so we also need to be more imaginative to make any funds go further.

As part of my work with Virgin Unite, I am also fortunate to have met many inspiring people who are at the forefront of these changes that are really at the heart of Capitalism 24902. As we've been on this journey with the Virgin businesses, we've learnt a lot from compassionate business entrepreneurs like Bill Gates and visionary social entrepreneurs such as Auret van Heerden, who played a role in ending apartheid, and Jeff Skoll, who started Participant Media and the Skoll Foundation, and Boudewijn Poelmann, who runs the Dutch Postcode Lottery, which has given many billions to good causes – and companies like Innocent Drinks in the UK and PUMA globally, about which you will hear more later in this book.

Once Virgin Unite was up and running I was immensely excited by the incredible entrepreneurial energy and the collection of people who were gathering around this new Virgin community, from leading business people to those in the social sector, philanthropists and governments working with Unite to form collaborations to help drive a new way of capitalism and new entrepreneurial approaches to global issues. The great thing is that this was not just coming from celebrities and well-known figures in the social sector: this community was a wonderful melting pot of people from all walks of life. What binds them is their willingness to listen to and learn from people on the front line to create new entrepreneurial approaches, and their firm belief that we should never accept the unacceptable. I was coming across many small examples of individuals prepared to expound this philosophy all the time, and what was interesting about them was that they revealed a remarkable cross section of ideas. Successful entrepreneurship comes in many shapes and sizes and, as I tell those who ask me what my secret is (apart from saying I have no secret), there is no great mystique about it. Have passion for what you do; believe in yourself and your product and your customer; persevere; delegate; listen. Have fun. Today, I add – 'Do good'. Ultimately, Capitalism 24902 is all about people, finding the right entrepreneurs to shift to a new way of doing business and getting every single person in the company excited about playing their part in making a difference. Here are a few stories which I hope will bring Capitalism 24902 to life, starting with the two small businesses I mentioned at the beginning of this chapter.

Jempson's is the store I came across in Sussex during my attempt to kite-surf the Channel. It was founded by the Jempson family over seventy-five years ago. They started small, as so many do, with a tiny shop, and over the years gradually expanded, never outstripping their capital, their resources or their customer base. Now Andrew and Stephen Jempson are the third generation of the family at the helm. Their ethos and brand are very clearly defined and pretty laudable. They state: 'We have sought to bring traditional, home-made foods to the public. Built on honesty and good value, our intention is to become the most prestigious food retailer in the UK in terms of innovation, design and fresh food excellence ... This is our guarantee. This is our mission.'

But lest you think that only a tiny corner shop could possibly achieve this level of service, in their case they now have four stores, all in the same corner of the same county, Sussex, and serve 100,000 customers a week. They have achieved this by being passionate about their support for local farmers and producers, and currently have thirteen suppliers who are deemed Jempson's 'Local Heroes' who supply their stores with quality, fresh local produce and services, and they spend £3.5 million annually with this band of local producers and suppliers. They believe in good, honest, ethical trading supporting local producers and service suppliers wherever possible. They are also advocates of the Fairtrade Foundation. It is a very people-based business where local people are employed and trained on simple but effective apprentice schemes in-store, with traditional food counters run by skilled local butchers, fishmongers and bakers and not – as is so often the case – people who just work there for a pay packet.

The store's 'Go-Green' initiative is an on-going project. Jempson's scrapped the use of disposable bags and estimate that they prevent on average two million bags a year from going to landfill. Boxes received from suppliers are passed on to customers to carry their shopping in, and all plastic wrapping is collected and returned to the original supplier. Customers have the facility in-store to recycle batteries and carrier bags and there's a comprehensive recycling centre in their car parks. In addition, they operate a bus service that runs daily, enabling those with mobility problems, families without access to a car or those who, in the current tough economic climate, find it too expensive to run their car to visit the store for their weekly shop. Through the Jempson Foundation they support local charities. I was interested to see that their model is very much like the one we are establishing with Virgin Unite. The staff join in challenges to raise funds and they willingly volunteer in many different ways in order to serve the community. Both Andrew and Stephen agree that doing good has increased their profits and brought new customers – the very philosophy that sits at the core of this book.

* * *

The world is full of extraordinary, heroic people doing heroic, extraordinary things. I think, however, that we can make the world better just by doing things differently, in a day-to-day, more or less ordinary way. This book isn't just about 'doing good'. It's about *doing better* – and it's about having fun on the way. One company that has 'Fun' at its core of branding is Finisterre, an award-winning, ethical clothing company that specialises in fabric innovation. Tom Kay, the founder of Finisterre, is a keen surfer and a small businessman with strong ethical values. He has lived by the sea almost his entire life, originally in Norfolk and now in Cornwall. He studied marine biology at university and afterwards, like many people, he went to London and found an average sort of job. But he started to think about the things that were really important to him and how he could build them into his life.

Tom's idea was simple and, on the face of it, not particularly radical: to sell truly well-designed garments. That meant design, and craft, but also responsible and ethical sourcing. He says that's what the Finisterre brand is. 'You can put anything that's important to you into a brand. You can, and I think maybe you should.' He'd buy from local sources where possible and support manufacturing initiatives that helped people and the environment. They always have an eye, in everything they do, for ways in which they can support environmental causes based around the sea. They're not the first clothing company to try something like this – there are some big companies out there now doing great work – but when Tom and his sister started out they were the only surf brand addressing these issues, something which struck them as strange when you consider that surfers feel so connected to their environment and care a great deal about it. Eight years ago, British surfers were being fobbed off with non-durable, badly made products that would spill out of a factory somewhere with no information about the origin of the materials from which they were made. There was virtually no recyclable fabric out there and very few natural fibres. So that became Finisterre's niche.

'Niche' is an important word for the business entrepreneur. Identifying the brand and then the niche and knowing the customer are all crucial to success. Finisterre started with a warm, waterproof fleece. Something surfers could slip on when they came out of the water and would get them as far as the car without dying of hypothermia. Tom didn't have any experience with this sort of thing, so he did all the initial testing on himself. According to Tom you can go a lot of the way on just blind optimism – and that is something I certainly identified with, having started *Student* magazine at the age of fifteen when still at school. Finisterre's products have since made it to Everest.

Tom Kay believes in involving customers and telling them what's in the clothing they're wearing, where it comes from and what its ethical qualities are. They get out regularly to share this message – again, much as I do with Virgin. If people trust the face behind the product, if you're open and honest with them and if they know there are no secrets, then they trust the brand.

Tom is clear on always delivering good value for money – that also protects the planet. 'Our stuff adds up. You can see where your money's going.' Eighty per cent of the carbon footprint of the garment is in its life – how often it's washed and reproofed, for example – so they try to make their garments long-lasting and relatively care-free. And they try to educate the consumer. If you're going to the trouble of buying an ethical product, you may as well look after it in a way that supports those values. And then, hopefully, when it finally gives out, they can help recycle it and close that loop. For the jackets, they have a great supplier who uses recycled polyester from Japanese workers' uniforms. Obviously they have to ship these from Japan (which is where most Japanese workers are to be found), which adds something to the garment's carbon footprint, but they think it's worth it since the customer can return a worn-out jacket. It's sent back to the supplier, and the supplier turns it back into a brand new jacket by adding just a very small amount of virgin (small v) polyester. That's streets ahead of the old way of doing things: then one simply took fresh ingredients, wore them out and dumped them in some landfill. If you log on to Finisterre's website you can click on their traceability programme. You can trace their entire production process from there, see where stuff comes from, how it moves about the world and gets put together. If Finisterre expanded, would they preserve the character of this great little company? The brand is a vehicle for their passions and they are ambitious and have got where they are by innovating. In the future the challenge will be for them to remember that they innovated in response to real-world problems. If they do expand, they say they have to preserve the values that were there when they started, which was to make the best product with minimal environmental impact.

It's really pleasing to see these wonderful small businesses making a difference, but what about the responsibility of some of the larger ones? One of the companies that certainly has taken this challenge on board at the core of their business is Marks & Spencer. M&S, the huge UK-based retailer with £10 billion in annual revenue, with whom just about everyone in Britain is familiar, has set out to be the world's most sustainable retailer by 2015. In 2007, they launched Plan A (obviously because there is no Plan B!). This plan is not just a simple advertising campaign with no teeth: it includes a dizzying and ambitious 180 commitments focusing on every aspect of their business, from decreasing waste through to the health and wellbeing of their staff and communities. With over twenty-one million customers visiting their stores each week and a supply chain consisting of tens of thousands of farms and factories, even a small shift as they 'screw business as usual' can have a dramatic impact.

M&S also put even more weight behind Plan A by allocating £50 million for an innovation fund. All these efforts are already paying off. As I write, they've achieved 95 of their 180 commitments and are on track for most of the others, including recycling 94 per cent of the waste generated by their stores, reducing carbon emissions by over 13 per cent, shifting to sustainable supply sources such as 90 per cent of the wild fish they sell. And the list goes on …

Stuart Rose, then CEO of Marks & Spencer, and Mike Barry, Head of Sustainable Business, did not see this as a one-off marketing campaign; they saw it as a platform to deliver business outcomes and an opportunity to improve their bottom line – which it has done. Plan A was cost-neutral in its second year, made £50 million in 2009 and £70 million in 2010. Mike summed it up really well in an interview with the *Business Green* website in November 2010: 'People are now getting the mindset that says, we're not at the top of this little hill called Corporate Social Responsibility, we're at the bottom of this big mountain called sustainability.'

* * *

I started this chapter talking about how people are really at the core of Capitalism 24902, so I want to finish by telling a couple of stories about some of the wonderful people we have in the Virgin Group who are making a difference every single day.

Jackie McQuillan has been working with us for eighteen years. She truly lives and breathes the Virgin brand and has helped me to build it. Back in 2003, during the Iraq war, I got a call from Jackie saying that she'd been contacted by a wonderful Iraqi gentleman (living in the UK) asking if we could help get medical supplies that his community had collected to the devastated people of Iraq. It just so happened that only the evening before I had been contacted by Air Marshal Brian Burridge asking if we could send a team from Virgin Atlantic to Basra to help to get the airport reopened. Watching the daily news bulletins it was becoming increasingly clear that hospitals had basically run out of life-saving drugs and the situation was now crucial. This was at a point when most people thought that the war was over and that the British troops would soon be coming home – so why not help get Basra airport opened but at the same time bring in a 747 packed full of vital drugs and medical equipment. Jackie, in her true, never-mind-the-bollocks style, decided that we had to do this relief flight, and she knew that I would be right behind her.

Over the next two weeks Jackie spent almost twenty-four hours a day on the phone to medical companies, the UK Defence forces, the British military and a whole host of other characters to make the flight happen. If you have ever tried to get the Chief Executives of major pharmaceutical companies on the phone you'll know this is no mean feat – but, with a potent mixture of charm and persistence, she did and once she had them talking, they bent over backwards to help and provided the much needed medicines for the hospital. Once Virgin people have made a decision to help they don't hang about! We were truly astounded by the company's generosity and how quickly they galvanised their teams to get the supplies to us at Gatwick airport. Michael Burke and Serge Allsop-menist from Virgin Atlantic hotfooted it to Iraq and started working to help get the airport cleared and reopened for the flight – they didn't even blink at being sent into what was still effectively a war-zone.

So on Thursday 1 May we boarded a plane loaded down with 60 tons of medical supplies worth over £2 million and, along with some eminent Iraqi doctors (again, now living in the UK), we flew into Basra. When we landed, our pilot, Mike Abu-Nayla, an Iraqi national, burst into tears; this was the first time he had been back on Iraqi soil since he'd left as a young man. It was quite a surreal experience to enter a deserted Basra airport where the British troops were camped out and getting ready to leave (or so they thought at that time). We drove to the hospital and were all shocked by the desperate circumstances where children with severe injuries did not even have access to simple painkillers. Cancer patients had not been treated for quite some time, because when Saddam Hussein had realised war was imminent, he had stopped vital supplies getting to hospitals. It was heart-breaking – these sights you never quite get on the evening news. Yes, every day we are bombarded with images of bombings and the hideous injuries inflicted by the horrors of war but what we rarely see are the effects that it has on people with cancer, premature babies that don't have incubators, the lack of heart defibrillators and ECG machines. The equipment needed in every hospital in the world to save lives on a daily basis.

As we made our way back to the aircraft, I could not help thinking how lucky I was to have companies like Virgin Atlantic and people like Jackie, Michael and Serge in the business who simply would not accept the unacceptable, who were willing to give it their all and use the tools we had in the Group (our planes and wonderful pilots) to make such a great difference and make the people in the Virgin Group incredibly proud. Grassroots Capitalism 24902 at its best. Since that trip, we've made a number of other relief flights, to the Far East after the Christmas 2004 tsunami, to Pakistan after the 2005 earthquake, to Australia during the 2010–11 bushfires and flooding. More recently we helped fly in supplies to the victims of the Haitian earthquake and the Japanese tsunami. And of course back in 1990 we flew to Baghdad to help rescue hostages during the first Gulf conflict.

* * *

Another person at Virgin who is making a difference is Peter Avis, who works at Babylon, a restaurant owned by

Virgin Limited Edition at The Roof Gardens off High Street Kensington, which is the place where I usually choose to eat out when I'm in London. I remember The Roof Gardens from when I was young because they were on the top of Derry & Toms and housed Biba. For those who were around in the sixties and seventies, Biba – more precisely Barbara Hulanicki – practically invented the miniskirt and tights. In fact, Mary Quant sold them first, but Biba pushed them with gusto. The Roof Gardens were legendary, going way back to the early 1930s, when they were *the* place to go for terribly chic tea dances. During the Second World War a German bomb had landed on the roof of the store but because it was set to detonate on contact with buildings it was clearly confused by landing in the deep soil of a roof garden. Derry & Toms tea room had the (properly defused) bomb on display for many years – something that fascinated me greatly on my visits there with my parents.

Anyway, years later the person who owned The Roof Gardens had run into financial problems and offered it to me for £400,000. I had no money, but the brewer supplying the bar at The Roof Gardens gave us an interest-free loan if we would agree to continue stocking his beer. It seemed a very good deal and I jumped at it and immediately set about restoring The Roof Gardens to its former glory. There are three themed gardens, covering one and a half acres, and within them you can find a stream, a belfry with a bell, Tudor-style galleries and even mature oak trees and fruit trees.

But apart from the obvious pleasure the gardens have

brought to thousands of people over many years, they also play their part in our effort to do things better in our businesses. No chemicals are used in maintaining the gardens and as much as possible is recycled and sustainable. For a garden in the centre of London the wormery is amazing ... These are some of the best fed worms in England as every scrap of waste food is fed to them, which then turns into rich black compost. We use this to grow the herbs and vegetables used in the restaurant. So when the chefs need fresh rosemary, or mint for the new potatoes, or chard, or rhubarb for some special pudding, like rhubarb fool, it's all there. There are fresh salads in season, as well as new potatoes, tomatoes and apples. Obviously, not everything can be grown on the roof, but we source as much as we can from markets as near to London as possible to reduce our carbon use. Meat, game, fruit, vegetables – all are organic. Fish comes from sustainable sea stocks – for example, we won't use blue fin tuna.

Peter, the manager of Babylon, is the young man behind this enterprise. He's a remarkable young Liverpudlian who has been with us for ten years. I believe that it's very important in a business to take a keen interest in the people who work there. Their happiness reflects on their performance as well as on the pervading mood of the business. I had known Peter since he first started at Babylon at the age of twenty-four, although often my visits would be infrequent, depending on my work and travel schedule. When I walked in one day, after a highly unusual two-year gap, I immediately noticed that he'd had a haircut. Where once his fair hair had been quite long, now it was short and stylish.

'You've been scalped,' I said.

'Why, yes, I have had it chopped off. Do you like it?' he replied. We chatted a little more, but I was slightly fazed to notice that he looked quite emotional, though he said nothing. Had I overstepped the boundary between friendly comment and intrusion? Some time later I learned that he was touched because, despite my not having seen him for some two years, I had immediately noticed his haircut. He said it had made a huge difference to him that I had noticed such a tiny detail. 'I resolved to do the same,' he told me. 'I wanted to show that I cared enough about the members of the staff at Babylon and anywhere I go; to notice *them*, as people, not just as employees.'

Like me, Peter is dyslexic. His headmaster at the secondary school he went to in Liverpool had taken him to one side when, at the age of seventeen, he was looking at the various career options open to him and had said: 'Some people are made to sweep the streets and, unfortunately, you are one of those people.'

It was like a bucket of cold water in his face, but it gave Peter the spur he needed. 'I had to prove him wrong.'

He went to London, started work as a dishwasher in restaurants and in time was elevated to trainee manager. But every time success stared him in the face, as soon as he thought his dyslexia might be discovered he did a runner. Eventually he arrived in the United States and started all over again, finding work in the restaurants of some very exotic hotel chains. But once again, every time he became worried that people might discover his secret he was gone. I had been given such huge support as a boy with dyslexia, and I found this story sad. But Peter was a survivor; a fighter. He never stopped trying, certain that one day he would make a breakthrough. This happened when he applied for a job as an under-manager at Babylon when he was twenty-four. He got the job and did well – until the manager asked him to handle spread sheets, to show profit and loss and cash flow. As someone who is still ill at ease with such things, I fully understand how Peter felt: once again he quailed and gave his notice. This time however the People director wouldn't accept it. She knew enough about Peter to understand that there was more in his resignation than met the eye. A little gentle probing revealed his secret.

'It wasn't that I was ashamed of being dyslexic, it was that I thought it would be a firing offence because I couldn't do my job. That's why I always left first – before I was given the boot.'

The People director put Peter's mind at rest. She had a word with the general manager, who put Peter in charge of the budget for uniforms, which stood at £6,000. He was shown how to do a very limited spread sheet that related just to the uniforms. Being able to handle it boosted his confidence. He realised that in all those years of running away from some very high-flying jobs he'd been fighting a dragon that didn't exist.

It's the Virgin ethos to take care of staff and to be considerate. At Virgin we always try and ensure we promote from within the company. The head of Virgin Unite in Canada started as Virgin Mobile's receptionist. The woman who was the managing director of Virgin's recording division started work for Virgin at the Manor Recording Studios; she was the cleaning lady. Peter never forgot the kindness he was shown and vowed that it, too, would be a major part of his job when he became a manager – as he eventually did. He not only made sure that we got the basics right at Babylon, he also embraced Virgin Unite's wider global community initiatives, from working at a crèche for orphans in the community surrounding Ulusaba, our private game reserve in South Africa, to creating various initiatives that raised funds. He was working at the crèche when he saw a baby days away from death from AIDS. He was so moved that he knew he had to help. As soon as he returned to London he and the staff at Babylon came up with the idea of creating the Red Edition cocktail. It's made of champagne, rose water and red hibiscus – red for the Virgin colour – and not only is it delicious and fun, but £1 from every cocktail sold goes to charitable causes.

Mentoring young people from Kids Company in London is something else Peter has devoted much of his free time to. He goes to Kids Company in south London to chat to young people there about work experience, and a group comes regularly to Babylon to learn more about how to run a restaurant. Peter also realises that he gets back as much as he gives to these young people.

Appointing Peter to the position of manager when it came up was inspired, as I soon discovered. In 2008 and 2009 he won two separate major awards, the first when he was voted Restaurant Manager of the Year and the other when Babylon was named Toptable Best Restaurant. Peter was praised for his 'complete dedication to the role of restaurant manager, his enthusiasm for service and his ability to inspire and lead his team'.

I was in Miami when I got the news and I was delighted. It reinforced everything that I believed in. *Do good – and the rewards will come.* Virgin people are happy people – the happiness factor – and because of that they love their jobs and stay in them. It's not just that the staff like working at Virgin – we value and respect them, another lesson I tell entrepreneurs. 'It's not about you, it's not about the business even – it's about staff and the customer. Those two are what drives a successful business.'

Hearing about the award I asked Joan if she would call Peter at once, to invite him to stay with us at Necker as our guest. When she got through to him, Peter was outside the Langham Hotel with his mother, who was up from Liverpool. He was recovering from an emotionally charged evening, where he had received his award. When Joan hung up, she said, 'When I invited him, he broke down in tears. I heard him say, "Mum, it's Richard Branson's wife, Joan, inviting me to stay on Necker. Oh my God, I can't believe it."'

There was a moment later, on Necker, when Peter was sitting at the long table with us – Joan, Holly, Sam and myself – and he started to sob. 'Are you all right?' Joan asked, concerned. I jumped up to give him a bear hug. 'I'm fine,' he said, through his tears. 'I'm so happy I can't stand it. I never thought any of this would happen to me – the dyslexic boy from Liverpool who was told he was only fit to sweep the street.'

To me, that is what running a successful business is all about.

Web: virginunite.com/screwbusinessasusual
Twitter: @virginunite #sbau
Facebook: Facebook.com/VirginUnite

2

Stop Saving, Start Reinventing

'I'm a big dreamer, always wanting to achieve more than what is expected. Passion is what drives me and I believe that nothing is impossible because impossible is nothing' – Bongani Tshabalala (Branson Centre entrepreneur), founder B&M Football5's

'The Branson Centre has contributed to my success. I can now create jobs for people that I've hired and the impact this has on their lives, and the lives of their families and their communities, is enormous' – Yashwin Mohan (Branson Centre entrepreneur), founder of Game Over

'What makes entrepreneurs different from other people is that they are self-motivated and self-driven. They can identify opportunities that others cannot see and they also want to create employment and help society' – Musa Maphongwane (Branson Centre entrepreneur), co-founder of Gaming Zone

For far too many years we've been trying to solve the world's issues by pouring trillions of dollars into aid. While this has been (and still is) absolutely necessary to ensure we stop human suffering in times of emergency, we all need to start looking beyond the emergencies, to stop constantly trying to save the world and instead look at reinventing how we live in the world. It can no longer be about putting sticking plasters on issues and hoping they will go away; it has to be about creating opportunities for people so that they can build the lives they deserve.

And who better to create opportunities than entrepreneurs? Every time I visit our Branson Centre of Entrepreneurship in South Africa I leave feeling that I just emerged from the epicentre of hope in the world. These young people have battled all kinds of adversity in order to create their own businesses. Each time I meet one of them I'm humbled by their focus on uplifting their families, communities and their country. It's not all about money or self-interest; it's about economic freedom for the community. Watching the financial crisis continue to unfold around the world, we certainly have a whole lot to learn from them! I thought, therefore, that it made sense to start this chapter with some words of wisdom from these incredible entrepreneurs. Throughout this chapter we will be celebrating people from all walks of life who are reinventing how we all live, but first a bit on how I started on this path myself.

When I was fifteen I decided I'd been educated enough in formal ways and needed to get out into the world to continue my education in life. Even as a boy of eight or nine I'd been a budding entrepreneur, although I doubt the word 'entrepreneur' was one I'd ever heard of; and even if I had I wouldn't have been able to spell it because I was dyslexic. Perhaps it was dyslexia that drove me to be entrepreneurial in the first place, because I knew instinctively that I'd never pass exams and go into a profession, such as the law, as my father and his father before him had. I'd never be a teacher, a doctor or a banker – or so I thought. Ideas and good schemes to set up a business that didn't require much formal learning seemed to be one of my best options.

'Ricky's money-making schemes' is what my mother rather charitably called them. Some of these schemes were doomed to failure. It's hard breeding budgerigars when you're away at boarding school; and, while digging up half of one of our paddocks to plant Christmas tree seedlings proved that I invested in futures – the trees would have taken at least three to five years to grow to a harvestable size – ultimately it wasn't a good idea if you weren't around to chase off the marauding rabbits that found them rather tasty.

Rather bizarrely for someone whose spelling wasn't a strong point, I nurtured a secret ambition to be a journalist. This was partly fuelled by my desire to get people talking about issues facing young people in the sixties, like the Vietnam War, racism, sexual health, and so on. I was further encouraged in my journalistic dream when I won an essay writing competition. Nobody was more surprised than I was that I'd entered it in the first place, but my parents had always taught me to believe in myself. Winning such a prize was a big deal. It proved I could write. Even so, not many newspaper proprietors would hire a fifteen-year-old reporter, so, together with a fellow pupil, Jonathan (Jonny) Holland-Gems, I created my own job by starting a national magazine for students. This was an audacious plan for a schoolboy with no capital, no office and, more importantly, no typewriter. Undeterred, I scavenged a large bag of loose change from Mum and, using the payphone in the main hall of the school (which became my office), set about selling the advertisements that would be needed to pay the print bill, negotiating with a printer to give me credit before the advertising money came in, and asking successful or interesting people if I could interview them. Had I known the pitfalls, I might not have been so chirpy, but I was brimful of confidence and the conviction that I could do it. My first step was to produce a business plan – I still have it. It lists all the necessary people we'd need to approach, from distributor and printer to contributors and advertisers. I calculated the potential profit and the possible loss and did my sums, all neatly tabulated.

Having done my homework, I thought it would be plain sailing. In fact, more than a year later Jonny and I were still pegging away with the same amount of enthusiasm, still trying to get the magazine off the ground while trying to fit in lessons and dreaded exams. I'd given up all subjects but one – History – in order to find more time for my passion to launch *Student*. I handwrote all my begging letters to would-be advertisers, and posted them to Mum for her to have them typed by a generous neighbour. My chutzpah was amazing, when I think about it. But 'nothing ventured nothing gained' is one of the creeds I live by and I was jubilant but somehow not totally surprised when Barclays Bank bought space and even sent us a cheque in advance that was enough to pay the print bill. In the blink of an eye *Student* magazine went from being one of 'Ricky's schemes' to a reality. It still wasn't that easy. There was a vast amount of work to be done and school work continued to be a distraction. Finally, I sat my one and only examination (A level) – frankly the result didn't seem important, just doing it and moving on was all that counted. Then I was off to London to make my fortune and my own way in life. I was still sixteen.

I have never forgotten the lessons I learned in those early years, the ups and downs and the downright terrifying moments when things looked as if they were about to go pear-shaped. I learned to grasp opportunities and the nettle with equal passion. I learned that if you see a bright idea – go with it. If you see a problem – deal with it. Do good, don't do harm. Give back if you can. The funny thing is that it was not until many years later that I realised how much that magazine had given back. Last year I was on a flight with Jean and happened to have a stack of old *Student* magazines with me. Secretly I gave her the stack to avoid working on the whole flight; somehow, whenever we are on a flight together, I end up with a rather long to-do list by the time we get off! As Jean looked through them, she kept on saying: 'Wow, you were already looking at this issue years ago.' It was then that I realised how powerful this simple magazine had been in shining a light on issues that were not being talked about, and how it had instilled in me a passion never to accept the unacceptable. The sad thing is that Jean was right: many of the same issues we were talking about in the sixties are still around today, making me even more passionate about turning upside down the way we approach issues and reinventing the way we live in the world.

* * *

One thing I did want to try and fix immediately in my teenage years was the limited access young people had to sexual health advice. I did this by opening the Student Advisory Centre, although it wasn't always plain sailing. One day, aged nineteen, I heard a loud knock on my front door. Two plain clothes policemen were standing outside. I asked them in and they told me I was under arrest for mentioning the words 'venereal disease' in public. We had a leaflet that asked people to 'Give Us Your Headaches' so we could help them with various problems. One young person's problem was obviously VD. Bizarrely it turned out it was illegal to mention VD in public under the Indecent Advertisements Act of 1899 and the Venereal Disease Act of 1916. I asked if I changed the words to 'social diseases' whether they would drop the charges. They agreed to do so, but we got people contacting us with pimples and acne and not VD so we put the words VD back on the leaflet.

I was promptly arrested! The court reluctantly found us guilty and fined me £7. We decided to take Her Majesty's Government to court for having their own VD posters on the backs of lavatory doors in order to get these laws changed. Reginald Maudling, the then Home Secretary, wrote to me asking me to drop my case, and promised to repeal the laws if we did so and offered me an apology for having taken me to court. We were right to make a stand. Since then, hundreds of people have been helped through the hard work of the team at the Centre, in the early days with sexual health issues and today problems linked to mental health.

Looking back, I believe that having at least the foundations of a more formal education, going to a school that taught good manners, the benefits of debate, respect for other people's ideas and for each other and broadening your outlook is very important in shaping the person you eventually become. My parents set me on the path to being adventurous and self-sufficient and to being considerate to others. They believed you could achieve whatever you wanted if you worked hard enough. But it was Stowe, my old school, that built on what I'd already been taught and took it to the next level.

All this came back to me as I flew over Stowe one sunny day in 2008. It was the first time I had been back in forty-three years. There had been times when I had almost dropped in when flying to Goodwood races in Sussex from my home in Oxfordshire. I'd glanced down as we'd flown over Stowe and wondered what it would be like to drop in unannounced, but my nerve had always failed me. There's something about your old school that can make you feel like a kid again – rather ineffectual and bumbling – so I'd just shrugged and carried on to Goodwood.

As the helicopter banked and turned for its landing I took in the rolling parkland, the pristine green lawns, the playing fields, the lakes, temples, fountains and follies. It was magnificent. As a boy I had found it too formal. Now, with hindsight and a love of history, I saw a wonderful place that nurtured learning, that put pupils first and built strong leaders and players of the future. We put down on the front lawn before the soaring neoclassical pillars of the main façade of a building that had been designed by Sir John Vanbrugh as a grand palace for the Dukes of Buckinghamshire and I jumped out. I felt apprehensive. Would it feel the same? Would I feel very estranged from the boy I'd been? Of course I had been sent invitations down the years, but I had always found excuses to decline them. I was busy and, anyway, I felt you couldn't go back. When it came to selecting a school for my own two children, Holly and Sam, I did consider Stowe because it was a great school, with a strong liberal ethos. I'd even discussed sending them there with the then headmaster, but in the end Joan and I had decided to send both children elsewhere, mostly because we wanted them to go to a school that was close to home.

Waiting on the steps of the main building was a crowd of boys and girls in plain grey uniforms. I quickly picked out a small group of five South African pupils who were standing together. They were the very first Branson Scholars and the reason I was making this visit. Seeing them standing there filled me with pride and hope that we were perhaps changing their lives in a very positive way. I have to confess that it wasn't really my doing, though, or even my idea. The person who had made this happen was Mike Parsons, founder and CEO of Barchester Healthcare, a company that owns some two hundred nursing homes in the UK. Mike and I have developed a good rapport since we met. We're the same age, with birthdays just two weeks apart, and we have a shared interest in South Africa. I first met him when he came along to one of the annual Fast Track 100 dinners I give in conjunction with the *Sunday Times* at my Oxfordshire home. These events are held to enable leading entrepreneurs to get to know each other, to network and exchange ideas and to join in the Virgin Unite auctions to raise funds for the Branson Centres of Entrepreneurship. Mike had won a Virgin Unite trip to South Africa to see the work we were doing at the Branson Centre in Johannesburg, and then travel due east for about 250 miles to stay at Ulusaba, the 10,000-acre private game reserve I'd bought in 1999.

We went to Johannesburg first, accompanied by Jean Oelwang and the Virgin Unite team, to introduce Mike to the Branson Centre of Entrepreneurship, where he was to be part of a panel reviewing the plans of some of the inspiring young entrepreneurs and to say a few words to the group.

There was an amusing little incident on the morning of our visit. Joan, my wife, was with me but had other business elsewhere, so we left her at the hotel and headed for the school. Mike was with his partner, Sara, a slender woman with long blonde hair (I don't often comment on people's appearance, but this has some relevance). The big room was mobbed with some two to three hundred chattering, excited young people. When they settled down, Mike and a couple of other visiting entrepreneurs said a few words, then one of the young entrepreneurs stood up and thanked us: 'Thank you, Mike, and thank you to Richard and thank you to Joan.'

I knew we had left Joan at the hotel so I did a double take, as did everyone else. But some two or three hundred pairs of eyes focused on a slender, blonde woman and they all chorused, 'Good morning, Joan.' Suddenly Sara was the centre of attention and she looked disconcerted, to put it mildly. Since then, whenever I meet up with Mike, I always ask him, 'How's my wife?'

In order to understand where the idea for the Branson Centre came from, it's necessary to introduce Taddy Blecher, the co-founder of South Africa's free university CIDA (which stands for 'Community and Individual Development Association'). Taddy is a true reinventor. He did not want to set up education programmes for the poorest in South Africa that relied solely on charity – he wanted the programmes to pay for themselves so that they would never disappear. He's hoping to use education to build entire economies that will lead the revolution in the way we should live in a changing world with fewer resources to go around.

As a qualified actuary, Taddy Blecher had an assured future. In 1995, he was on the verge of taking up a more lucrative job in the United States. He bought an airline ticket and packed up his life. He was about to leave South Africa, when it occurred to him that he was leaving his home behind. He was rich and his homeland was poor – was he copping out? He tore up his air ticket. A week later, he felt driven to visit a township, the kind of place he'd never been to before. His first reaction to the poverty around him was to open his wallet and hand out money, but even as he did this he knew it was the wrong thing to do. He wasn't helping people, he was humiliating them. These people didn't want charity, they wanted choices in life.

In January 2000, Taddy typed up a letter from his office in Johannesburg and faxed it around the country, announcing the creation of a new kind of university especially for young people from low-income families. It would be virtually free. It would offer a degree in business administration – and it would be 'the best business education in Africa', fully accredited and taught by some of the finest commercial minds in the country. Such was Taddy's enthusiasm for his idea that it didn't occur to him that he'd written his letter on the letterhead of his employer, Monitor Company. The company went ballistic. It received 3,500 applications for a university that did not exist. Security would be saying: 'Who are these people outside?' And the students would be saying: 'Your university building is so beautiful.' And security would say: 'Go away, it's not a university, it's a consultancy company.'

Undeterred, Taddy and a handful of colleagues managed to borrow a building from a company. Two weeks later, the first students arrived. There were no computers: the students made do, learning to type on photocopies of a keyboard.

Taddy kept costs down by empowering his students to run the school and do all the cooking, the cleaning and the administration. He wrote to the country's top businesses for help teaching the course. Poor children from the townships or rural communities who never stood a chance before were being educated to degree standard for around $350 for the full course, including books and accommodation, a cost to them of less than one tenth of traditional universities. In 2011, CIDA's business degree graduates working in the marketplace will earn in excess of R100 million ($13.5 million) in salaries. Over the course of their careers, these same graduates will earn in excess of R3 billion. And many graduates are taking the skills they've learned back to their homes in the most disadvantaged parts of Africa, where their communities are hungry to learn from them. About 600,000 people have so far benefited from the informal teaching undertaken by CIDA students.

Taddy says, 'The really exciting part of this work is that you can predict, with real certainty, the scale of the change you're ushering in. If all our 5,500 degree and other graduates who are already working can just keep working now, rather than being unemployed or working in a supermarket packing boxes, together they will end up earning just over R9 billion – about $1.2 billion. As the years go by, that money will work its way through their families, as they see that their children get educated, and that their brothers and sisters train and get good jobs, and that their parents have a real house to live in at last. And the fact that over half our graduates are female makes us even more certain of this outcome, because it's been shown time and time again that when you raise a young woman above the poverty line, you change the whole destiny of her family for good.'

Taddy has a unique way of inspiring people. It was Taddy who inspired me to set up a school dedicated purely and simply to entrepreneurship. I was leaving CIDA after attending an incredibly inspiring session with the Dalai Lama and a whole host of students, when Taddy ran out after Jean and me, grabbed me by the elbow and blurted out his idea for the Branson Centre of Entrepreneurship. These days we always joke that the birth of the Branson Centre happened right there on the street in downtown Johannesburg! Virgin Unite and CIDA worked together to make the idea a reality, and the Centre opened in October 2005. Taddy really helped us to get this Centre off the ground and train thousands of young people how to become entrepreneurs. Over the years we became independent from CIDA as we realised that the biggest difference we could make was to focus on supporting entrepreneurs who already had some success under their belts with their small business and just needed help in taking it to that next stage. Our investment in the Centre was matched by a group of successful UK entrepreneurs – people like Mike Parsons and many others who joined me in the belief that job creation must play a critical role in eliminating poverty. Each group made a donation to Virgin Unite to join us on a trip to South Africa and learn more about the issues.

Equally as important as these funds has been the time that these entrepreneurs have put into mentoring and learning from the budding young entrepreneurs, as well as the spin-off programmes they have created.

We're not there to churn out employees. We're there to get people to develop businesses and employ others. How lucky we are that there are loads of aspiring young entrepreneurs who just need to be given the chance to shine. Their businesses range from a transport company, to a design company, to internet cafés; some are chicken farmers, others fashion designers and we even have one lovely entrepreneur, Cleopatra Simelane, who is following in my earlier footsteps and has set up a student magazine called *Recess*. It's an alternative to celebrity-filled magazines and focuses on positive role models for young people in South Africa. Cleopatra is an unbelievable dynamo who blew me away the first time I met her. She has entrepreneurial energy in spades. Her magazine is already distributed in hundreds of high schools, with more on the way. She is the kind of person you just know will never give up, no matter what obstacles get thrown in her way as she starts this journey. The Centre is partly a place that provides training, partly a networking hub that connects young entrepreneurs with established businesses that might want to invest in their ideas. In my opening speech I said: 'The South African economy is dependent on entrepreneurial activity for creating future economic growth and jobs. But the economic contribution to South Africa's entrepreneurial sector is below the average. I believe that increasing entrepreneurship in this country is the golden highway to economic freedom.'

Each year we have a bit of a 'pitching session' with the young African entrepreneurs presenting to successful business people from all over the world. Having walked in their shoes I know that the graduates are often very nervous, so I always try to add a little lightness and humour to these sessions. When, for example, Lere Mgayiya, another young South African, pitched his business idea of offering townships much-needed access to baths and showers – with an ambitious sales target of R2.9 million, I asked, 'Do you get a discount if you shower with your girlfriend?' Everyone burst into laughter and the ice was broken.

The Branson Centre is one of the most satisfying projects I've ever been involved in. Part of that is to do with my long love affair with South Africa and its people, and part of it is simply the pleasure of seeing ideas take shape and start to work. This is why I ended up in business in the first place, and it's still what gets me out of bed in the morning. Part of what motivates me now is that I'm absolutely convinced that if we want to take capitalism to its next stage and *screw business as usual*, then the best way forward is to give more people everywhere greater power to build their own destinies. Even as I write these words I'm on the brink of opening a Caribbean Branson Centre of Entrepreneurship, in partnership with Virgin Holidays and Virgin Unite, and I have future plans to open more in areas where they are most needed and will have the greatest impact for local communities and for the economy. The Caribbean Branson Centre is a great example of how one particular business, Virgin Holidays, which has committed more than $3 million over ten years to the project, has woven change into its core to support this Centre. This change will ultimately help support the growth of businesses that could in turn become suppliers linked to tourism, that in turn gives opportunities to people and protects the environment on the beautiful islands in the Caribbean. My old friend Chris Blackwell, who started Island Records and launched many artists such as U2 and Bob Marley, has also joined forces with us at the Centre. He has always had a strong focus on giving people a chance in life and so his ethos fits perfectly with what we are trying to do at the Centres.

After spending time in Johannesburg, where Mike Parsons and his fellow entrepreneurs talked to and mentored students, sharing their plans and offering them advice – bear in mind that Mike runs one of the most successful 'people' businesses in the UK, has a degree in economics and has set up a leading advertising agency and PR company, so he knows his onions – we headed to Ulusaba Private Game Reserve. It's in the heart of the wild and beautiful Sabi Sands Reserve in north-eastern South Africa, near the vast Kruger National Park. But the purpose of the trip there wasn't just to have an exciting and unusual holiday, watching elephants and zebra from the decks of the lodge or exploring the bush and photographing lions and rhinoceros – but to experience at first hand some of the work of Virgin Unite in partnership with our hotel collection, Virgin Limited Edition, and our private game reserve, Ulusaba.

Ulusaba – the name means 'place of little fear' because once it was a kind of warrior citadel on top of a massive rock – is surrounded by small villages. Many of the people who live in these small local communities work for our game reserve – which is run as a tourist hotel – so have become part of our extended Virgin family. Ulusaba is a business but it's firmly embedded in the community and does a lot of good in the district. Tragically, the scourge of HIV/AIDS has badly hit the communities and life is a great struggle, especially for the many children orphaned when their parents died. To work with and among this community Ulusaba and Virgin Unite started Pride 'n Purpose. We have built a clinic, schools and a crèche, as well as helped establish market gardens and incubate small businesses. There's also a shop where many traditional goods are made and sold, and other similar businesses are being developed that give people work and a living.

As we walked through one of the villages, Mike was taking it all in, asking questions, discussing the work, suggesting ways he could contribute. Unite doesn't believe in throwing money at problems. We try to find ways to help people help themselves so that their future becomes secure. Out of the blue as we walked in the bright sun, Mike started talking about Stowe. It seemed a strange contrast to the simple village schools and way of life in Sabi Sands. He said: 'My son's at Stowe, you know. He loves it.'

Casually I said, 'I must go back to school. I have never been back.' I had mixed views but inwardly thought it might take a lot to get me there. I felt like Shakespeare's reluctant schoolboy, creeping like a snail, unwillingly to school.

'I know the head quite well, Dr Anthony Wallersteiner,' Mike said, conversationally. 'Anthony's a nice chap, very inspiring. These public school charitable foundations have social responsibility written into their manifestos. Stowe helps underprivileged people.'

I nodded.

'I think it would be a good idea to give the opportunity to some really underprivileged kids in South Africa to spend some time in Britain.'

'What would they do?' I asked cautiously.

'I was thinking that some of them might attend Stowe.'

'I'm not so sure,' I said slowly, my mind going into overdrive.

Mike persisted, 'It's a very progressive school. The headmaster is very open to new ideas. I think it would gain perhaps even more than the pupils from here would benefit. It would definitely be a two-way street.'

'Are you thinking of sending students from the Branson Centre? They're a bit old – most of them are well past schoolleaving age.'

'I was thinking of finding a good school with a compatible standard of education. The pupils would have to fit in for it to work. I have one in mind, one I know. It's the Dominican

Convent School in downtown Johannesburg. It's co-ed – mixed boys and girls. Many of the children there are very deprived and many of them have been affected by the AIDS epidemic. Many live in the townships. Yet the standard at the school is extraordinarily high.'

I felt myself warming to the idea. It was a good one, and I could see it working, but, while I'm the last person in the world to put difficulties in the way of good ideas, I felt concerned about doing the right thing. We discussed how it might be for these young people, uprooting them from their familiar environment and putting them somewhere as extraordinarily privileged as an English public school. In the end it was the quality and character of the children themselves that put my initial doubts entirely to rest. South Africans are strong and resourceful. All they need to flourish are the opportunities that most of us take for granted.

By the end of Mike's trip to South Africa we had ironed out the basis for such an undertaking. He generously offered to contribute the entire fees for five pupils, and the fees for another two years' worth of pupils; I agreed to cover the overheads, such as airfares back and forth for school terms and holidays. Later, Stowe itself agreed to chip in with a bursary for one child each year, leaving Mike with the job of funding four. It took less than nine months to set up the entire project.

After the initial group of students had settled down at Stowe, Mike managed to get me to actually make that visit to my old school that I had reluctantly agreed to back at Ulusaba. Afterwards, I said I wondered what had kept me away for so long. On my arrival I was presented with a folder that I was terrified to learn contained my school records. In a lengthy report, I instructed the then headmaster, R. Q. Drayson, in no uncertain terms just how I felt he should have been running the school. I covered many areas, from the menu to changing the way we ate (from formal tables to a cafeteria-style diner) and so on. Boldly, I said money would be saved by my plan and this could be put towards my next proposals. I found this both funny and relevant – because today I am still looking for ways to save money. When you consider that schools, whether private or state, are run as businesses, it all becomes crystal-clear to me that I haven't changed at all. I always was an entrepreneur.

One thing in the Stowe folder that did move me deeply was a letter written and signed by my dad, Ted, in his firm and elegant hand. At prep school I'd not done too well and it was doubted that I'd pass the entrance exam to get into public school. I had to go to a crammer to bring me up to scratch. My father decided against the school I was down for and looked around with great care for a school that would understand and nurture me. Stowe was suggested, and Mum and Dad went along to inspect it. They really did love me and had my concerns at heart. I knew that, of course, but this letter brought it home to me:

30.4.64

Dear Mr Drayson,

We were very impressed by all we saw and heard on our recent visit to Stowe and agree with young Richard who is quite decided that it is the school for him!

If I may therefore accept your offer of a firm place (subject to his Common Entrance papers) I will tell Mr Milligan that we are making Stowe our first choice.

Yours sincerely
Edward J. Branson

Another thing that was in the file was a number of letters from Mr Drayson in support of my idea to start a magazine. He had typed out several letters, introducing me to useful people. One letter read: 'I think you will probably have heard from Richard Branson, a 16-year-old in Cobham House, who is a budding magazine editor! He has spent hours and hours on this project of his, and undoubtedly has achieved something fairly substantial in the way of preparation for his undertaking. I have spent literally hours trying to help by talking with him and introducing him to various people. There is, however, as I have warned him all along, the fact that at his age he cannot really possibly cope with organisation of such a magazine and with all the financial commitment involved ...'

In another, dear old Mr Drayson wrote: 'I have a 16-year-old boy here ... this boy, whose name is Richard Branson, is editing a new national magazine for students throughout the British Isles. He has already approached many well-known personalities and has received articles from the following: John Le Carré, Vanessa Redgrave, Col. Henriques, Lord Russell, Yehudi Menuhin, Paul Ferris and Julie Felix amongst others ...'

What's quite striking about these old letters is that they express exactly the same thing I would tell a budding entrepreneur today: discuss your plans, talk them through with a mentor, achieve 'something fairly substantial in the way of preparation' – then ignore the naysayers if you really feel you have something good to offer and have the financials worked out – and *just do it!* I did. The letters from my headmaster were written towards the end of 1966. During the Christmas holidays I had made up my mind to leave school and get going. I'm amazed by my self assurance, even though it's the same confidence that has carried me through life, and which I press upon all entrepreneurs and, indeed, everybody, who asks for my advice. A month later, in January 1967, I carefully composed a leaving letter to Mr Drayson: '... The fact that I am asking to leave may well sound gutless and inexcusable, after all you and Stowe have given me. I fully appreciate and am extremely grateful to you for *everything* you have done. ... By leaving this summer I feel I can give more to Stowe and Britain ...' I filled a few more pages with my reasons and then wrote: 'I feel that it is here that I can best repay Stowe for all that it has given me. By giving a platform to students and others, we aim to spark off enthusiasm and a new drive in Britain, beginning with its young.'

This was food for thought. In fact, there was quite a revolution taking place all over the world in the 1960s and 1970s and it was led by the young. In spring 1969, I wrote an editorial in an issue of *Student*: 'The views of any person must be tolerated, not only because some of them may, for all we know, be on the right track, but because it is only through the conflict of opinion that such words as knowledge or wisdom can have any meaning. For however depressing are the setbacks suffered in conflict, they are infinitely better than the sterile silence of death that follows when people are stifled and silenced.'

I believe that the same could be said today. Young people are demanding change; they know we can't continue as we are. They really are saying *screw business as usual* in all directions. They want peace, they want a cleaned up world. They want to inherit the earth, not a desert. There is an eagerness and an energy, a clear vision in young people that is so powerful that, if not tapped and supported by the community to point it in the right direction, can become counterproductive and destructive, as we saw in the recent (2011) riots in London. Every young person is entitled to have a fair start in life – and, when they don't, it's up to those with good fortune to see what they can do to help out. I glanced up from reading those old documents at the boys and girls on the steps looking expectantly towards me – at the smiling faces of the five South African Branson Scholars, who were starting their own journey in life – and I felt very cheered. This was the new generation and in them I could see the future.

I first met Mark Christophers when he came to one of our Fast Track 100 dinners. He described how he had been working in the City as a venture capitalist when he got a call from two close friends. They'd grown up together in the same small town in Cornwall and shared a passion for snowboarding. With their father Ken, the brothers Gavin and Arron Cocking had started a Cornish pasty company with the modest capital of £2,000 and initially slept in the basement to save overheads. They expanded to five shops, all in profit, proving that the concept was good, but with cash flow pressures and no external funding, they were forced to dispose of all but one outlet. They then asked if Mark, with his City expertise, was interested in investing and working with them on developing a new pasty business. Mark went back home to Cornwall to work with them on a new business plan. He thought the idea of a genuine Cornish pasty company based in Cornwall and run by Cornish people was worth another go and he agreed to invest £40,000. The brothers' former girlfriends, sisters Victoria and Sarah Barber, with whom they were still on good terms, chipped in £5,000 each and, with a solid business plan drawn up by Mark, they set to work. Because they were all friends and had surfing and snowboarding in common, and had bags of energy and a sense of fun, they worked and played hard together. Branding the company was important; they named it the West Cornwall Pasty Co. It gave it an identity as a good regional brand with a solid British tradition behind it.

They opened their first shop in 1998 and rapidly expanded until they had shops throughout England and Scotland. Mark continued working in London, but he was convinced that, when a small business is growing, keeping everyone happy, from staff to suppliers, is the key to success, and part of their business plan was that one of the directors would telephone the shop managers every day to check in, partly to iron out any problems before they could escalate but also because they believed in keeping in touch. 'It was a family business and people are very important. We wanted that ethos to continue as the company grew.' They started a company magazine so that the staff could feel like part of a family. They also established very good relationships with their suppliers. It wasn't just about getting the best price; it was also about loyalty. If the suppliers felt valued, then they would go the extra mile for the company.

This all chimed with me as, when I was Chief Executive of a company, I'd make sure I wrote to all our staff once a month, keeping them in touch with what was going on and always making sure I thanked them. My letter would cover everything, from large strategic decisions to small things that affected a particular group at the company. I would always give my personal address to enable people to contact me. In that way I could jump on issues or suggestions quickly. Here's just one of those letters that I sent out many years ago to Virgin Atlantic's cabin crew:

Dear All,

I know I'm a little late but many congratulations! For Virgin Atlantic to once again be on top of the world with awards for best airline, best business class, best transatlantic, best food, best wine, best entertainment and best ground staff is incredible enough. For cabin crew to beat 125 other airlines and only to be pipped to the post by Singapore Airlines crew in a year with all the extra pressure you've had to contend with is remarkable.

All this has resulted in us having a good year at the airline so we've decided to celebrate by relaxing on one or two areas where we perhaps squeezed a little too hard in the depths of the recession. More on that next month.

On an immediate basis, we've decided to celebrate by having another two weekends of parties at my home. We'll try to roster you so that as many of you can make it as possible. Sundays will be more for families with kids. Saturdays more for those without. For those coming Saturdays, bring a tent so you don't have to worry about how much you drink. There will be great bands, bonfires, fireworks, dancing, the lot.

We delivered a bombshell to some of you last week with the news that we were going to be the first airline to introduce non smoking. We've had so many complaints from non smokers that we decided to bite the bullet and have completely smoke-free planes. Personally I think other airlines will copy us in time. I do think it will help those of you who smoke give up. I know it's easier said than done having given up for the third time myself six months ago. I seem to have finally cracked it but my other vices seem to be worse since! I do hope you all cope okay. At least the non smokers amongst you will be very happy. More about that next month too.

We're also planning to be the first airline to introduce seat back videos in all our seats. More about that next time.

I had hoped to announce a number of new routes to you today but I'm afraid the Heathrow scheduling committee gave us very little in the way of slots. We're still battling with them.

I do hope you all like the new hotel we put you in in central New York. If you have any problems with it drop me a line at my home address. Likewise, if there is anything you don't like about the new staff travel policy.

Anyway, once again a thousand congratulations!

All the best,
Richard

The West Cornwall Pasty Co grew rapidly and suddenly the surfing days Gavin and Arron had loved so much seemed few and far between. Eventually, they wanted to move abroad, so when they got the offer of a management buyout they accepted. Mark's original £40,000 investment yielded him a very healthy return when the business was eventually sold in 2007 for over £30 million.

After hearing Mark's story at a Fast Track evening, I knew he was of the right calibre to advise the Branson Centre entrepreneurs. Luckily, he wanted to go to Africa with us to see what he could do to help and kindly bid at one of our auctions to make such a trip. I'm sure he wondered what he was doing when he ended up with me at the Branson Centre in Johannesburg. In at the deep end, it was a baptism of fire but he had a great time and I think he saw very quickly what we were about. At least, he enjoyed his experience so much that a couple of years later he even returned for two months.

'I like the fact that you don't just hand out money like so many charities do,' Mark told me. 'You're hands on and come up with sustainable solutions. It's a virtuous circle.'

A virtuous circle. I liked that and made a note in the notebook I always have to hand.

After a bright start, a few of our young entrepreneurs can sometimes get stuck in a bit of a rut and need a little help to show them where they are going wrong and what can be done to kick-start them again. Mark said he was interested in working with two of them to see what he could suggest by way of improvement, based on his expertise and experience. He was a bit apprehensive because he had little experience of the micro level of these businesses and didn't want to be a hindrance; but he was very eager to do what he could to help, even in a modest way. The Virgin Unite team worked with Mark to select two small businesses that could benefit from his experience. The first was a young man who created artwork from wire and beads.

Cornelius Maluka was desolate. A self-taught bead artist, his work was amazing and much admired, but it just wasn't selling. He came from rural Mpumalanga in the Sabi Sands district where our game reserve was situated. Through Lindsay Hanekom, Pride 'n Purpose's manager, we'd mentored him into starting his bead business in the first place. He needed to sell his artwork because he was responsible for his brothers and sisters, as are so many young people in South Africa, thanks to the devastation of AIDS. Cornelius had started out selling directly to tourists who came to Ulusaba and then he put some of his lovely artworks in the small curio shop we'd established there. By the time Mark was introduced to him Cornelius had learned that the shop no longer wanted to stock his work. Now he had no outlet.

'Why have they stopped stocking your things?' Mark asked.

Cornelius looked perplexed. 'I don't know.'

'Have you asked them?'

Cornelius was alarmed. 'I didn't ask. What could I say?'

Mark was surprised when he learned that Cornelius had never even been in the shop. He was too nervous and shy. He'd never left Sabi Sands, never used the internet, and yet he was a brilliant artist.

Cornelius was almost dumbstruck when Mark took him to the shop, worried that somehow he was being offensive when Mark asked why they had dropped his work. The manager explained that she hadn't wanted to drop Cornelius, but his work took up too much space, space for which there was a lot of competition. 'Nobody wants his things,' she said bluntly. 'But it's so good,' Mark protested. Patiently, the manager explained that Cornelius made animals – such as elephants and giraffes – out of cleverly worked wire and beads. It was stunning, but simply too cumbersome for tourists to take home.

Cornelius listened intently, but remained silent. Mark had to speak for him. 'What can you sell?' he asked.

'Small, everyday objects, useful things, like coasters and table mats.'

'I can do that,' Cornelius said shyly. 'What about necklaces? Could you sell those?'

'Definitely.'

'Well, let's do it!' Mark said. 'What do you need?'

Cornelius needed more beads to start, so Mark flew him to Johannesburg. He bought forty kilos of beads and you could see Cornelius's mind working on overdrive as he planned how he could use them. Pricing was another area that Mark helped with. Cornelius hadn't allowed for a profit and sold for a very low price in the first place, often for a mere R100 that was so low that shopkeepers weren't very motivated to push his work. He gave the shop what they wanted, then expanded into making bowls, necklaces, bracelets, pens and wall hangings that are being sold for up to R1,350, and by using the internet and Skype he was able to sell to other shops and to mail order. Within two months Cornelius was employing four people, a wonderful achievement in a region in which there is so little work. Mark still keeps in touch with him on a monthly basis.

This reminded me of an encounter I once had a few years ago. One day I was visiting Ulusaba when I heard someone calling my name. 'Mr Richard' she said. It was a woman from the village, dressed in a KwaZulu gown of bright reds and yellows. 'I've heard you are a very generous man. Can you lend me money to buy a sewing machine?'

I've been asked for money hundreds of times over the last thirty years, but rarely with such directness. You've heard of the elevator pitch? This was the elephant-pool pitch. She told me she was a talented seamstress but that she needed cash to buy a sewing machine to get her business going.

'So how much do you need?'

'Three hundred dollars would be enough,' she explained. 'And, what is more, I'll repay it within three months and employ six people full-time.' The woman's determination and ambition were fantastic. So was her focus: she knew exactly what she wanted, and why. She got her $300.

And as I walked away I said to myself: That's money I'll probably never see again. I wasn't being cynical. I simply had experience of how the odds were stacked. At Ulusaba I had come to know many local people who were working on the game reserve and looking after our visitors. And believe me, they have big fears. Malaria, tuberculosis and HIV/AIDS stalk their daily lives.

Three months later I was invited back to the village to open some of the community projects supported by Virgin Unite, including crèches, orphans' homes and an AIDS-awareness clinic. When I got there, six women came up to me, and gave me a gift of the most exquisite cotton pillows and tribal clothes which they had made. And, to complete my surprise, they returned the $300.

But where was the original entrepreneurial seamstress? I asked.

'Mr Richard, she is so sorry she can't be here personally to see you. She is off to the market selling the products,' they told me.

I've thought of her often since that day: a confident, direct, intelligent woman, using a sewing machine to better her own and others' lives. If you want to meet entrepreneurs, come to Africa. It's a continent full of opportunities for the creation of wealth, enterprise and future prosperity.

The second business that Mark Christophers selected was the Gaming Zone, an internet and gaming concern, co-founded by Musa Maphongwane and Amos Mtsolongo of Soweto. It appealed to him because it seemed a great idea, one that gave more than a hundred township children a safe place to play every day and provided them with internet access. The 'arcades' were nothing more than discarded shipping containers and very easily set up. All they needed was spray-on graffiti, and some advertising on the outside and inside, screens and playstations and a row of accessible computers in order for them to be able to access the internet.

Mark liked it because it was a good mix of social and business enterprise. But the business simply wasn't expanding. Part of the problem was lack of capital.

Mark found that although the gaming business was not his background, business strategy is pretty much universal – something I have found time after time in the wide range of businesses under the Virgin umbrella. It's not a case of one size fits all, but of using the tools that work across the board and adapting those that don't. It's possible that by knowing too much a mentor can be a bit cocksure and bossy, something to be avoided! When you come across a new business in which you have no experience – as Mark did with the Gaming Zone guys and Cornelius – you have to listen more carefully. This is good for you, and you often learn new ideas and ingenious tricks of the trade.

Mark went with Musa and Amos on a tour of the arcades and instantly saw a few ways to improve things. One was to make the graffiti outside work harder. But the biggest problem he spotted was that the cash desk was right at the front, blocking the approach to what was a fairly narrow opening. This was also very off-putting to some kids. He explained that you have to sell what you have to offer, you have to show people your wares and draw them in. 'As the kids walk by, they don't see their friends playing right upfront where they can spot them, they don't hear them laughing and having a good time. They see a cash desk and an adult manager looking back at them. So make it more accessible.' The very simple expedient of siting the cash desk at the back – where, incidentally, it was also a lot safer from a hit and run robbery – and having the playstations right up front was a huge improvement. Mark also suggested incentivising the managers by offering them bonuses and building a database of their customers. During the month he was in South Africa he saw sales increase by almost 30 per cent. By the time he left, the first outlet showed an increase of 50 per cent. Needless to say, Musa and Amos were over the moon. Their plans for the future expanded rapidly. Greatly excited, they visualised having a thousand containers right across South Africa. It wasn't long before they were able to employ fifteen people.

When Mark and I spoke about it later, he said that while he could give a framework to the businesses he mentored, he couldn't dictate strategy. That had to come from the people whose business it was. Most of all, while the environment was far different from what he'd expected and was a bit of a shock, it was a good one. He had gained enormously from the experience and was looking forward to returning on future trips with Virgin Unite to help other entrepreneurs. Mark's experiences in Sabi Sands and the things he had seen were so humbling to him personally that before he left he made a ten-year promise to support one of our HIV positive orphan's private medical bills. It's seeing this warm, human response that moves me deeply. To me, quiet heroes like Mark, Mike, Taddy and all the wonderful Branson Centre entrepreneurs learning from each other and using entrepreneurial skills to create jobs is a shining example of one of the most important things we can do to reinvent the world to lift people out of poverty and enrich each other's lives. And importantly all these heart-warming success stories always remind me that you invariably end up getting back much more than you ever put in!

As we are seeing with the Branson Centre, entrepreneur-ship in its own right can change the world through simple, straightforward job creation. On top of that, there is an exciting new breed of entrepreneurs emerging who are using the power of entrepreneurship to start businesses that not only create jobs, but that also help solve social and environ-mental issues. We will explore some of the great new frontiers later, but for now I want to celebrate a few entrepreneurs who are reinventing how we think about entire industries and re-engineering what is generally known as 'charity'.

In the late summer of 2006, former US Vice President Al Gore came to breakfast at my home in London – a house I have since sold when I came to the conclusion that I didn't need such a large base in London – in order to give Will Whitehorn, Jean Oelwang and myself his remarkable presen-tation on climate change. His initial ideas on climate change would later lead to the making of the film *An Inconvenient Truth,* in which Gore expressed his conviction that we are blindly walking headlong into what could be a global disaster. The movie would become a huge influence on millions of people around the world. So I was keenly aware of the power of film when, shortly after that breakfast with

Al, I met Jeff Skoll, who was turning the film industry upside down to see how it could play a larger role in driving change in the world.

I already knew something of Jeff Skoll's background – that he had been the first employee and first president of eBay and had founded the Skoll Foundation, the largest supporter of social entrepreneurship in the world – but I was less aware that he had set up Participant Media to get behind social change and had been instrumental in making *An Inconvenient Truth*. Jeff said, 'I first saw Al do his slideshow presentation on global warming in May of 2005. I met him afterwards and suggested we turn it into a film.' Participant then went on to distribute it. Neither of them expected the film to do anything more than maybe get a screening on PBS, the American public television network, but gaining wide distribution and theatre outlets through Participant made a huge difference to getting Al's message out. Participant also distributed or fully funded and produced a host of other films such as *Charlie Wilson's War*, *Countdown to Zero* and *Waiting for Superman*.

All these films had one thing in common: they had a message which sought to encourage people to do good and to drive change, and Jeff even set up an organisation called Take Part that helped people take action. When I met Jeff I laughingly said that Participant based its entire business model on telling inconvenient truths and Jeff – a pretty shy guy – said he hoped so. Even inconvenient truths can make popular and successful films, as Jeff found. In fact, we had a great deal in common. I had just pledged a significant amount from the Group's share of the future profits of our transport companies to invest in renewable energy which hopefully could have amounted to up to $3 billion at that time – because I believed that these investments could make a difference. Jeff felt the same. He wasn't looking to make money from Participant. Many business people are driven to make money, but in Jeff's case he put the message he was delivering above profit. What he hadn't anticipated was that his movies would make money – quite a lot of money in fact – simply by doing the right thing. One of Capitalism 24902's founding premises: doing good is good for your business.

I've always been curious about people regardless of their background. However, people who achieve a great deal can be good role models, so it's worth telling Jeff's story as he told it to me over the five years I've known him.

When Jeff was young, his family used to spend summers camping in upstate New York. There was little to do, so he spent much of his time reading. By the time he was a young teenager, he had formulated a view that the world in the future might be a scary place, with terrible new weapons, disease, and insufficient resources to go around. He decided that he wanted to tell stories that would get people interested in the issues of the world, and motivate them to take action.

At the same time, he realised that telling stories about important issues might not be the best way for him to make a living, so he resolved to become financially independent first. That led him down an entrepreneurial path. He started a systems engineering business, then a computer rental business in Toronto in the late eighties. The rentals company was called Micros on the Move, which unfortunately was aptly named because people kept stealing the computers! He realised that he needed to go to business school if he wanted to run a business.

While Jeff was at Stanford Business School, he became friends with Pierre Omidyar, and, soon after he graduated in 1995, Pierre pitched Jeff the idea for a person-to-person website with an auction format. By then, Jeff was working for a big newspaper company and it struck him that theoretically newspapers should be jumping on this kind of thing given that they owned classified advertising. But after a number of meetings with the newspaper heads, it became clear to Jeff that newspapers were not about to put classified ads online because they were a cash cow that they didn't want to mess around with. In 1996, Pierre and Jeff left their respective jobs to work on Pierre's idea full time. That company became eBay and two years later it became a public company.

All of a sudden, Jeff went from living off his credit cards and sharing a house with five guys to having a rapidly growing fortune in the bank. It was unreal in many ways. Jeff didn't feel any different; he was still the same person. The money didn't seem real either. He began to think about how to share this blessing with the world. He spoke to John Gardner, the architect of the Great Society programmes under US President Lyndon Johnson in the 1960s, asking him, 'What am I going to do with all this money?' John told him, 'Bet on good people doing good things.'

This led to Jeff setting up the Skoll Foundation. Many of the social entrepreneurs it supports, including Muhammad Yunus, Ann Cotton, Paul Farmer, Victoria Hale, Wendy Kopp and Taddy Blecher have gone on to make a huge impact in society.

By the early 2000s, Jeff had more time and he revisited his dream as a kid to tell stories that would change the world. He thought about the movies that had inspired him, 'Films like *Gandhi* and *Schindler's List*'. He wondered, *Who is there now making those kinds of films today?*

In 2003 he began making regular visits to Los Angeles to engage with people in the movie business to see if there might be a way of using film to tell the sort of meaningful stories he had in mind. He discovered there wasn't a specific company that was focused on the public interest – everyone he talked to, from actors to agents, lawyers to business leaders, all wanted to make movies about subjects that had personal meaning for them, but not unnaturally the Hollywood system was skewed towards films that were safer from a financial perspective. Hollywood studios were investing a lot of money in action thrillers, superhero stories and sequels. This constant search for that next blockbuster left little interest for investing in independent films with any kind of social mandate. In other words, if you had a message forget it if you were looking for funding or support from Hollywood.

In the past it was easy to plead ignorance about certain world issues. If you hadn't heard of an issue or problem, then you certainly couldn't be expected to deal with it. Today, we find ourselves in the unique position whereby just about anything going on in the world can be reported at any time. The now no longer so 'new' media and communications, from cell phones to the internet, have brought the world closer together and have made 'full information' readily available to all. When the earthquake struck Haiti in 2010, the world was quick to know about the disaster and governments and aid agencies were able to mobilise fairly quickly, especially compared to other disasters in the past. However, modern communications alone are not necessarily enough to mobilise people. For example, the floods in Pakistan in 2010 that displaced twenty million people did not prompt much action from the international community although the event was widely reported. The big studios just wanted to entertain because they thought that was all its audience was interested in, and bad news didn't sell tickets.

Jeff founded Participant Media in 2004 and in 2005 their first slate of movies was released – *North Country*, *Syriana*, *Murderball* and *Good Night and Good Luck* – collectively gaining eleven Oscar nominations. Each film had an advocacy and activism programme built around it, so that not only would people talk about important issues, but they could look further and discuss issues through Participant's online social action network and its partners in the social sector. *North Country*, starring Charlize Theron, for example, helped influence the successful renewal of the Violence Against Women Act in the US.

Jeff is justifiably proud that his company has carved out a unique niche in the film industry, just what he dreamed about as a kid – to tell stories that would get people interested in the burning issues in the world and incite them to take action. As an example of how new media can make a difference, Participant conducted a social action campaign for the movie *The Cove*, about the mass slaughter of dolphins in Japan. At the end of the movie, they inserted a short code 'text "dolphin" to 77177' for people to send a text message from their cell phones. Once the code is sent, some information is returned to the phone, with a website address and the opportunity to sign a petition. To date, almost two million people have signed the petition and the advocacy work has led to a slowdown and at times even a cessation of dolphin hunting in Japan.

Whenever social change is being tackled there is inevitably opposition from those who would like to maintain the status quo. This was certainly the case when Participant released *An Inconvenient Truth*, where entrenched interests in the oil and coal lobbies rallied furiously to debunk the movie and its message about climate change. When they then released *Fast Food Nation*, the fast food industry ran ads to counter the movie's portrayal of them and their products. And with the release of *Waiting for Superman*, a documentary about the state of the US education system, Participant has seen significant pushback from teachers' unions. Participant's goal is to shine a light on social issues and facilitate a conversation about the problems, but in almost every case such issues have caused those entrenched interests to shuffle their feet uncomfortably. Social change is rarely easy.

All Jeff Skoll's organisations share a common vision of living in a sustainable world of peace and prosperity. They have developed an amazing issue matrix that they call 'THE PIE'. THE PIE stands for 'Tolerance and human rights', 'Health', 'Environmental sustainability', 'Peace and security', 'Institutional responsibility' and 'Economic and social equity'. Under each of these categories are subcategories, such as 'oceans', 'pollution and toxins', 'diversity of species' and so on. Where they choose to focus their efforts depends on a variety of factors, including the breadth and scope of the issue, the timing, the relevance of the organisation or project that will deal with the issue, and sometimes just being opportunistic and entrepreneurial. The Skoll Global Threats Fund, for example – a foundation that Jeff launched in 2009 to address major issues such as climate change, unrest in the Middle East, proliferation of nuclear weapons, pandemics and water – very early in its life played a role in accelerating deployment of a vaccine for swine flu. They worried that traditional producers of injectable vaccine, which took a longer time to develop, would see their stocks swallowed up by orders from the developed world leaving the poorest countries most vulnerable. As it turned out, Skoll's team joined other foundations in offering to place a large order for a nasal 'mist' or 'drops' vaccine, which is usually used only for children but which could be made ready months before the traditional injectable vaccine could be available. Sometimes it is just the offer of a large order that stimulates production, as in this case, and that creativity helped catalyze earlier availability of vaccine.

I know from personal experience that many of the harder and more altruistic goals I have set myself are very difficult to achieve and will play out over time. Good things and worthwhile things aren't always quick or easy to achieve. In the same way, Jeff's philosophy is that the vision of a sustainable world of peace and prosperity is a long-term goal. It is not something that can really fully be realised anytime soon. But, working together, all his organisations are trying to move things along. For example, the Skoll Global Threats Fund is acting as a consultant on the Participant Media film *Contagion*, a film about a pandemic made with Warner Bros. Participant almost always includes social entrepreneurs from the Skoll Foundation in their social action campaigns around the movies. Their financial organisation, the Capricorn Investment Group, invests in companies like Tesla or Nanosolar that are viable businesses with a social mission. Together, all these organisations combine to maximise their contribution to social change. It would be what the Japanese might call a 'keiretsu', a set of companies very much like the Virgin Group, with interlocking business relationships and shareholding, but in this case a 'social change keiretsu'.

Jeff and I share the belief that people are basically good

and, if you can only give them the opportunity to do the right thing, they generally will. This applies to business as well. One of the more devastating theories of the 1970s was that no matter what it took to achieve it, the primary purpose of business was to maximise value for its shareholders. This principle has led to a variety of social ills where businesses discard employees (at the drop of a hat), pollute our air and waters, or create short-term gains that are unsustainable. It is important for people in business to recognise that long-term shareholder value is more likely to be created by companies that value their employees, act as good environmental stewards and think long term in general. Jeff has proved that by making films that make a difference and entertain people you can also build a solid business. Through the 'keiretsu' he created he has also reinvented the way we look at issues and shown that, by connecting his business interests with his desire to change the world, all his initiatives have thrived and made a difference to millions of people's lives.

I'm thrilled and proud to be able to report that my son, Sam, is following in Jeff's footsteps. His passion to do something that will make a difference has grown over the years and so he has decided to start up his own company. 'Dad, for my production company I want to educate people on important topics through the medium of film in an entertaining way. I want to tell stories that demand to be told,' Sam explained earnestly to me. 'That's the plan, but I realise that a small new company has to take on work when offered. However, I'll try to make sure we only accept ethical commissions. Our aim will be to be selective.' That made sound sense to me and I watched as Sam's ideas evolved over the next two years.

In 2009 he named his company Current Sponge, which reflected his business philosophy of soaking up new and current ideas and sharing them with a wider audience via television and film. Ultimately, Sam wants to make what he calls his passion projects: documentaries that educate and change people's mindsets on current issues. Films that are thought-provoking or create debate – a little bit in the same way as *An Inconvenient Truth* sparked debate on climate change. But he doesn't want to lecture or preach to people on how to live their lives – he just wants to put forward a cogent argument and let people make up their own minds. Some day, too, he dreams of making movies with impact – very much like the ones that Jeff Skoll makes through Participant. As I write this, Sam is working on a feature film called *Taboo* which calls for an overhaul of international drugs policy.

Through my work with Virgin Unite I have been blessed with the opportunity to meet some quite extraordinary people from all over the world. I wanted to share with you an inspiring story about one such entrepreneur who is reinventing how poor people get energy, and he is creating jobs at the same time.

Gyanesh Pandey was introduced to us by Jacqueline Novogratz, the visionary founder of Acumen Fund. Several years ago, Gyanesh came to the conclusion that it was unacceptable that over 1.4 billion people in the world have no access to electricity. Four hundred million of those people live in his homeland, India, and eighty million of them in one of India's poorest states, Bihar. This lack of power not only slows down economic growth, it also causes significant health problems as people burn fuel in a very small space for cooking and light.

Gyanesh and a partner founded Husk Power, an innovative company that is delivering eco-friendly, reliable electricity to families for only $2 per month. They did this by going out and listening to people in communities throughout Bihar and working out how they could turn something that was discarded as waste into something valuable and reusable. They generate electricity using rice husks, a waste product from rice manufacturing in the region. Even as optimistic entrepreneurs, they were also very practical and realised that the best way to deliver this service would be to operate at a village level. This brilliantly simple idea has also served as a platform for the creation of jobs.

Today Husk has installed sixty-five micro-generation units run by three hundred people in rural India giving power to more than 30,000 households. By 2014, Gyanesh and his team want to reach one million homes and create 10,000 jobs. I suppose this could be categorised as a truly rubbish solution!

Web: virginunite.com/screwbusinessasusual
Twitter: @virginunite #sbau
Facebook: Facebook.com/VirginUnite

3 If You've Got It – Use It!

'For those who think business exists to make a profit, I suggest they think again. Business makes a profit to exist. Surely it must exist for some higher, nobler purpose than that' – Ray Anderson, founder of Interface Inc.

Several years ago I had the great pleasure of meeting Ray Anderson, the founder of Interface Inc. While I was working on this book, Ray sadly lost his long struggle with cancer. It seems appropriate, therefore, to open this chapter with a quote from him: he was one of the few leaders who truly turned his company upside down and put doing good at its very core – and (I hope you are detecting a recurrent theme here) once again proved that it was good for his business. Ray had the vision to realise the urgency of the environmental and poverty challenges we have been facing for many decades and the part that business has played in continuing to exacerbate those issues. He knew that a critical part of the solution had to be transforming existing businesses so that they could use all they had for a purpose other than just generating profits for shareholders.

In this chapter we are going to go on a journey to celebrate some of the companies that are already going down this path of change.

The phrase 'Dr Yes' was coined for me by the team at Virgin. As many Virgin staffers seem to know, when I get hold of an idea and it looks good, I want to do it now! David Tait, who was one of the people who helped make Virgin Atlantic a success once described me as 'the ultimate don't confuse me with the facts person'. Essentially I'm not into protocol or meetings for the sake of meetings and I'm definitely not into looking for ways *not* to do something. 'Screw it, let's do it' is a personal mantra that really kind of says it all. So when I was chatting to Professor Muhammad Yunus about how he found himself in a 'screw it, let's do it' moment, I was intrigued.

This magical moment occurred in October 2005, when he was due to fly to France to deliver a lecture and receive an honorary professorship at HEC, one of the leading business schools in Europe. Muhammad was renowned for the invention, some years earlier, of the principle of microfinance. It had come about by chance. Born into a large family in Bangladesh, one of the world's poorest countries, he had scraped together a good education – with difficulty, since his mother had died when he was twelve and his father a jeweller, wasn't well off. Eventually, he won a US Fulbright Scholarship and gained his PhD at Vanderbilt University in Nashville, Tennessee. He stayed on in the US at Middle Tennessee State University as a professor of economics. He returned to Bangladesh in 1972. In the aftermath of the Bangladesh famine of 1974, he met a group of very poor village women who made bamboo furniture to help provide for their families. They complained that they found it hard to buy bamboo because they had no spare cash, and no banks or reputable moneylenders were willing to lend to people with no property and no expectations. On the spur of the moment, Muhammad pulled some money out of his trouser pocket – $27 – and distributed it to forty-two families so they could buy bamboo. That sum of $27 became the stuff of legend. To his astonishment, the women later repaid it.

Deeply touched by their integrity, Muhammad looked into how he could help them and similar groups and discovered a very real need for cash flow. These women were often the sole bread winners in their families and, while willing to work, they just didn't have the capital to get started and then fund any kind of enterprises. Moneylenders were more a part of the problem than the solution – often charging usurious interest rates of as much as 2,000 per cent.

By turning it into a university research project, Muhammad managed to find a way of setting up a project specifically for the purpose of lending small sums of money to these women. He called the system microfinance and named it Grameen (meaning 'village bank' in Bengali): a legend was born. Some $10.89 billion in tiny sums has been lent to borrowers since the bank's inception and the repayment rate is 96.89 per cent, a remarkable figure compared with the default rates of borrowers in other parts of the world. To put it into even greater perspective, there are no written contracts between Grameen Bank and its borrowers; the system is based entirely on trust. Grameen's investment account – the amount of money it lends – is partly built from savings accounts. Borrowers are expected to save small amounts as a kind of insurance against contingencies. In a country in which few women may take out loans from large commercial banks, 97 per cent of the Grameen Bank's borrowers are village women.

This was the background to Muhammad's trip to France that October in 2005. Shortly before his departure, he received the following message from the office of Franck Riboud, CEO of international yoghurt manufacturers Danone: '*M. Riboud has heard about the work of Professor Yunus in Bangladesh, and he would like very much to meet him. Since he will be travelling to Deauville shortly, would it be possible for him to have lunch with M. Riboud in Paris?*'

Professor Yunus was always curious when a leading entrepreneur wanted to meet him, especially if it somehow might help him in his goal of eliminating global poverty. He agreed to the lunch date provided it could be fitted around his lectures. On 12 October, Yunus walked into a private room at La Fontaine Gaillon, a smart new restaurant, and shook hands with Franck Riboud. Seated at the long table were seven other high-level officers of Danone, some of whom were board members and others senior executives. After an excellent lunch, Monsieur Riboud invited Professor Yunus to tell them about his work. His presentation concluded with the words: 'By the end of next year, we hope to announce at the Microcredit Global Summit that one hundred million poor people around the world have been the beneficiaries of microcredit.' He then explained how the initial small loans to help fund small enterprises had expanded to help poor people pay for a range of things, from housing to education. 'In fact, we now lend money to beggars.'

'Beggars?' Monsieur Riboud raised an eyebrow. 'How do they pay the bank back?'

'They use the money in an entrepreneurial way to set themselves up in business. It doesn't matter how small or basic it is, it's a start. They grow and before long they've paid for a room, they're no longer living in the street. They've become small businessmen and women.' He explained he believed that poverty is caused by failure at the conceptual level, rather than any lack of capability on the part of people. 'I firmly believe that we can create a poverty-free world if we collectively believe in it. In a poverty-free world, the only place you would be able to see poverty is in the poverty museums.'

The audience was impressed. Yunus then asked Monsieur Riboud to tell him why he had invited him to lunch.

Monsieur Riboud gave a brief rundown of the company. Danone was founded in 1919, producing yoghurt which was sold in chemists to treat intestinal disorders. It remained small and specialised. Other kinds of food businesses were developed and the company expanded. When Franck inherited the chairmanship from his father, Antoine, in 1994, he set about focusing the business's core value on manufacturing wholesome, healthy food – Danone yoghurt – and dispensed with everything else that he thought wasn't pulling its weight.

He was mindful of a landmark speech his father had once made at a conference. Antoine Riboud had said: 'There will not be sustainable economic value creation if there is no personal development and human value creation at the same time.' At times, though, when Franck inherited the business he thought the board was losing its way. It put pure profit above sustainability and doing good.

Professor Yunus began to understand why the meeting had been called.

Franck continued. He explained that Danone yoghurt was an important source of food in many parts of the world, including many developing countries. 'We don't only want to sell our products to the well-off people in those countries. We would like to find ways to help feed the poor. We hope you can help us find a way to do this.'

Professor Yunus immediately grasped the amazing opportunity he was being offered. Usually he thought long and hard about ideas and new concepts but, just as he had spontaneously pulled out that $27 from his pocket to help the village women thirty years earlier – thus launching the revolutionary concept of microfinance – now he grabbed this opportunity. He had no idea what Franck Riboud wanted to do, or how far he might go, but Professor Yunus was no mug. In a flash over that lunch table in a Paris restaurant he created the model they would follow and an entirely new entity: Grameen Danone.

He proposed that, between them, Grameen and Danone could develop a food – more than likely yoghurt – that could be packed full of extra nutrients and sold door to door by the good ladies of Bangladesh for pennies, a cupful at a time. They would recover the cost and the hungry, especially children, would be nourished. He thought this might be the start of something – the basis for weeks, maybe years, of discussions. It would probably fizzle out, as so many spontaneous ideas did. Much to his astonishment, however, Franck Riboud simply said: 'Let's do it.' They shook on the deal.

Yunus was confused. Had Riboud understood what he meant? That Danone would be committed to building a huge new organisation that would need funding to the tune of a million euros? An organisation that would make no profit, but would use the core strengths of Danone? Now it was his turn to backtrack. He started reiterating his words and elaborating on the detail, as if to make sure that Riboud really had understood what he'd just agreed to. Riboud stood up.

'Professor Yunus, did you not say that when you lent money to your ladies it was secured on a handshake? No contract?'

The professor nodded.

'Well, then, we shook hands. We have a deal. I hope you're not trying to backtrack ...'

As Muhammad told me this story, I was lapping it up. Franck Riboud was a man after my own heart. 'And did you do it?'

I already knew that they had, because Grameen Danone is an existing business, one that is making waves as a model of social entrepreneurship, but I wanted to hear the detail. *How* it was achieved.

Muhammad said that he still couldn't believe it had been that easy. Danone was a major international corporation, worth some $16 billion, with a heavyweight board and shareholders who only understood one word: *profit*. How would Franck Riboud manage to pull it off and convince them that they could sell one of their products to millions of poor people and not be concerned about the sacred cow of profit?

Yunus had another appointment near Paris that afternoon. On the way to it after lunch he sent Franck a quick email, what he described as the 'get out' clause. In essence his email said: 'Are you sure about this?'

'I'm very sure,' Monsieur Riboud emailed back. 'We shook hands. The deal is final. Let's do it.'

He put the enterprise not just into motion but into rocket fuel-propelled turbo drive. That very afternoon, Professor Yunus received a telephone call from the Shanghai office of Emmanuel Faber, the head of Danone's operations in Asia. He was thrilled about the project, looked forward to meeting Professor Yunus and discussing it, and he added that he was fully committed on a personal level to social business and asked Yunus to send him his initial ideas on the proposed enterprise so that they could start to drive things forward immediately. He added, 'I'm only forty years old. Still young enough to think I can change the world!'

'I couldn't believe how fast they were moving!' Muhammad said to me as he described the breakneck pace at which things were moving. 'I was still stuck in France, fulfilling speaking obligations; while, metaphorically speaking, all hell was breaking loose in Asia. Teams were flying in to set the ball in motion, emails and faxes were flying back and forth. It was incredible.

'We created something new under the sun: the world's very first consciously designed multinational social business.'

'Business as usual' went out of the window for this ground-breaking new concept. Instead of huge factories in the usual Danone international model, they designed a new small model to suit Bangladesh's small-scale environment, where roads were poor and power supplies so erratic they couldn't depend on large-scale refrigeration. Yoghurt goes bad quickly if not cooled down fast and kept chilled, so everything had to be small and with a rapid turnover. Engineers and architects who initially scoffed that it was physically impossible, not to say wasteful and extravagant, to set up boutique factories were soon swept along and recognising a new zest for life as they designed the perfect buildings. What was particularly exciting about the enterprise was that a great deal of milk was needed – and over the years many of the Grameen ladies had already used their loans to buy a few cows. Selling milk door to door was something they knew about so selling fresh yoghurt wouldn't be that different. Turnover would be quick and on such a small scale the yoghurt would stay fresh even in temperatures of a hundred degrees and more.

They would make 10 per cent commission. In order to make the yoghurt more appealing to a culture that likes very sweet drinks and desserts, and to disguise the taste of the added vitamins, a little molasses and some cane sugar was added – both of which just happen to be locally produced and grown. The yoghurt was named Shokti Doi – which means as 'strong as a lion' – with a motif of a cartoon lion that appealed to children, and it was sold for €0.06 a cup. At that price, even the poorest could afford to buy it regularly. This might enable them to buy a few more cows, a little more land, and earn more money for their families. More children would be educated, more houses would be built, impoverished people would move up a notch or two in the social scale. At the moment the yoghurt is sold in disposable plastic cups, however future entrepreneurial plans involve ongoing research to create an edible cup. Developing a cup made from rice that can be eaten along with the yoghurt – much like an ice-cream cone – would be both ecological and a nutritional bonus.

Exactly a year later, in October 2006, Grameen Danone was up and running. Millions of people were receiving additional nutrition at minimal cost, working women were making more money and in Sweden the Nobel Prize Committee was taking note. In October 2006, Muhammad Yunus and Grameen Bank jointly received the Nobel Peace Prize. In his acceptance speech, Professor Yunus said: 'To me, poor people are like bonsai trees. When you plant the best seed of the tallest tree in a flower pot you get a replica of the tallest tree, only inches tall. There is nothing wrong with the seed you planted; only the soil base that is too inadequate. Poor people are bonsai people. There is nothing wrong in their seeds. Simply, society never gave them the base to grow on. All it needs to get poor people out of poverty is for us to create an enabling environment for them. Once the poor can unleash their energy and creativity, poverty will disappear very quickly.' There are many aspects of Grameen Danone that could be applied in other ways to existing businesses to help drive change for the better in the Capitalism 24902 model. Not every company has $16 billion behind it, as Danone has, but even a small or a medium-size company could look at different ways to use its resources to be proactive in some way and to support the communities and environments in which they operate. Many have already done so. There are some fantastic examples out there of businesses that are truly using all they've got to make change happen in the world – from their people to their products and services to their suppliers.

* * *

The quest for world peace is something else about which I am passionate, for, while conflict rages in a country, businesses can't thrive, people can't grow healthily and it is almost impossible for anyone to lift the country out of poverty. We started The Elders some years ago both to help stop conflict arising and to help resolve it where it had begun. Some businesses have been brave enough to help create opportunities in post-conflict countries.

Political uncertainty is perhaps no greater anywhere than in Southern Sudan, a newly formed country that has emerged from decades of conflict and civil war and gained independence on 9 July 2011. I was fortunate to have travelled to southern Sudan in 2007 with members of The Elders and was shocked at the state of the refugee camps. Lying in bed at night watching the cockroaches crawl over my bed and listening to the sound of gunfire, I reflected on the strength of the people we had met earlier that day and was humbled by their positive spirit in the face of such dire circumstances. Again and again, we saw how excited people in the camps were that former US President Jimmy Carter, Archbishop Desmond Tutu, Graça Machel and Lakhdar Brahimi had taken the time to come and listen to them. They clearly felt that the world had forgotten about them.

In 2009, a couple of years after my trip, I was heartened to hear that SABMiller, the global brewing and bottling giant had the guts to put everything they had into creating opportunities for people in Southern Sudan. Their first step was to invest $37 million in a state-of-the-art brewery in Juba that has created two hundred jobs and a local ownership model that provides ongoing royalties to the community. They then teamed up with Farm Africa and the African Enterprise Challenge Fund and are working with two thousand smallholder farmers to turn cassava, a tuber that is traditionally a subsistence crop, into a cash crop. The cassava will replace some of the malted barley now imported for beer-making. This initiative will also ultimately benefit more than fifteen thousand people in Southern Sudan.

But these were not the only benefits from the company committing to Southern Sudan. They've also paved the way for other investors as they have helped to establish the regulatory framework and encouraged the government to set up a ministry for investment.

Entrepreneurs all over the world are reinventing the way we do business to serve communities and protect our natural resources.

One of these business leaders, Yin Guoxin, exudes an almost hypnotic sense of humility. He is so self-effacing it is almost embarrassing. You immediately want to help him and support him in whatever way you can, and that feeling only grows as you get to know him better, despite his accomplishments. Over the last thirty years he has worked himself up from the shop-floor of a small state-owned garment factory in China to the head of the Chen Feng group of companies, which produce nearly 400 million garments a year for major brands in Europe, the US, and Japan. To grow a business this big is an amazing achievement in itself. Yin Guoxin was able to purchase the factory where he worked with a small group of associates, and now Chen Feng is a global player in the garment industry. Beyond this incredible success, what I've been really impressed by is the environmental awareness that Yin Guoxin has embedded in his business.

He was harvesting rainwater for use in his factories and recycling his waste water long before any factory I know of in

China, and before any buyer imposed those conditions. The same goes for energy consumption. He started measuring energy consumption and reducing the energy intensity of his factories early on and is now well ahead of government targets for energy reduction. These types of environmental initiatives are very sexy nowadays, but for Mr Yin and Chen Feng, this was simply the right thing to do and not worth boasting about. It therefore came as no surprise when Chen Feng became the first Chinese company to join the Fair Labor Association. My friend Auret van Heerden, the head of the Fair Labor Association, said that Mr Yin's approach to sustainability made him an ideal candidate for membership, especially because he has continually helped to promote the organisation and environmental and social responsibility in China.

If business people consistently acted in such socially and environmentally responsible ways, I firmly believe that the world would be a better and fairer place. Justice would prevail. Poor people would be helped out of poverty, business as usual would be well and truly screwed, and everyone would have the means by which they could improve their own lives without depending on charitable handouts for years on end. The great thing is that all of this will also be good for business and, ultimately, will be the only way that businesses can thrive in the future.

About six years ago I had dinner with the late C K Prahalad, who coined the expression 'the fortune at the bottom of the pyramid'. He believed that poor people all over the world wanted and deserved access to products and services but simply could not afford them. He also believed that this lack of access was keeping them in poverty. I remember him telling me stories about companies like HLL, a subsidiary of Unilever, which successfully designed new products such as soap to serve the needs of the poor and created new business processes to make their products affordable by all. They did this through innovations like the creation of local manufacturing, packaging with smaller quantities, lower-cost ingredients and local distribution.

According to the World Resources Institute, the bottom of the pyramid market in Asia and the Middle East is made up of 2.86 billion people, with a total income of $3.47 trillion. In Eastern Europe it's $458 billion; in South America it's $509 billion. In Africa it's $429 billion. That's a *five trillion dollar market*, and yet most Western business investors – investors steeped in the habits of 'business as usual' – won't touch it because it is considered too risky. The good news is that research has shown that poor people are more likely to pay back their debts, with interest. People might feel a bit squeamish about making money on the backs of the very poor – but if a loan helps the poor, if they make enough money to pay back a loan and then go on to earn a decent living, isn't it worth it? Many of the products being sold to the poor, such as HLL's soaps, also have great social benefits, in this particular case reducing diarrhoeal diseases that kill over two million children all over the world each year. Today, companies and banks are suddenly waking up to the fact that they can *ethically* do business with the very poor, make money and help people to create better lives for themselves and their families.

When I was in South Africa a few years ago, I was reminded of C K Prahalad's advice to look at viable opportunities for the poor where you least expect them, and to think about how they can often do far more good than charitable dollars in lifting people out of poverty. I thought of this opportunity immediately on meeting Nora, who would have benefited from a bank loan to set up a business that would help her structure her amazing benevolence. But she could not get a loan because, not only did she live in a tin shack, but as I saw when I met her, she spent every cent she could find on feeding the orphans in her community. In the midst of the AIDS epidemic, I was visiting small communities with my mother Eve and the Virgin Unite team to see what needed to be done to help, knowing well that any contribution, however modest, could mean the difference between life and death for people who had less than nothing.

We came across Nora in a small village some forty-five minutes outside Johannesburg. In the middle of a clearing of beaten dirt was a tiny tin shack, and seated patiently cross-legged on the earth were dozens of children who had been orphaned by AIDS, waiting to be fed. More children were slipping in from who knows where, almost like shadows, to sit in the circle alongside the others. Meanwhile, Nora was in her stifling tin shack, cooking up a storm. She had a couple of enormous pots and was stirring what appeared to be mealie porridge – what the local people called pap. It's their staple diet and very cheap. She also had some kind of vegetable stew, but no meat. Nora never had meat, but she was still able to rustle up enough nourishment as if out of nowhere to keep body and soul together for well over two hundred incredibly needy children.

Nora had dedicated her whole life to using entrepreneurial ways to support those hungry and homeless children from her community. She had taken in many of them, who slept in her crowded shack. Without Nora these young children would have starved to death.

My mum asked, 'Where does the mealie pap come from, Nora?'

She laughed her big laugh. 'Oh, it comes. I walk here and I walk there, and I return with food,' she said, sweeping out her arms to indicate the distance she covered. South Africans are tenacious. I had seen how they walk miles to get work, water, schooling and medicines. Most of us, who take so much for granted, who pop down to huge supermarkets with a wallet full of money to spend, have no idea what goes on in more than half the world. Talking to this big-hearted woman and watching her cheerfulness and warmth when she had so little herself, seeing how good she was with these homeless children, I was humbled and resolved that we had to do something. If she could feed over two hundred children every single day from thin air out of a one-room tin shack, I had little doubt what she could do if she had resources behind her.

After that visit, Virgin Unite funded Nora through a charity called Starfish to help upgrade her facilities – that is, to set up a couple of small buildings around her existing very cramped hut to provide meals and a place for the young people to go during the day and to sleep at night under cover. Starfish bought food supplies and helped Nora to create gardens for fresh vegetables. The idea was to sell or trade some of the excess vegetables for mealie and other essentials.

Telling Nora's story reminds me of a trip that Virgin Atlantic undertook with their staff and customers to Kenya a couple of years ago. Virgin Unite connected them to 'Free the Children', a wonderful not-for-profit that supports communities to set up schools, but goes well beyond that to create gardens for food, wells for water and small businesses for ongoing income for the community.

I was fortunate enough to join them on the trip and was blown away by the commitment of the people in the community, which was fully matched by the commitment of our staff and customers. Since then, Virgin Atlantic has continued to have a wonderful partnership with Free the Children.

Capitalism should help organisations like Free the Children and people like Nora. So why couldn't she borrow money to set herself up in business? She was doing the job that governments usually perform – she proved that she had entrepreneurial skills yet banks weren't willing to invest in her. It makes no sense not to invest in people like Nora who take the pressure off government. As Ralph Nader wisely observed, 'If we had justice, we wouldn't need charity.'

There are so many really interesting opportunities like this for Capitalism 24902 to bring together businesses, governments and the social sector to create brand new business delivery models that take far better care of our communities. Companies have a wonderful opportunity to reinvent their charitable giving to look at how they can help kick-start and pilot some of these new models. Using the best bits of governments, business and the social sector with new entrepreneurial approaches is a really exciting area of opportunity. Sadly, as yet there are very few foundations out there creating these new hybrid business-based models which leverage everything they have to drive change, but one exception that we've found that *is* doing some very exciting stuff and turning corporate philanthropy upside down is the Shell Foundation.

One of the areas that Chris West of the Shell Foundation has addressed is the 'missing middle' – small entrepreneurs who lack access to core business inputs as they are too big for microfinance and too small for larger financial institutions – by coming up with GroFin, a social enterprise that aims to kickstart a major engine for economic growth in the developing world. It's where philanthropy meets small business – by *screwing business as usual* and inventing a new working model to provide finance and skills where they are most needed.

At the time of writing, according to *Forbes* magazine, Shell is the second largest energy company and the fifth largest overall company in the world. The combination of vast wealth and small entrepreneurs is an unlikely one, yet Chris

West had the vision to see that Shell could harness a wider range of its assets – business thinking, functional expertise, networks and of course its brand to support the work of its foundation. GroFin is the fruit of one of Chris's earliest entrepreneurial partnerships back in 2001. The business is to Africa the logical extension of what the Grameen Bank is to Asia; whilst the Grameen Bank offers small loans, GroFin offers a combination of medium-size loans and business support to help small businesses to grow. Very few lending institutions are willing to risk these medium-size sums, yet there is a huge need for investment at that level.

Shell's aim to do more to help the very poor developed after accusations that the company wasn't giving enough back to society. Their response was to set up the Shell Foundation in 2000 with an endowment and governance structure that means, whilst funded by Shell, it isn't answerable to it. This autonomy gives it the freedom to pursue the most effective routes to achieve its charitable goals and to pilot some riskier ideas that would not fly in its parent's mainstream business. I realise that Shell (like most businesses) is not a perfect company and, like other oil companies, has had a negative environmental impact. But at least they are trying to do more to address some of the tough issues they are having to face.

Chris West's appointment as director was an inspired one. He'd never even sold a can of oil in his life. Having set up and grown a small environmental consultancy in the UK in the 1980s, he sought to apply his own experiences in Africa. But he was ahead of his time. He realised his own experiences in setting up a new venture, being underskilled, and underfinanced – were pretty much the same encountered by the kind of small entrepreneur you find throughout Africa today, struggling to get something started. Chris came to realise that entrepreneurs the world over faced the same two questions: how do I fund my growth *and* how do I develop the skills I need to succeed? Whilst in the UK you're likely to find answers, African entrepreneurs are not so lucky. Years later Chris was invited to help mould the shape of Shell's new foundation and he remembered this lesson. It's one that resonates with me too.

Chris describes his appointment as Director as 'pure luck'. In an almost serendipitous way, he says, luck rather than competence took him from the struggles of starting a business, to living in Africa, to the Shell Foundation. He was in the right place at the right time. I appreciated this candid aspect of Chris's story because many of my own opportunities have come from being in the right place at the right time. In fact, most of the most successful entrepreneurial businesses have come about by being in the right place at the right time – and seeing the opportunity and grabbing it. This is quite a different animal to what many people like to designate as 'pure luck'. I have always believed that luck is something you manufacture, it doesn't (generally) just happen. Someone who sits at home or in their office waiting for 'luck' to strike is not likely to be in the right place at the right time. Put another way, being overly cautious does not make for a good businessman or woman. You have to be bold, while not being foolish. Quickly weigh up the odds, but don't gamble is the best advice I can give to a new entrepreneur.

Chris immediately saw the potential to use his experience in the field to help start-up and growing businesses in Africa – but with the objective from the outset to do so in ways that were innovative, market-driven, scalable and sustainable – that is, financially viable. This became the foundation's mantra. He uses an interesting term for his role. With the business venture he had he was a 'social entrepreneur'; but by working to change the corporate social responsibility practice of a large corporate he became a 'social intrapreneur'. To start with, though, it took time to work out how the foundation should operate to do the most good.

I first met Chris in New York at the Clinton Global Initiative. There were quite a few people in a big room discussing how we could get more investment into business-based solutions to social and environmental issues and, at the end of my opening speech, I threw the question to the floor by asking, 'What can be done for these global challenges? Does anyone have an opinion?' Nobody wanted to be the first to speak. Let's face it, there is no easy answer to the question. Then, to Chris's horror, Jean turned to him and said, 'Chris, you've already been doing some great work in this area – why don't you kick off?' Jean had already been talking to Chris for some years about finding solutions, so she must have thought he was a good, sensible man who could voice an opinion that would open the forum and he didn't disappoint. He proved that he's a bit of a rebel by speaking a lot of sense, eschewing all jargon.

He said that he certainly didn't see the role of philanthropic organisations as being one of throwing money around, as many charities still do. Money is a sticking plaster, not a solution. People in Africa, just like anywhere else in the world, say, I want a job. In many parts of Africa there are not enough jobs. That's why there's so much poverty. How can people survive when they quite literally don't earn money and there are no social services to give them the kind of benefits we take for granted when we're unemployed? Chris is not a great fan of corporate foundations. 'I'm sick to death of receiving their self-glorifying reports, every one of which shows some smiling poor person standing beside a well. Most of these outfits have grossly underperformed. They've not made enough difference in the world, and they've had next to no influence on their parent companies. So when I agreed to join Shell's foundation, it was with the view that we didn't want to wander down the same path.'

Right from the early days Chris saw his role as adopting a business-based approach, to tackle a few big global development challenges that were relevant to the energy industry – by viewing these challenges as market failures and the poor as consumers, with choices, rather than victims. Back then few others were working like this. At first, despite being very specific about the types of things they wanted to support, they found out quite quickly that they weren't delivering nearly enough, for long enough, in ways that would make any real difference. That forced them to change their strategy. Shell felt they should be businesslike – they were business people, after all – but, rather than try and be all things to all people, they decided to offer business services to people who were trying to solve the problems they were concerned about. Again they hit the buffers. They found it was no good looking out there in the market and expecting there to be ready-made solutions that with a bit more support could really spread, grow and make a big difference. It was disappointing, but they found that it's almost impossible to expand an organisation that never sets out with an ambition to grow.

Chris says he doesn't want to knock not-for-profit outfits, because clearly they've gone into places where the regular markets fear to tread. The trouble is, not being businesses, they've never made expansion one of their objectives and sadly all of us have made the mistake as donors to encourage this type of limited thinking. Often, they're geared around being drip-fed by philanthropists and foundations, usually on a project-by-project basis. If you operate this way, the best you're ever going to be is an island of excellence. You're never going to be in a position to build the capacity that you need to make a big difference. So while they didn't use these exact words, their attitude then became 'Screw development as usual'!

Chris realised they were going to have to grow new kinds of businesses, social businesses, from the ground up. In the years that followed (and after as many failures as successes) a new model for identifying new market-based solutions, finding the right partners and helping them to scale their businesses began to emerge. Shell Foundation found that their partners needed much more than money for success – they needed support, networks and strategic guidance. They also needed patience. Chris and his team leveraged the Shell brand to secure further investment from a range of sources (for example, GroFin's investors include the International Finance Corporation, the Skoll Foundation and even some African banks) to help their ideas grow and have impact. Ideas that will be around ten or twenty years from now – businesses that address everything from sustainable transport and financing small enterprise in Africa, to tackling indoor air pollution inside tiny huts generated by wood-burning stoves by replacing them with a cleaner alternative way of cooking.

Shell's GroFin offers risk capital and business assistance to small and medium-size enterprises in Africa whose owners may lack the track record or the collateral to get a regular bank loan. Since it began in 2004, the company has built an impressive portfolio, helping enterprises tackle everything from water management to electricity supply, animal feed distribution and student housing construction. It operates in nine African and Middle Eastern countries and is expanding further into the Middle East. So far, it has secured over $260 million in funding and supported over 3,000 SMEs. Over 90,000 people have benefited as a result. As Muhammad Yunus found with Grameen, the repayment rate is good. Grameen's lending model is rather clever: they lend to individuals in a group of five borrowers, where the members collectively support each other, though each is responsible for their own loan. Peer pressure discourages members from defaulting. GroFin's individual loan system carries a default rate that is a lot better than the default rate of the average main street bank loan in the West – largely due to the extensive support their clients receive to more viable business plans before they receive funding. Small entrepreneurs in the developing world treat money with respect because often it's the difference between starvation and survival; they want to remain in business, not grab the money and run.

The bad news – and something that needs to be addressed – is that there's a limit to how far and how fast GroFin can grow. Microfinance took twenty years to reach its current level of development. Organisations need to grow faster because the need is there and pressing, much driven by the problems of climate change. No matter how successful GroFin is, it will never be able to finance all the potential start-ups and growing businesses across Africa. Chris thinks that they need to start promoting GroFin as a solution. Just as Grameen became the poster boy of microfinance, GroFin should become the template for a new kind of investment vehicle – one that's different from the loans banks provide, and less risky than private equity: *growth finance*. It's a new asset class. One of the difficulties is that collateral is a problem in a continent where land ownership is a very grey area and where property deeds simply don't exist. GroFin cuts through the usual red tape and lends on different values – such as the business itself or book orders.

Shell can make a big difference. It's big enough and powerful enough that it can drive market reform debate at a very high level. That's really important. Little islands of excellence are great, but they will not save the world. For a second, Chris says, you sit back and think, 'Another successful partnership – great!' And in the next second you're thinking, 'Bloody hell, the world needs *hundreds* of these things.'

Yes, it does. You can let the overwhelming odds defeat you, or you can see it as a challenge with a solution. This is why I say, *screw business as usual*. We have to change the rules and fix things now, not wait for another twenty years. Jean and the team from Virgin Unite have listened to Chris and learned from his honest perspective on the successes and failures they've had at the Shell Foundation. In setting up Virgin Unite we had a similar philosophy: we wanted to look at how we could use everything we have as a group of businesses to connect people to create entrepreneurial approaches to some of the tougher issues in the world. Everything is built on a core belief that businesses really can and must do better in the world to take care of people and the planet. Seven words say it all: '*Doing business like there is a tomorrow*'.

We've learned a great deal over the last seven years about what we do well, and what we don't do so well. Today Virgin Unite focuses mainly on three things: working with our three hundred businesses so that they put driving change at their very core, the incubation of new approaches to global leadership, like The Elders and the Carbon War Room, and the building of a community of people that never accepts the unacceptable. Across all our businesses, we are still learning every day about how we can do better and are fully aware that we are far from perfect. What we do try to do is listen and learn from people facing the issues, find the gaps, work with brilliant people to come up with entrepreneurial solutions and make them happen as quickly as possible. Frankly it's pretty much the same approach that we adopt when starting up any one of our businesses.

*   *   *

I've always looked on my businesses not just as money-making machines, but as adventures that can, I hope, make people better off. The older I get the more I'm inspired to make business investments that can also change the world. There is a real opportunity for businesses and foundations to look at how we can use our investment portfolios as vehicles for change in their own right. There are tremendous opportunities in this area. At the moment, the buzz word – the new phrase – in the world for this type of investment is 'impact investing'. I remember when Ben Cohen and Jerry Greenfield (of Ben & Jerry ice cream fame and both Virgin Unite Trustees) were recently on Necker where someone was presenting something about 'impact investing'. Ben immediately stopped them to ask what the hell they were talking about – making me smile because all the jargon (which can often be a nice word for BS) in this sector drives me mad too! The reality is that Ben and Jerry have actually been doing 'impact investing' long before it became fashionable. They based their business on investing in an ethical supply chain and ploughed much of their profits back into investments that would make a difference in their local communities and the world. A good reminder that many people have already been working on changing the way we do business for decades. Most of the ideas are already out there but we just need to get the right momentum behind them to make them work.

During one of the leadership gatherings on Necker, Alex Friedman, who had recently left his job as CFO at the Gates Foundation, gave an inspiring presentation about the work he was doing to shift philanthropic dollars into investments that would deliver social and environmental impact.

Alex wrote in a recent article in the *Financial Times*, 'These days, it has become something of a trend to demonise capitalists and praise philanthropists. But if we are to make true progress in tackling our most pressing social problems and live up to our moral obligation to help those in extreme poverty, these two seemingly polarised groups need to come together in fundamentally new ways. We need to stop separating investment decisions from philanthropic giving; the building and giving away of wealth should not be seen as disparate sets of skills. The world's problems cannot be solved either by unfettered markets or by limited pools of philanthropic dollars.'

At a broad level, he wrote, four steps are needed. First, foundations could carefully lend against a small portion of their assets not given away each year. Second, financial institutions have a unique opportunity to work with foundations to syndicate grant-making opportunities. Third, banks could develop a wider range of social sector finance products. Finally, governments could provide tax incentives for high quality social impact investments both nationally and internationally.

Inspired by Alex, we've been working with Virgin Unite, some large family foundations, financial institutions and the governments in the UK and the US to look at how we can help encourage financing to flow into investments that will be good for the world. We have the chance to encourage a whole new philosophy around this type of investment, one that gets people excited about meeting a need and delivering a solution – and making money at the same time. Everyone wins. In a recent article in Spear's Wealth Management Survey, economist and author Michael Green said, 'I get frustrated in the development world when people have this idea that there's giving money away, which is doing good, and there's making a profit, which is taking money away, and that just isn't true. People are just hostile to profit, and we have to change that debate.' Venture capitalist Michele Giddens agreed. 'Historically the accepted theory about investment was that you make the maximum financial return with your money and then you might take some portion of that, perhaps much later in your life, perhaps for the next generations as a foundation, and you give it away for social purpose alone, with no financial return. Over the past decade, there's been a seismic shift in people's understanding and increased belief that there is a space in the middle.'

The opportunities are not just in the emerging markets, but also in our own backyards. In the UK venture capitalists and social entrepreneurs had already identified these hybrid investments many years ago. For example, Faisel Rahman founded Fair Finance in London's poor inner city borough of Hackney in 2005. Its purpose was to offer small loans at reasonable rates to the same missing middle. Many had no credit rating so high street banks wouldn't touch them, while loan sharks were happy to grab their custom at a massive 2,500 per cent APR. As Faisel told the Spear's Wealth Management Survey, 'It's a market, it's an opportunity.' Some Fair Finance clients, for example, want to borrow modest sums to set up as driving instructors, a job they can fit around the school run. This resonated with me because some of the entrepreneurs the Branson Centre supports in Johannesburg are women who have set up local taxi services they can fit around their family duties.

One of the reasons I wanted to get into the banking industry is because I saw the money markets and finance as a way to build bridges between the social sector, big government and business. It's the natural way in which Capitalism 24902 should evolve for a fairer distribution of wealth.

I've known Jayne-Anne Gadhia since she helped Virgin enter the financial services sector back in the mid 1990s. The business prospered and grew and in 1997 we launched the Virgin One account with RBS. RBS bought us out in 2001 and Jayne-Anne and her team stayed with the bank. I was sorry to lose them, and I said to Jayne-Anne, 'If at any time you find you don't like corporate life, give me a call.' Six years later, she did just that.

She had stayed close to her team, and there was a core of old Virgin people still working together at RBS when the culture at the bank started to change. When she called me she said, 'I'm falling out of love with RBS – we are being pushed to drive profitability in a way we don't think is right. One Thursday morning my marketing director and finance director came in to see me and said, "You know, it's time to pick up the phone to Richard."'

I told her I was glad she had, and I meant it sincerely. The timing couldn't have been better for us. Virgin Money had by then developed three successful product lines: insurance, a credit card and a savings and investment division. But there was no real connection between them, either in the way they were organised or in the way they were marketed. So Jayne-Anne's first and most important job was to come up with a holistic marketing message for those products.

'I initially started with a marketing thought – what is the thing that binds all these products together? And as we started to think about that, we realised we were looking for our "glue" in the wrong place. The products were the products; what bound them together was the people.

'Looking at Virgin Money as a *community*, rather than a

profit-making vehicle, made the job of creating a distinctive brand that much easier. It freed us up to think about what we wanted the bank to feel like. Because no one – *no one*, not even bankers! – leaps out of bed in the morning just to open an envelope or read an email or answer the phone. They get out of bed to make a difference. We wanted to make a difference we could be proud of and over a few weeks of discussions we hit upon a one-liner that summed up our aspirations. What we actually want to do is make everyone better off. We want to find ways of doing business that benefit both parties. We want to establish win/win business relationships.

'Making this happen throughout the company had an extraordinary effect. In saying to the whole business, "We're here to make everybody better off", people were able to make their own decisions within a clear context that's normally quite hard to pin down. If you say to people developing a new product, "You need to tell us how this makes everyone better off", it actually sets them thinking along lines that are good for the stability and sustainability of the business. We can't charge one group of customers more than another or less than another. We can't find a way to tack on a hidden charge. We can't give duff or ill-considered advice. Why? Because none of those things make everyone better off.'

At a time of huge turmoil and a deepening lack of faith in banking and bankers, Jayne-Anne and I discussed the way banking should go. We were convinced that Virgin should always remain a retail bank, and that the big banks should be broken up, separating their investment and retail functions. The problem with running a mixed model is that you're ramming together two very different businesses, who entertain very different expectations. Given a decent year, the investment bank is *always* going to make more money than the retail bank. If they're under the same roof, what happens is that the investment bank begins to attract all the attention, all the kudos, all the best people. And as a result the retail customer gets the second best deal – at best. This was what happened at Royal Bank of Scotland – all the capital investors started courting the investment bank, and regular customers were let down. At Virgin Money, all of our talent and all of our focus go into retail banking.

Virgin Money's brand value also made a difference to the way the company chose and developed its own people. We spent quite a long time working out what we think are the key competencies and attitudes that people in our business have to have, in order to make everyone better off. We need really strong technical experts, of course, because people are entrusting their money and their livelihoods to us. But more than that, we need people who naturally factor others into what they're doing, and who have a wide and generous definition of who their community is. When we judge performance and pay out bonuses – yes, we do pay bonuses, though not quite on the RBS scale! – we weigh their 'hard' and 'soft' competencies together, because both are essential to delivering on our brand promise.

Virgin Money's clear brand goals have been like spectacles, bringing the whole operation into focus. Now they've begun to notice ways of using their existing business to drive quite unexpected change. Take, for example, the curve ball I threw at them in 2006. The London Marathon was looking for a new sponsor and one of my closest personal friends, Andy Swaine, mentioned this to me. I thought this was a great idea, as did Alex Tai from Virgin's Special Projects Team – if only we could tie it in some useful way to a Virgin brand. Sponsoring a world class race and the world's biggest annual fundraising event is not something you take on lightly, and certainly not something I would just drop into someone's lap!

Also, every Virgin company is very different. Some have long-standing philanthropic commitments elsewhere; others are start-ups that are devoting every spare hour to their survival; some lack the resources to take on a task of this scale. All I could do was ask, 'Jayne-Anne, the London Marathon sponsorship is available. Would you be interested in taking it on?'

Her silence spoke volumes. I have to admit my first reaction had also been 'What has the London Marathon to do with a financial services business?' Yes, the marathon is the single biggest annual money-raising event on the planet. It raises over £50 million per year. But that in itself was a problem. Virgin Money is typical of the Group in that it punches well above its weight. It has three million customers, but only 450 staff (even fewer when I phoned Jayne-Anne that day in 2007). The London Marathon was a major invest-ment. Unless the fit between Virgin Money and the London

Marathon was watertight, Jayne-Anne could be staring at the loss of a lot of money.

There was another problem which made the idea even more tricky. Small though it was, Virgin Money was still employing too many people. So how could Jayne-Anne consider asking people to go and at the same time take on a major philanthropic cause? Money is always tight, especially in relatively small companies. How could we actually make that very significant investment work for us and help our brand?

Pondering it, Jayne-Anne suddenly had a light-bulb moment. Virgin Money wasn't a health business or a clothing company. They did handle money, though, and they knew how to handle deposits and withdrawals. How did the runners who took part in the marathon handle money? How were all those thousands of individual sponsorship efforts processed?

Jayne-Anne discovered that many of those transactions take place through an online charitable donation site called JustGiving. If you're going to climb a mountain, or run a marathon, or bathe in beans, you can ask your mates to sponsor you through JustGiving. Your sponsor can make their financial donation through JustGiving's online engine. It's a nice idea, but there's a problem. JustGiving is a commercial enterprise. It doesn't 'just give'. It makes a profit. Most people assume that all the money they're sending through JustGiving is going to their cause. It isn't. What with the costs of setting up their operation, paying salaries and making a profit, Jayne-Anne found that JustGiving were taking 6 per cent of the total charitable donation before they pass the money on to charity.

For Jayne-Anne it was a heaven-sent opportunity. She realised that Virgin Money could operate a much better online donation engine. We had the hardware, the know-how, and we had the people – people who, only the day before, we had been thinking of making redundant. It was a brilliant solution – if she could get it to work.

I love it when our Virgin machine moves smoothly into action to solve problems and make things work. In record time, we set up Virgin Money Giving with a wonderful woman, Jo Barnett, at the helm. The operation was set up as a not-for-profit and would be paid for out of people's donations, like JustGiving was, but because it was supported by our commercial business, Virgin Money, it wouldn't need to take anything like 6 per cent of everyone's generosity. People's gifts would go straight to the charities of their choice, with less than 2 per cent covering overheads and hopefully over time by finding additional sources of revenue bringing this down to zero. The value to Virgin Money is promotional: it gives thousands of people a good feeling about Virgin Money, in the most authentic way possible, by providing a great service.

So, rather than put a lot of friends out of a job, we set them this great task of developing a not-for-profit online charitable donation system, and we made that engine, Virgin Money Giving, the sponsorship engine of the London Marathon. This provided a service for the runners and their charities, and made the Virgin Money brand really visible in a meaningful way. It justified and explained our involvement in the marathon. It gave us the natural, watertight fit we needed between the event and the brand. Virgin Money Giving has already grown to be the online donation platform for over 4,000 UK charities across many thousands of organised events and personal challenges.

The 2010 London Marathon collected more sponsorship money than it had in any previous year. It even got me running. Ever since my kneecap and I parted company on the playing fields of Stowe when I was a schoolboy, running is not my body's favourite activity. We sponsored one of my favourite charities – Kids Company – and in no time the young people Kids Company supports were having a great deal of fun stitching a giant caterpillar for Sam, Holly and Princess Beatrice and some thirty of their friends to wear, in their bid to become the longest 'tied runners' in marathon history. I had the great pleasure of running alongside them dressed as a butterfly with giant butterfly wings.

In the first year Virgin Money Giving collected £25 million in donations. The Virgin Money Giving website gets up to 25,000 hits a day. And thousands of pounds have gone to charity that would have been paid out in profit to JustGiving. All of our people are enormously proud that we've done it. It's been a real demonstration of what we mean by making money while doing good. At a time when banks were perceived as just being in it for as much money as they could screw out of the customer, Virgin Money was showing that profit wasn't our only motive. They gave back and they had fun. Truly a win-win that once again illustrates how doing good things can also do good things for a business and the morale of its most important asset, its people.

My wife Joan had noticed that every time I came home from an overseas trip I put my loose foreign change in my top right hand drawer and the drawer was beginning to sag. She said, 'If it happens to you it must be happening to every business person who travels. Why not get them to empty their pockets when they get off the plane? You could raise millions for charity and the money wouldn't go to waste.' I spoke to our commercial team at the airline and suggested we start telling our passengers about this as they exited the plane and shake them loose of their foreign change.

Coincidentally, that very same week David Tait, who ran Virgin Atlantic for us in the US from the very first flight got a call from someone at UNICEF's UN headquarters asking for our help on an almost identical idea. It seems they'd been unsuccessfully pitching to all the big airlines of the day like Pan Am, TWA, Eastern, and what's that British airline? Oh yes, British Airways. As David told it to me, 'All the others had bounced them around from department to department and they just couldn't get anyone to say maybe, let alone yes. I think we were well down their call list so when they actually got the senior guy on the phone I could sense they were already surprised. When after a five minute description of the concept I said "Sure, we'll work with you on it – let's do it", I think the guy on the other end of the line was so taken aback he almost fell out of his chair.'

One of the first steps we ever took in the 'change for good' business was actually called exactly that. We had the little donation envelopes in every seatback within weeks and even got Phil Collins to record an on-board promo for us. Over the coming years Change for Good raised millions of dollars for UNICEF which was eternally grateful to Virgin for giving them their start. Eventually our cabin crews and others started to ask me if there wasn't some way we could have a greater level of say as to where the funds were being used. By this time UNICEF had recruited a number of other airlines and so we eventually had a very amicable split with them and we morphed the programme into our own Change for Children on-board appeal.

UNICEF still runs Change for Good to this day and one of their many airlines is now, you know, ehm, whatever they're called!

Over the intervening years, with the commitment of Virgin Atlantic's wonderful cabin crew – and the driving force behind our Community Investment programme, Jenny Bridgen – our passengers have donated many millions of pounds to small grass roots charities for children and young people. More recently, we realised that to make a real difference, we needed to support sustainable change through adopting a longer term approach, which we have done by partnering with a wonderful organisation called Free the Children. Recently, my beautiful daughter Holly made a short video, played onboard all our flights, in which she explains that Change for Children aimed to raise over £1.5 million for Free The Children between 2010–12.

It really is a great example of an almost painfully obvious opportunity to put cash to good use that otherwise was destined to end up residing forever in bedroom drawers and at the bottom of briefcases.

Owning an airline may seem like a bit of a contradiction in terms considering the environmental work I'm so passionate about. To be pragmatic, people are always going to fly, whether with Virgin or not, so we made a commitment that if we were going to continue to fly aircraft, we needed to do everything we could to be a leader in sustainable aviation. The team at Virgin Atlantic, led by Jill Brady, Sian Foster and Emma Harvey, have been spending their lives looking at how we can reduce our environmental impact. More than 99 per cent of our measurable carbon emissions are in our aircraft operations, which means we've spent a lot of time focusing on fuel efficiency (like buying new aircraft, reducing unnecessary weight onboard and maximising efficient route planning) as well as working closely with the Carbon War Room and other partners to find renewable fuels that will work for aviation. We've set ourselves an ambitious target of reducing our carbon emissions by 30 per cent for every passenger and cargo kilometre flown by 2020 – and our shiny new, more fuel-efficient aircraft (A330s and Boeing 787s) are going to help us get there.

* * *

Over the last few years, as Virgin Unite has been working with the Virgin businesses across fifteen different industries to help them embrace a philosophy of doing what's right for people and planet, a common theme has emerged among many of the businesses around creating opportunities for young people. In South Africa the businesses have rallied behind young entrepreneurs through the Branson Centre. In Australia, Canada and the US they have focused on ensuring that no teenagers are forced to live on the streets. Virgin Media in the UK have used two of their great assets: being part of the entrepreneurial world of Virgin, and the ability to harness the power of their digital platforms for budding businesses. They launched Virgin Media Pioneers, an online community for young entrepreneurs where they can develop their ideas, gain new skills and create mutually beneficial networks. The community is growing stronger every day. Virgin Media has also spent the last few months listening to and learning from young people. They are getting ready to launch a major initiative that will use all of Virgin Media's assets to help amplify the voices of these young people and help bring to life some of their solutions to the issues they are concerned about.

When I was recently looking through a rare stack of *Student* magazines from the late sixties, I stumbled upon a story that was very relevant to what was happening around the world four decades later. As I read, I realised that these words could be from any newspaper front page today, all you would have to do is change the names and the places. To paraphrase the famous French saying, 'The more things change, the more things stay the same.'

'This summer the American ghettos once again exploded in violence, cobblestones flew in the streets of Paris, Russian tanks moved into Czechoslovakia, and the bombs continued to fall in Vietnam.

'Each day the gulf between students and the rest of society grows a little wider. With each demonstration and protest meeting another section of the non-student world turns away in disgust. After each newspaper report, another adult begins to believe that a student is a thing apart, his attitude mindless and destructive, his life centred around sex and pot, his contribution to society absolutely without value. The wider the gulf becomes the more do both society and the student suffer.'

Following the summer 2011 riots in the UK, there has never been a better time to ensure that we understand the issues facing this next generation and learn from young people themselves what can be done to support them. As a community, we've not fulfilled our part of the bargain for these young people, leaving many of them jobless, with very few options in life.

One of our partners, Camila Batmanghelidjh, of Kids Company, has dedicated her life to giving young people in the UK a chance. Camila has become an expert on using advocacy – active support – as a brand. Every successful business should be branded – that is, given a distinct identity. Strangely, some people seem to find it odd when social entrepreneurs do the same thing to draw attention to their charity or organisation. But if it makes sense for a business, why not across the board? Social entrepreneurs are well ahead in this particular game. You only have to look at the way Kids Company has become one of the best known and best loved charities in Britain – and they've done it not by marketing, but by generating headlines and stories of real substance, as they run around the UK's lawmakers, making hay of the shoddy compromises and double thinking that surround the country's attitude to young people.

Camila recently wrote an article in the *Independent* about the riots in London which was spot-on. With great insight she wrote: 'Working at street level in London, over a number of years, many of us have been concerned about large groups of young adults creating their own parallel antisocial communities with different rules. The individual is responsible for their own survival because the established community is perceived to provide nothing. Acquisition of goods through violence is justified in neighbourhoods where the notion of dog eat dog pervades and the top dog survives the best. The drug economy facilitates a parallel subculture with the drug dealer producing more fiscally efficient solutions than the social care agencies who are too under-resourced to compete.

'The insidious flourishing of anti-establishment attitudes is paradoxically helped by the establishment. It grows when a child is dragged by their mother to social services screaming for help and security guards remove both; or in the shiny academies which, quietly, rid themselves of the most disturbed kids. Walk into the mental hospitals and there is nothing for the patients to do except peel the wallpaper. Go to the youth centre and you will find the staff have locked themselves up in the office because disturbed young men are dominating the space with their violent dogs. Walk on the estate stairwells with your baby in a buggy manoeuvring past the condoms, the needles, into the lift where the best outcome is that you will survive the urine stench and the worst is that you will be raped. The border police arrive at the neighbour's door to grab an "over-stayer" and his kids are screaming. British children with no legal papers have mothers surviving through prostitution and still there's not enough food on the table.

'It's not one occasional attack on dignity, it's a repeated humiliation, being continuously dispossessed in a society rich with possession. Young, intelligent citizens of the ghetto seek an explanation for why they are at the receiving end of bleak Britain, condemned to a darkness where their humanity is not even valued enough to be helped. Savagery is a possibility within us all. Some of us have been lucky enough not to have to call upon it for survival; others, exhausted from failure, can justify resorting to it.'

I first ran into Kids Company in November 2007. I was launching Virgin Mobile's 118 918 directory enquiry service that was going to be a vehicle to help drive donations for a select group of charities focused on vulnerable young people. Virgin Unite had made sure that one of those organisations was Kids Company. At the launch, I met this extraordinary woman, as tall as I am, in a red turban and a black, red and blue dress. I had no idea who she was; all she wanted to do was talk football. There was a table football game in the corner of the room and she reckoned she could beat me. 'I have a mean left hook,' she said with a twinkle in her eye. This was Camila Batmanghelidjh, Kids Company's founder. Like me, Camila is dyslexic. I had always been good at sport – even table football. I grinned across the table at her.

'You won't beat me.'

'I will.'

'You won't!'

There's nothing like a healthy dose of competition to get me going. One of the odder aspects of dyslexia is how easy it is to confuse left and right but it didn't stop us running round the table, neither of us quite sure in which direction we were supposed to be shooting the little plastic ball.

Camila won. Soundly thrashed, I knelt and kissed her feet. We became instant friends.

Camila has always been socially motivated. When she was only nine, before the revolution in her home country of Iran, Camila announced that she wanted to run an orphanage. She got her mother to join the Child Development Society so that she could read the journals. The trouble was, her dyslexia prevented her from reading anything. While working part-time as a therapist for family services in south London, twenty-year-old Camila realised why so many children were missing appointments: they didn't have a parent or carer capable of bringing them. So she reinvented her job. She cleaned up a broom cupboard in a primary school and called it 'The Place 2 Be'. Children who needed her just had to roll up outside the broom cupboard. Five years later she left The Place 2 Be, which became a national charity reaching 100,000 children a year based on a replication model she wrote for them before she left, to set up Kids Company. Today, Kids Company looks after some 14,000 children mostly in London. This is in just one wealthy city in the Western world where billions of pounds over many years have been thrown at the problem and childhood poverty and deprivation are supposed to have been solved.

'People just don't see what's going on,' Camila told me over that table football game. 'We had to act.'

Kids Company takes children from the worst circumstances you can imagine – some of them have been psychologically scarred for life from the abuse they've suffered – and get them to engage as a community with the outside world. Camila believes in these young people and realises the great value they have to offer society, if we give them the chance.

According to the New Economics Foundation and Action for Children, a shocking 1.5 million children are abused and neglected in Britain every year. Another 1.1 million children are living with drug-addicted parents. The groups overlap, but it's pretty safe to say that there are about two million *British* children who, one way or another, live extremely vulnerable lives. On average, 550,000 of them are referred to social services every year. It's at this point, according to Camila, that things get silly.

'If you look at the Office for National Statistics, its figures have stayed the same for the last eight years. Each year, between 35,000 and 38,000 of those half-million children are placed on the child protection register and given a social worker. The figure never gets above 38,000. This is because, if you put a child on the register, then by law the government has to stump up the cost of a social worker and intervention. So almost the same number of children are deregistered within the year to make room for new kids coming along. Last year nearly a quarter of those had to go back on the register, because they were prematurely removed. Politicians can get away with this because these abused children can't hold them accountable.' They don't have a vote yet either, which sometimes has a lot to do with just who gets the attention and who gets ignored by our elected representatives.

And this is why Camila Batmanghelidjh is arguably the highest profile youth worker in the country and practically has a seat reserved for her in the BBC newsroom. She's been getting judicial reviews for child after child and winning every case. She's hasn't lost one yet. In fact, she doesn't have time to handle all the cases she knows she can win.

Camila and I have both been shaped by dyslexia. I've never regarded it as a disability, but as something that has forced me to engage with the world in a special way. None of us is perfect, and a difference can be a strength, if we can find a way to approach it positively. For Camila, as for me, dyslexia helps because we can't get stuck in the detail of things. We develop a very global view of everything. It makes you value voices, stories and conversations. It makes you listen.

For myself, being dyslexic might explain why I've been so lucky at spotting opportunities in so many different markets. Detail is vital, of course, and I've always surrounded myself with great people who can drill down to it. The most able people I know can do both, drilling down while not losing sight of the big picture. It would be good if strategic thinking – *entrepreneurial* thinking – were to be taught in schools. Not every child is an academic; not every child is destined to work for someone. Entrepreneurship could open many doors to a different kind of workforce. Entrepreneurship is what made Britain great and set up the US. It's not really valued at all in the modern educational syllabus and it should be.

Our businesses in the UK have been giving all they have to help support Camila and other organisations working with vulnerable young people. Our staff have mentored (and been mentored by) the young people, we've raised millions of pounds, we've loaned our professional skills, we've woven their voices into our communications, we've created products and services for them, we've trained the young people how to work in our businesses, we've given them internships and, most importantly, we've worked with Camila and others as true partners, realising that in everything we do we are getting back as much or more than we are giving. This two-way experience has been great for our businesses and enriched the lives of everyone at Virgin.

Like Camila, Rick Koca, a former career naval officer in the US, has been helping children for most of his adult life. In January 1990, with his own money and the help of friends, Rick started Stand Up For Kids, an all-volunteer organisation based on a simple idea: 'We tell homeless and street kids we care about them. Then we go to the streets and prove it.'

He was largely working under his own initiative when Virgin Mobile USA came across him, thanks to Virgin Unite's focus on tackling tough issues with great front-line partners. Dan Schulman joined Virgin Mobile USA as founding CEO in September 2001, with Howard Handler, Peter Boyd and Bob Stohrer, from the marketing team. They had a light-bulb moment when, after working with the Virgin Unite team and doing some careful research, they realised that there was a problem that nobody wanted to address: the issue of homeless youth. They weren't talking about well-heeled kids, whose parents paid their bills, but the vast number of youngsters who had nobody to help them. Usually they have no fixed address, no bank accounts, no education and no jobs.

Over two million young people face homelessness each year in the US. But we didn't at that stage know anything about how and why youth homelessness is such a problem. How could we begin to engage with that community?

That was when we came across Rick Koca.

Every quarter, Virgin Mobile USA got its staff together as a way of sharing stories, successes and problems. These meetings injected some soul into the operation. On one of these get-togethers Virgin Unite brought Rick Koca along to talk to them. As he spoke, the hairs stood up on the back of Dan's neck. Rick told the hushed room how meaningful the partnership with Virgin was for them. He said it was validation for him after all those years of struggling on his own to help street kids that a company like Virgin Mobile had picked him as a partner. And as he spoke, he wept. Dan stood up afterwards to follow Rick with a quick state-of-the-business message, and as he looked out into the audience he saw about a quarter of the people were also in tears. It was a powerful moment.

Dan knew they had to harness this passion and Rick helped to show them the way. He took them out on the streets – an experience they'd never forget. It was a pure *Trading Places* experience. The guys among them didn't shave for a week. They turned up in torn jeans and unwashed T-shirts. They threw their wallets and keys on the table. And they hit the suddenly very unfriendly streets. For twenty-four hours they went about the city with no resources, nowhere to go, no one to phone, not even money for a cup of coffee. If they wanted something, they had to beg for it. Afterwards they all agreed it was one of the hardest things they'd ever done, and easily the most frightening – and it had lasted for only twenty-four hours. There were moments when they were terrified. They couldn't imagine it being permanent.

In the forefront of their minds was the knowledge that in twenty-four hours they could pick up their lives again. A quarter of the homeless people out there were kids. It showed Dan, Howard and Peter why the problem mattered.

It made them want to do something at once. Those few hours 'abandoned' in the city rocketed them into making it their mission that young people should never have to sleep on the streets. In 2006, with the support of Virgin Unite, Dan, Howard, Peter and the team created Re*Generation, a programme that gave Virgin Mobile's five million customers a way to make a difference to homeless youth. Since it began, Re*Generation has invested $7 million in time, resources and cash to help end youth homelessness. As Rick put it, 'More has been achieved in the last two years than in the previous seventeen with the support of Re*Generation.'

The beauty of what Virgin Mobile did was that it was not just a simple marketing campaign bolted on to their business; they built in a mission to tackle youth homelessness at their very core. They worked with Virgin Unite and got every team in the company to map out what tools they had that could be used to support these young people; then they spent hours listening to and learning from the young people about what they wanted. They used their text messaging service to connect their customers directly to homeless youths so that they could hear from them first hand what it was like living on the streets. They teamed up with American Eagle Outfitters so that every time a customer texted the word 'karma' American Eagle donated an item of clothing to a young person on the street. They raised funds and gave their time to help get them off the streets. They shifted their advertising campaigns to amplify the voices of homeless youth.

What strikes me most about the social media phenomenon these days is that so many talk about it, but few understand it. It's more than being socially present with a Facebook page or a Twitter account. It's about influencing and shaping conversations. Whether it's sharing someone's thoughts on a new idea or sharing the coordinates to trigger a movement, the power of social media has always been about the conversation. And in business, it's even more astonishing. There's a quiet renaissance happening in social commerce at the moment. These days, consumers (especially those under thirty) won't make a purchase decision without first consulting their friends online. And if their friends don't know the answer? They'll just ask a stranger. That level of power – or rather, 'empowered dependence' – is a rare thing. And businesses that understand that dynamic within their social audiences will be more successful at spreading awareness of social good than those that don't.

These days, the ability to share an idea is just as powerful as conceiving it. A business may innovate the most groundbreaking social cause, but without the ability to harness the power of social circles, its progress will remain stagnant. And you can't change the world by standing still.

That said, one must never underestimate the power of a good idea and relentless execution when promoting social change. The days of simply making a public announcement are over. I know this may sound harsh, but consider this: with all the wired and wireless distractions out there, no one has time in their day to look at black and white imagery of disenfranchised young people. If you want to get someone off the couch, you have to scream at them to get their attention.

Now led by Ron Faris and Felicia Hill, the Re*Generation team at Virgin Mobile launched a series of initiatives to stimulate awareness and funding to help homeless youth programmes with support from Virgin Unite. When Ron pitched me the idea to make the Virgin Mobile Festival in 2009 (host to hundreds of thousands of music fans across the US East Coast) free to the public in exchange for an optional $10 donation to youth homelessness (the normal price of a ticket is $100 a day), he said we had to 'earn the right to be discussed virally'. I couldn't say 'Yes' quick enough. The breakthrough idea is what you need to get the masses chatting about it. At a time when people were facing layoffs or swine flu, the free concert captured attention worldwide, increased awareness of the issue, and most importantly, put smiles on faces when fans needed it most. The crew at Virgin Mobile also initiated a 'FREE.I.P' programme, which allowed fans to volunteer their time at homeless youth shelters in exchange for a VIP ticket to the festival. Three years later, I found myself guest-bartending on the festival grounds at our third FreeFest with Cee Lo Green at our now legendary 'Karma Bar', with every dollar for a drink sold benefitting youth homelessness. We uploaded the video on a simple flip cam and watched as bloggers and Facebook fans shared with millions in their newsfeeds.

Consider the following example that leveraged the power of a social audience to inspire social change (both also created by Ron and his team at Virgin Mobile USA in partnership with Darin Spurgeon at Virgin Unite). First, we partnered with Lady Gaga – the woman with the most Twitter followers in the world – and inspired her to join our cause to combat youth homelessness. This wasn't easy. Not because she isn't philanthropic. On the contrary, there isn't a single person in the world today who fights harder for gay rights. But that's just the thing. Typically, it's hard to get a celebrity to join your cause because it tends to dilute the attention they need to give to their own charity. And sometimes their passions – no matter how magnanimous they are about pursuing them – just don't align with yours.

But then it hit us. We found a common ground. It turns out one of the top reasons kids are homeless in the US is due to homophobia in the household. And if you visit Green Chimneys in New York City, you'll find an unsettling number of children who were kicked out of their homes for simply trying to express themselves in the most authentic manner they know how. So we were off to the races, as they say. Gaga would encourage her throngs of fans to donate to youth homelessness. Then we Facebook-broadcasted clips from her tour when she would actually stop her show and call a Virgin Mobile fan in the crowd to announce that a donation to youth homelessness would be made in that fan's name. These videos have been viewed by millions who are now aware and are actively donating their time at homeless youth shelters to earn tickets to her shows. Behold, the power of viral. Social celebrities can do wonders for social good if partnered and aligned correctly.

These moments make up the bedrock of success for Virgin Mobile USA's Re*Generation initiative, and most importantly are helping stop young people from having to sleep on the streets.

These are big ideas that earn the right to be discussed virally. And social networks are the engines that fuel our work. Companies can break through and *screw business as usual* by leveraging this social phenomenon. Virgin Mobile, in partnership with Virgin Unite, was successful because they found the right cocktail of fusing social networking with a social message. Twitter, Facebook and foursquare are weapons we can use to wake up masses of people and get them to engage. In short, we need to give more love to the word 'social' in 'social good'.

Through all this, Virgin Mobile USA gave thousands of opportunities to young people across the US. As a company they also got a tremendous amount back from this 'good karma'. Everyone took more pleasure in their work. They got involved and connected at a deeper level – frankly, a more *interesting* level – with each other, with our customers, with homeless youth and with the wider community. The bottom line is that they felt proud of what they were doing and learned more than they could ever dream from the young people that they were privileged to spend time with. We found that our customers also got involved and felt part of something bigger.

This momentum has been building with Virgin Unite's initiatives across the entire Virgin group. Our 50,000-strong employee group does feel like a big family. We're happier, we all feel as if we belong to something special.

These days I think you've got to talk about your value proposition – why are you so proud of your product? And you've got to communicate that pride in ways that add up to a young generation that's very well informed and very idealistic. The young care about where products come from. They care about what the company that makes the product actually does in the world – or not. Virgin Mobile proved that a company can do these things. But you can't fake it. You have to say, *screw business as usual* and just do it.

As a postscript, to show how much value doing the right thing added to Virgin Mobile USA, we went from a small, struggling company trying to carve out a tiny niche market in 2001 to going public in 2007. By the time the company was acquired by Sprint Nextel in November 2009, we had more than five million customers and $1.3 billion in annual sales. *That* is the power of Capitalism 24902, the power of doing good – and you don't have to be a huge corporation to have this power. It's something everyone has – they just need to unleash it.

Businesses also have the power to work with governments to make larger systems changes that are often the root cause of the issues. Virgin Mobile and Virgin Unite did just that, by teaming up with the musician Jewel to build awareness in the US about the issues and the need to change the system.

Jewel hitched a ride with me at the end of a trip I'd made with Sam to the Arctic Circle in 2007. The 101 Expedition had been organised by legendary explorer and sled dog trainer Will Steger to highlight global warming. It was an incredible experience, although unfortunately I had to leave early. However, I returned with Jewel for the celebratory concert at the successful conclusion of the expedition. Hearing her sing in a snowy wilderness at an Inuit party, at which a typical feast of raw fish and elk was laid out, was something I will never forget.

At this stage, Jewel had been a Virgin Unite ambassador for some time; she had once been homeless herself and felt passionate about ensuring that no young people should endure what she had experienced on the streets. At one point, suffering from recurring kidney infections, homeless and destitute and with no means of paying for treatment, she was turned away from an emergency room one evening because she had no health insurance. She almost died of blood poisoning as she threw up in her car in the hospital parking lot, and no one would help.

Her experiences made a huge impression on Jewel. When she eventually found success, secured a recording contract and became a big star, and finally had money to spend on causes close to her heart, she set up Project Clean Water, conscious of her personal experiences when her own health was suffering. So far, she has helped provide clean water for thirty communities in thirteen countries worldwide, where fresh, clean water is not a given. Together with Unite she's doing a lot more.

I was mesmerised by Jewel's story. She made everything sound so matter-of-fact, but from meeting so many street children over the years I knew how hard it was, especially for a girl, to survive. Working with Virgin Mobile and Virgin Unite, Jewel has made tremendous headway towards making a difference for young homeless people in the US. Along with Dan, she was invited to speak before a Congressional subcommittee on underage homelessness. She spoke candidly, relating her story in her own words and certainly made a deep impression. After this, the American government declared November a month of awareness building to get everyone behind ending teenage homelessness. But the task is enormous; there is a great deal more work to be done and certainly neither Virgin Mobile nor our other businesses will give up until we ensure that young homeless people are no longer a fact of life.

Web: virginunite.com/screwbusinessasusual
Twitter: @virginunite #sbau
Facebook: Facebook.com/VirginUnite

4 The Next Frontier and Beyond

'Doing well is the result of doing good. That's what capitalism is all about' – Ralph Waldo Emerson

Reinvention does not need to be complicated. It's all about listening to people who are impacted by an issue, learning from nature and working out how you can put the power back into the hands of the people at the village level. There is no better listener in my world than Jane Tewson. Her whole life has been about listening to people who are directly impacted by issues and then helping to amplify their voices by involving them. She is one of the true reinventors of 'charity'. Shifting the focus from old donor vs giver relationships to respectful partnerships; from top-down to bottom-up approaches and from misguided sympathy to empathy, celebration and empowerment.

Jane is best known in the UK for Comic Relief (famous for Red Nose Day), Timebank and her recent work with Pilotlight Australia. As an entrepreneur, she has always pushed the boundaries to look at how you can inspire (on the whole new) people to philanthropy by bringing people from all walks of life together. Or, as she says, 'igniting change by combining extraordinary people'. With Pilotlight Australia, she works behind the scenes to bring individuals and businesses together with some fantastic organisations working with people on the edge. When I first met Jane she was an impressive twenty-something who had the idea of using comedy to raise money for entrepreneurial approaches to some of the major issues the world was facing. I immediately liked and trusted her and absolutely loved the idea, so I paid her salary and overheads as she got Comic Relief off the ground. That meant she was able to say that 100 per cent of any money raised went to good causes – as we do with Virgin Unite today. As we all know, this seed of an idea that Jane nurtured and brought to fruition raises tens of millions every year. In March 2011 in one evening alone it raised an amazing £74 million. Jane has remained a close friend and Trustee of Virgin Unite, helping Jean, Unite's Chair, Patrick McCall, my sister Vanessa and me shape the foundation over the last seven years.

Her mission has always been not so much to raise money as to start productive dialogues. Jane Tewson lives to set up conversations that inspire those people in a position to help to talk directly to those who need help. When you witness this in process it's quite remarkable – you can almost see the sparks fly as the new creative ideas for change emerge. She thinks you can tell a lot about a society's problems from what it *doesn't* talk about. Recently she published a book called *Dying to Know* – bringing death to life. 'People said, "Whoa! What has a book about death got to do with social change?" Well, it has *everything* to do with social change.' In Jane's words, '*Dying to Know* seeks to break the silence around death and dying and stimulate a discussion that genuinely connects people on the most profound level, not as experts, but as people with the same dreams, hopes, fears and concerns.' Jane reckons the book is a natural extension of her work creating Comic Relief. 'It's a talking point. It gets people engaged. And it brings a bit of passion to things.'

Jane believes conversation is one of life's great pleasures; that the solutions to our problems can only come when we truly involve and connect with people needing help and by empowering them and resourcing their ideas. I think she's right. Actually, I *know* she's right. She has been instrumental in setting up many conversations over the years to help get Virgin Unite's work off the ground. One of the initiatives inspired by Jane is the successful Champions Programme, where Virgin staff in Australia are mentoring and being mentored by former homeless young people. The conversations that are taking place between the young people and our staff are life changing, for all of them. Our staff are learning from these inspiring young people who have years of wisdom under their belts from having to survive in circumstances we cannot even imagine. Some true friendships have been formed and everyone agrees that their lives have been enriched by this unique programme.

It was while I was on holiday in Australia that Jane thought I might like to meet thirty-five young prisoners in Melbourne's Port Phillip Prison maximum security young offenders unit. Aged eighteen to twenty-five, they were involved in an in-house social enterprise programme, learning how to manage businesses. The inmates' company, called Doin' Time, produced T-shirts, and they donated the money they raised to charity. Of their determination, I said to Jane: 'This project is unlike anything I've ever seen. I'm blown away. We need to see how we can try and replicate this in the UK and get our businesses to support these social enterprises by employing former offenders.'

Jane wasn't surprised by my response. 'When we first started visiting I found it difficult to make eye contact with the young men and to gain their confidence. As with all Pilotlight Australia projects we listened to them and heard directly from them what would make the difference in their lives. This led to the creation and development of the small business programme spearheaded by Doin' Time. The young men are highly inventive and entrepreneurial. This programme harnesses that potential and teaches them responsibility, decision making and leadership in a positive way. Part of their rehabilitation is to show them the value of caring – first for themselves and then for people and the environment around them.' I realised as we went through several steel doors to get into the unit that there is a very fine line between these young people and all of us. In fact any of these prisoners could have been my child. They just happened to take a wrong turn along the way and now very sadly many of them will call prison home for the rest of their lives.

Two years later I met one of the inmates again: a guy called Roger who now works outside the prison to help get ex-offenders into jobs. Generally, employment is a huge problem for former inmates. Without a wage or any real prospect of regular work, many revert to crime just to get back into the relative safety of prison. The young men involved with Doin' Time, however, have had a bit more success: many of the inmates involved in these programmes do not reoffend. If you follow the prison and crime statistics on the news at all, this is a huge achievement: a vindication of the power of entrepreneurship and business to help people turn their lives around – and make society as a whole a better and safer place. (And let's not forget the T-shirts – the Virgin Group in Australia now buys its promotional T-shirts from Doin' Time!)

The beauty of Doin' Time is that it proves that a new, humane, entrepreneurial approach to prison reform works. There are now three social enterprises up and running at the Unit – the latest being Stories from the Inside in which the inmates tell their stories through film in an attempt to help young people like themselves on the outside avoid making the same mistakes they have made. Historically, people services such as prison reform, health and education have all been the domain of the government with some spillover into not-for-profits. This is an example of how a tiny innovative project can be the spark for a new way of thinking – as was Jane's first idea that led to the phenomenal Comic Relief.

We've started to look at how we can support young people who have run into trouble, by employing ex-offenders in our businesses (at the time of writing not one one of them have re-offended since working with us, which is great for society and for themselves). We're also trying to help train people whilst they are in prison by purchasing products in our supply chain, like the foam portion of the earphones that Virgin Atlantic uses, from social enterprises in prisons. We've learnt a lot from organisations such as Toll in Australia and Pathways in London who are working in this area.

'It's about a shift in how we respond to issues in the world,' Jean Oelwang says. 'Firstly we need to wake up and realise that we can no longer operate in silos, that is, in isolation; everything is interconnected and it is no good saying that's the role of government or the role of charities, all of us must take responsibility for making the world a better place. What a brilliant opportunity to form some unlikely marriages between different sectors to create solutions that will drive positive change at a much faster pace than if any of us were working on our own. Although I'm not sure I can quite visualise the union of Richard Branson, Mother Teresa and David Cameron!'

I am not at all sure I would want to visualise that either, but I'm certainly not keen on silos so I was more than happy to agree that they had no place in the way we operate. The business of doing good for people and the planet is the most challenging frontier for entrepreneurs. As governments step back from providing basic services, and as the need to tackle our local and global issues continues to grow, we have an opportunity to invent new types of businesses that can respond to these needs and truly make a change. The opportunities are endless and they will come in all shapes; from the delivery of people services such as prison reform, and education to health and wellbeing to renewable energy to global connectivity. The list goes on. Some of these entities will be profit-making, others will put their profits back into helping solve the issue and many of them will be somewhere in the middle. Around the world many of these new types of business are emerging, starting with something close to my heart – health and wellbeing. Before we jump into the opportunities, I want to take a moment to reflect on a trip I took to South Africa in the midst of the AIDS epidemic that really was a turning point in my life.

There are some things that change you for ever. They have such an impact on a deep level that not only will you never forget them, but you know you have to do something. Standing in a hospital full of dying people in South Africa was such an emotional experience that I felt moved beyond belief. I began to cry and wiped my tears away. I was deeply moved – but I was also very angry. This shouldn't be happening.

This was in 2004, shortly after we had launched Virgin Unite. What didn't make sense was what I observed that bleak week as, with Brad Pitt, the international recording artist Estelle, Jean and Emily Sayer from the Unite team, we drove through the townships of South Africa on a mission to observe what was taking place in the midst of the AIDS epidemic. These were communities I remembered from when I had first come to South Africa back in 1999 with my parents. Things seemed very joyful and vibrant back then and we felt positive that this nation, that had been mired in problems for so long, would continue to send an inspiring message of hope to the world. Much of this inspiration and leadership had come from Nelson Mandela, the first black president and leader of the African National Congress. In 1999 he stepped down after a five-year term and Thabo Mbeki stepped into his shoes, having won the country's second multiracial, totally democratic elections.

'We will act together to build a South Africa that truly belongs to all who live in it, both black and white,' Mr Mbeki said.

With his words ringing in our ears, my parents and I felt confident about the future. We had found a wonderful game reserve, Ulusaba, adjoining the Kruger National Park. It was up for sale, and we had a vision of building a splendid lodge on an amazing lookout spot where people could come on holiday and enjoy the best game viewing anywhere in Africa. I always like to learn as much as I can about somewhere new, so we travelled through the townships around Johannesburg and explored the endless horizons of the countryside. In 1999 the roads of the townships had been lined with signs for emerging small businesses – symbols of hope for a better future in the aftermath of apartheid. But that week in 2004, as we drove around, all we saw were billboards advertising funeral companies. Mile after mile of funeral ads. It was ominous and deeply disturbing. I really did feel as if we were travelling the back roads of hell.

Every place was the same. In the dreadfully crowded hospitals and hospices we visited we were shown around wards where people lay silently waiting to die. Having abandoned all hope it was as if they were resigned to their fate. The corridors were also crowded with the dying, waiting for someone to die so a bed could come free.

Our small party was stunned into silence. We walked out of the last ward into the lobby of the hospice, numb with shock and a sense of helplessness. A group of women were standing in the lobby and adjoining waiting room.

I was embarrassed when these women recognised me. What I hadn't expected was that they would see the pain openly etched on my face and in my eyes and that they would be the ones to offer *me* comfort. They spontaneously burst into song, dancing and holding out their hands. We all joined in and danced with them: it was both moving and life-inspiring. We were celebrating not death, but one another. *That* is one of the reasons why I champion Africa and Africans so fiercely – their hope and their belief in a better life is contagious and constantly humbling.

The problem was that the ANC – an organisation I had respected for years – refused to accept that HIV and AIDS were linked. I had seen what was going on with my own eyes, walked through silent wards full of the dying, and I couldn't understand how South Africa's first free and inclusive government could turn a blind eye to so much suffering. Things gradually escalated while I seethed at being able to do so little. They came to a head when a gentle man – a poet and artist called Donald – who worked at Ulusaba as a waiter, died of AIDS-related tuberculosis. He had left behind a deeply affecting letter to the other staff in which he bravely described his illness and how so little was being done to combat it. He said: 'I'm a songwriter who writes about HIV and AIDS ... Let us work together as one, to be proud of ourselves and have the same purpose in order to defeat the enemy. This is not a disease but it is a war that is in Africa, aiming to destroy our continent.'

Together with Dr Brian Brink from Anglo American, Dr Hugo Templeman, who had started another incredible clinic in South Africa, and the teams at Ulusaba and Virgin Unite, we opened the Bhubezi Community Health Centre in the district around Ulusaba to offer free healthcare and testing and treatment for HIV and AIDS for 100,000 people who lived around us. Bhubezi means 'lion' in Swahili.

One of the reasons I am so positive about bringing Assura Medical into the Virgin family is that as an organisation it is fast developing a fantastic track record in the provision of NHS sexual health services in the UK. It may be that we will be able to replicate this level of service in other parts of the world in the future.

After Donald's death, Joan and I called in everybody who

worked for us at Ulusaba and in front of them all we were tested for HIV. I urged everyone to take the test, so that if they needed it they could then seek treatment. But even free HIV tests and free medicine weren't enough since people were deeply suspicious of the retroviral drugs they needed to take to keep HIV and AIDS at bay. Another part of the problem was that the South African health minister, Manto Tshabalala-Msimang, had herself publicly declared – at an International AIDS conference in Toronto, no less – that beetroot, garlic, lemons and African potatoes were a cure for HIV. Her comments had sent shock waves around the world.

My frustration finally boiled over and I told Jean that, at a dinner at which Cherie Blair was to be a guest of honour, I intended to say that President Mbeki should be indicted for crimes against humanity for allowing so many of his people to die without treatment. While she understood my anger, Jean was worried that, like many other foundations before us, we would be kicked out of the country and all the people we were working with would be left high and dry.

Priya Bery, who was now part of the Unite family and with us during this discussion, looked on slightly shocked, but kept her counsel. Jean had stolen Priya from the GBC – the Global Business Coalition on HIV/AIDS, Tuberculosis and Malaria. Priya had been instrumental in setting up this coalition with Ambassador Richard C Holbrooke, one of the true entrepreneurial diplomats of our time. Harvard-educated, she'd worked for Fortune 500 companies and advised the US and India in health and rural development. She was young, bright, ambitious and knowledgeable and has played a key role in building Virgin Unite. She was as frustrated as Jean and I were, but openly accusing the South African president of such a crime was new territory, particularly given her passion for bridging collaboration and communication between the sectors, and she could also see our work here coming to a rapid end.

'We have to do something,' I said. 'I can't just continue to bury my conscience for political expediency.'

But I knew what I had to do – and I just did it. At the dinner, when I stood to make my prepared speech, I instead ad-libbed and said everything that I felt had to be said. Afterwards, I compounded my words by giving a press conference. I said that although I admired enormously what the ANC had achieved in uniting their country, by depriving them of antiretroviral drugs and killing millions of his own people, the president of South Africa was guilty of genocide for crimes against his own people and that health ministers who offered beetroots and not ARDs to be a cure were also guilty of crimes against humanity.

I have always felt that it is important to do what you think is right. Speaking out was right. It wasn't about me, it wasn't about business – it wasn't even about aid workers and charities. It was about millions of lives that were being lost when there was a solution. Doing nothing. *That* was criminal.

Everyone knows that compromise is part of business as usual. But I knew we had to *screw business as usual*. Putting my South African businesses on the line in order to embarrass a head of state was an extreme thing to do. I only did it because Virgin *was* involved, *was* implicated, *was* part of the country in which we operated. I felt that speaking out was my only option.

I didn't know what to expect after I'd made my speech and it was widely written up, but nobody was more surprised than me when President Mbeki magnanimously wrote me a very personal letter. It was pages long and reading it moved me deeply. It came from the heart. He wrote about his upbringing, his people and his country, and it was from these stories that I began to understand how he had come to make such a dreadful mistake. It at least gave us the foundation on which to build a positive relationship going forward and we agreed together that something positive should come out of our correspondence. I thought for some time that South Africa needed a centre for disease control. America had one, Europe had one, but the place where diseases were rife did not have one. President Mbeki agreed with this and we joined forces to set up such a hub.

One of the primary objectives of this book is to convince readers that they can gain in many different ways by doing the right thing. Certainly, Virgin Unite's initiatives have developed and scaled up. We grew our businesses and are still growing them. Our interests in South Africa range from health clubs, tourism, mobile phones, banking and, of course, an airline. We could have lost the lot, and were lucky that we didn't, but I would never have forgiven myself if I had not spoken out.

In June 2011 I wrote in my blog: 'Today, President Clinton,

the UN Secretary General, the President of Nigeria, the US Global AIDS Ambassador and a number of other leaders are meeting at the United Nations to work out a global strategy to prevent babies from contracting HIV in childbirth. Sadly I wasn't able to make the meeting but wanted to share a bit about this important issue. It's shocking to think that thirty years since the first case of AIDS was first found, thirty-four million people are still living with the virus and nearly the same number have died from the infection (UNAIDS). What's worse is seven thousand are newly infected each day, and nearly every minute a baby is born with HIV.

'There has been tremendous progress over the years and we truly have a chance to beat this disease. Now, more than ever, we have the tools and proven solutions that can give us an HIV-free generation but only half those in need have access to life-saving services. We can pretty much be sure that HIV won't be passed on to the baby by encouraging future parents to get counselling and testing, and by giving the right antiretroviral medications to an HIV positive mum during pregnancy, labour, and breastfeeding.

'Wouldn't it be just incredible if no more babies were born with HIV? Let's help rally the global community and support governments to fill the gap in preventing mother-to-child transmission. Each year there are about 1.4 million women living with HIV in developing countries who give birth. We can help ensure their babies have a healthy, HIV-free start to their lives.

'Even your voice can help make an impact. Join me in

raising attention to this opportunity of a lifetime. Through the Bhubezi Community Health Centre we're providing life-saving treatment to people living with AIDS, including pregnant mothers and soon-to-be-parents. Check out what world leaders are up to at the UN today, finding solutions for this critical issue. The US government has been doing pioneering work on mother-to-baby transmission of HIV/AIDS. Check out Ambassador Goosby's blog. He serves as the US Global AIDS coordinator.'

People have worked hard for the past thirty years and there have been great breakthroughs with antiretroviral drugs. The frightening thing is, despite the low cost, not everyone can afford them and therefore millions of people are still unnecessarily dying of AIDS. I find it of great concern, as do many others, that thirty years after HIV/AIDS was recognised as an identifiable illness, it's still with us. Twenty-five million have died, half of whom are women. There are sixteen million AIDS orphans. In 2009 nearly two million people died. Millions more are still getting infected.

The positive news is that many entrepreneurial models that bring together the government, business and social sectors are getting great traction in helping to stop AIDS and other diseases that should no longer be killing people. As we were working on the disease-control hub in South Africa, we had the great pleasure of working with Dr Ernest Darkoh, a founding partner of a healthcare company called BroadReach. Ernest took many a trip to Pretoria with us all crammed into a car to visit the South African health ministry. He is one of those rare individuals who is incredibly well qualified, yet impressively humble and compassionate – all of which comes with a very cheeky sense of humour.

BroadReach is a great example of a business that is a pioneer in the 'new frontier' and has done well by doing good. Ernest and his team of consultants are constantly bringing about unlikely marriages between governments, global not-for-profit organisations such as the World Health Organisation and businesses. He is a bit of a hybrid model himself, as a medical doctor who has worked at the consultancy company McKinsey.

In 2001, Ernest was tapped on the shoulder to lead a programme called Masa, supported by one of the most effective public-private partnerships of our time – the African Comprehensive HIV/AIDS Partnerships (ACHAP). At that time, a staggering 38.5 per cent of the inhabitants of Botswana were HIV positive. The government had the vision to realise they needed to bring together the right mix of partners to stop people from dying, so they launched ACHAP, a country-led, public-private development partnership between the Government of Botswana, the Bill & Melinda Gates Foundation, and MSD/Merck Company Foundation committed to enhancing Botswana's national response to HIV/AIDS. With $100 million and donated drugs in his toolkit, Ernest oversaw the programme's rollout countrywide. By 2010, there were over 170,000 people on treatment with a 90 per cent compliance rate in adhering to the right drug regime – which is almost unheard of. This was achieved by combining the skills and assets of all the different partners. This partnership has saved tens of thousands of lives and is now so successful that it is moving into its next phase with an additional $60 million donated by Merck and the Gates Foundation.

Another pioneer in this brave new world of health businesses for good is Victoria Hale, PhD. It was the year 2000, and Victoria was forty years old and working in the United States in drug development. For two years she'd been thinking about starting a different kind of pharmaceutical company, one that would target diseases that no one was researching. 'Many, many pharmaceutical professionals want to contribute to developing a new medicine, particularly a cure for a deadly disease. We're all well aware that the poorest among us have the greatest need for new medicines. There was simply no place for such professionals to gather to work together; there was no vehicle suitable to accept donated intellectual property.'

Victoria was in a taxi on the way to a pharmaceuticals conference in New York when her driver asked her what she did. When she told him, he laughed, 'and then he said something that was extremely painful, and it really was a turning point for me. It was: "You all have all the money in the drugs industry."'

Victoria was acutely aware that some people have medicines for everything while, a few thousand miles away, babies die of dehydration caused by diarrhoea. Over the years drug development has become incredibly expensive due to the many hoops companies need to go through to get a drug approved. It takes about a billion dollars to create a new product. This means that, to inspire efforts to find a cure, a disease has either to be extremely prevalent or particularly acute in places where there's lots of money. Approximately 10 per cent of the money the world spends on health each year is devoted to diseases or conditions that account for *90 per cent* of global disease. Of the 1,500 new drugs approved in the past twenty-five years, fewer than twenty were for neglected infectious diseases that disproportionately affect the poor. In addition to 'neglected diseases', many diseases – eight thousand of them, according to Victoria – are 'orphan diseases' that affect small numbers of people throughout the world, too few in number seriously to interest the large pharmaceutical companies. Together, these diseases affect millions. So Victoria Hale, stung by her taxi driver's provocative remark, set about designing a business that matched orphan and neglected diseases to orphan and neglected drugs: drugs that often already existed but that no one was developing or producing.

OneWorld Health was not set up to make money. In fact the conditions on the funding were specifically that OneWorld Health did *not* make a return. Instead, it would work to identify off-patent medicines, and have them manufactured by companies which would then sell them, at cost, around the world. The first cheque OneWorld Health received was for a million dollars. This, remember, is *one-tenth of one per cent* of the money required to come up with just one new medicine!

But that didn't matter: the shelves of the big pharmaceuticals companies are piled high with *old* medicines: incredible, tested technologies that just didn't make enough money to justify further investment.

In Bihar, the third most populous state in India, there is something called black fever. People there compare it to HIV. It wipes out your bone marrow and turns you into a walking skeleton. The drugs usually used to treat this condition are poisonous, ineffective and cost about US$200 a course – three generations of a family can go into debt to save one family member – so the disease usually goes untreated, and causes 200,000 deaths each year.

Meanwhile, there is an off-patent antibiotic called paromomycin, no longer manufactured because the company that invented it couldn't justify the low sales it generated. With the help of funding from the Bill & Melinda Gates Foundation, OneWorld Health took paromomycin through clinical development and trials to see if it could treat black fever. It could, and it does. It was OneWorld Health's first and most celebrated victory. Better still, the drug is so cheap to manufacture that the Indian government is distributing it in Bihar for free.

So, after setting up America's first non-profit pharmaceuticals company, Victoria decided she wanted to take on another challenge – setting up a profit-making company that could service the poor. Thus came about the birth of

Medicines360 which she describes as a 'hybrid non-profit'. In effect, it's two companies in one: a non-profit parent, with a wholly-owned profit-making subsidiary. The non-profit parent makes products. Its for-profit subsidiary sells these products and returns its profits to the parent. The parent then uses this money to market the same products to the poor at a fraction of the original cost. 'This,' Victoria says, 'is doing the real thing. We have actual commercial markets like every pharmaceuticals company does, but we also have at our core a non-profit that addresses the needs of the poor. Business models are human creations, just as technology is. So we innovate the heck out of technology. Well, let's do it with business models too.' For funders and investors, this attitude can be a bit of a challenge! 'I've been told, "Victoria, you're evolving your strategic plan all the time! Do you ever freeze it?" And I say, "No! We're always learning." I believe the most innovative and effective organisations figure out the best path and they work with their funders to say, "Come on, change is good, it'll be *fun*!"' Truly a woman after my own heart!

I could fill the rest of this chapter with wonderful stories about these new hybrid health models, such as our Virgin Unite project with our partners in Kenya that puts health workers on motorbikes to reach thousands of people every month with life-saving health services. One of the best bits is that they double as entrepreneurs who sell goods and services to earn an income for their families. Another interesting 'dual career' health model is Living Goods in Uganda, the 'Avon ladies' of pro-poor products. They've got a brilliant programme that employs hundreds of women who go door to door selling life-saving and life-changing products to consumers living on just a few dollars a day. But I want to shift gear for a moment and look at the opportunities in health globally for businesses all over the world. As pressure is increasingly put on governments to support growing populations with quality health-care, there will be more and more opportunities for business to play a role. The potential is enormous as, in 2007 alone, world health expenditure was over US $5.3 trillion.

I've always been very keen to see how Virgin Unite and the investments team at Virgin Management look at new business opportunities in the field of health, as I see that this fits perfectly with our focus on doing good to do well. It's still very early days, but we're looking at how we can build a strong portfolio of health businesses across the Group. Our journey in health and wellbeing began with a telephone call.

One evening in 2001 I was dozing in the bath at home in London at the end of a long day when the phone rang. It was Nelson Mandela, calling from his home in the Eastern Cape. 'Hello, Madiba, how are you?' I greeted him, using his affec-tionate family name. 'Well, Richard, we have a problem –' he started. He went on to explain that Health & Racquet Club, South Africa's biggest gym chain, had gone into administra-tion and thousands of jobs were at stake. It was important they should be saved. 'How many clubs are there, and what kind of money are we talking about?' I asked, my mind going into overdrive.

We had launched Virgin Active a couple of years earlier in the UK with just three clubs and one of the first things that happened was that there was a fire in one of them just as the builders were due to hand over the club. The delayed revenue meant that Virgin Active wasn't exactly fat with spare cash at the time. I learned that there were seventy-six South African clubs that were in serious financial difficulties that could be acquired for somewhere in the region of £30 million. 'I'll do my absolute best,' I told Madiba. I asked Matthew Bucknall, who ran Virgin Active UK, to go and check out the details. Twenty-four hours after I had spoken to Madiba, Matthew was in South Africa, and four weeks later we had reached an agreement. The team had visited all the clubs and put in place a substainable turnaround plan as the new owners of Health & Racquet Clubs. I was pleased that I had been able to move fast and had saved thousands of jobs and contribute to the health and wellness of this great nation. I was also pleased that I had answered Mandela's call. I would do absolutely anything for him.

In 2005 we had a letter from a grandmother who wanted her grandson to open a gym in Alexandra township to keep him and his friends out of trouble. Ikasi Gym was born. Virgin Unite worked with Virgin Active to help set up Tumi Masile with the right equipment and he provided the space in an alley next to his home. His granny's persistence and his entrepreneurial energy led to this small gym generating over five hundred members and a whole host of community outreach programmes. I'll never forget in 2009 taking my mum and a group of entrepreneurs to visit Ikasi. Tumi and his granny were in tears when they welcomed us to their beautiful gym. They had set up aerobics classes in the streets that all of us joined in (showing that Brits really can't move) and then out came the body builders ... They were twice my size! It was a magical day seeing how Virgin Active was making such a big difference to the lives of the people in this community. There are now a further two township gyms like Tumi's.

This summer, I'm looking forward to opening Virgin Active's first flagship health club in Soweto. The team have added all sorts of innovative touches that the community will love like a hair salon, a DJ booth, loads of free internet stations, a media wall with huge plasma TV screens and a café bar and relaxation area, plus the usual big pool and state of the art equipment. The team from Virgin Active in South Africa have continued to amaze me with their focus on using everything they've got to help people live healthier lives. They are about to launch a programme in local high schools to get physical activity back on the school curriculum. Unfortunately many schools in South Africa do not have adequate sports facilities and the majority of students are not active. Virgin Active will be adopting various high schools in their local communities and have prepared specific exercise programmes that the kids can do in their classrooms; they'll donate gym equipment to these schools and will offer high potential kids access to the Virgin Active Health Clubs. Ross Faragher-Thomas, the Managing Director of Virgin Active in South Africa, has also played a role in shaping the Branson Centre of Entrepreneurship. Once again, it all comes back to people – and, luckily for us, Ross certainly has doing good at his core!

What was interesting was how quickly the health clubs business expanded globally. Health and exercise is on everyone's agenda these days. People want to be fit; they want to live longer and healthier lives. We were in a prime position to grow fast, and not just in South Africa. We now have a current portfolio of 250 clubs in the UK, Spain, Italy, Portugal, South Africa and Australia and the team plan on opening many more. By 2011 Virgin Active had over a million members around the world.

About seven years ago we drew on resources across the group to create an incentive-driven wellness platform called Virgin HealthMiles in the US. Run by CEO Chris Boyce and his capable team, Virgin HealthMiles runs an incentive programme that rewards people for healthy choices, which reduces weight gain and other preventable health behaviours that result in chronic disease. They work with employers, who directly pay much of the cost of healthcare in the states to encourage and reward employees in member companies to exercise and live healthy lifestyles and provide employers with information to ensure that employees, health service providers and their operating units are all working together to improve health and productivity. The evidence is pretty strong that it reduces claims and companies and employees' rising healthcare costs, makes people turn up to work more often, and makes people happier. It's a small business but growing very fast. Currently health spending is 10 per cent of UK GDP. The UK population is increasing fast. People are living longer – while at the same time becoming unhealthier. We have sedentary lifestyles; we eat the wrong food; diabetes and obesity are on the rise. If nothing changes by 2040 health spending in the UK and the US could rise to 20 per cent of GDP. It's unsustainable.

Prevention is obviously better than cure. We want to keep people out of hospital and do more at the GP, non-hospital end, which is why we bought the medical division of a business called Assura Group in the early part of 2010 and asked Patrick McCall, the former commercial director of Virgin Trains and the Chair of Virgin Unite, to lead the purchase process. The idea is to provide primary care, urgent care and outpatient services, diagnostics and day care procedures outside hospitals, in the community. If you get an outpatient's appointment and Assura Medical are on hand, you won't have to travel so far, and you might actually find the place open at a time to suit you. And patients don't pay for this improved level of care: the NHS does. Crucially, however, Assura Medical provides these services more effectively and efficiently while at the same time improving their quality, meaning that taxpayers get a better deal. We thought this was a great model: a private company supporting the NHS with business services. We think we can extend the model, adding private and complementary services. We want to offer non-urgent complementary services that combine physiotherapy, dentistry, optometry, diagnostic testing and scans. This is where some people's hackles rise, as they imagine private medicine muscling in on the clinics themselves. That's not what we're about. Our complementary services are there to promote healthier lifestyles and wellbeing among the population at large and save the NHS considerable money.

After an inspiring conversation with Patrick about the potential for Assura Medical to support vulnerable young people in the UK, I suggested that my daughter Holly should talk to Kids Company and learn from them. I could see Holly taking my suggestion on board. I thought it was a really good example of where you can actually get a for-profit company working with a not-for-profit organisation and everyone's a winner.

The business sector can also support the health sector by taking on the risk associated with new advances. Stem cells, for instance, offer many possible medical breakthroughs, and are already used to treat eighty-five medical conditions. We set up Virgin Health Bank on the understanding that dividends to the Virgin Group or to me personally would be donated to not-for-profit initiatives that are helping to fully realise the potential of cord blood stem cells.

At Virgin Health Bank, which currently operates in the UK and Qatar, stem cells collected from the umbilical cord shortly after birth are stored at an extremely low temperature so that they will be available should they ever need to be used for a transplant. In the UK we offer a unique range of services; our Community Banking service allows families to donate part of their stem cell collection enabling us to offer those donated units to transplant surgeons free of charge. This is helping to increase the number of stem cell units available to treat a wide and expanding range of conditions. The other part of the collection – and this is what our customers are paying for – is kept in reserve for the family's own use. Virgin Health Bank offers the lowest-cost stem cell banking service available in the UK. Currently there are very few medical conditions that require the use of one's own stem cells, but many scientists believe that regenerative medicine, which would require one's own stem cells, could revolutionise healthcare in the future. In Qatar, we offer Family Banking, where the entire stem cell is retained for the family.

This is a smart use of private business. We can't expect public health services to offer universal access to every speculative medical technology as it comes along. Better that those who can afford it make a bet on the future, and prove the business case. If eventually regenerative medicine proves its worth, then it should absolutely be considered for the public health system. So we were delighted when the government of Qatar approached us to start storing cord blood stem cell samples there, particularly because there are only forty-five registered bone marrow donors and donated cord blood units in the entire Gulf region. Virgin Health Bank has relocated its international headquarters to the Qatar Science & Technology Park, where it operates a state-of-the-art processing and cryogenic storage facility. Qatar's parents are now able to have their newborn babies' stem cells collected, processed and cryogenically stored in a world-class facility.

There is and probably always will be controversy around the role of business in the health sector. My vote is that we need many different solutions, and we have to consider every one of them openly, practically and with enthusiasm – and be prepared to make mistakes. With our aging population and the millions of deaths each year due to treatable and preventable diseases, we don't have time to waste. Here more than ever there is a need for unlikely marriages and entrepreneurial approaches.

Another interesting frontier of opportunity is education. Long the domain of governments and some not-for profits, Jeff Skoll's Participant film *Waiting for Superman* showed that there is a great need to reinvent educational systems. As the world has rapidly moved to new forms of information sharing, sadly education has often remained stagnant, but this is all changing through the vision of some inspiring entrepreneurs. An example from *Waiting for Superman* is KIPP, the successful network of public charter schools in the US. I am impressed by KIPP's leadership model because KIPP school leaders are entrepreneurial and run social start-ups. First, KIPP identifies and recruits smart and passionate teachers who may not have had experience as principals but who have proven success at and dedication in the academic success of low-income students to start their own schools.

These school leaders then participate in immersive hands-on residencies where they get direct leadership experience, are mentored by school leaders and learn from their mistakes. They then work with financial, real estate and operational teams to help them start and lead their own schools. KIPP schools start out small, adding one grade each year, and stay small and tight-knit so that everybody is accountable and so that the school leader has the freedom from bureaucracy to make decisions in the best interests of the children. It's great to see that 88 per cent of KIPP's students go on to college, twice the number from the average in New York City schools. These KIPP school leaders are true entrepreneurs – except that their bottom line is educating children to become adults who have meaningful, productive lives.

Jean sent me a link recently to a TED video with a simple note, 'the education revolution starts here'. Intrigued, I watched the video and was totally inspired by what I saw. Sal Khan had created the world's first free virtual school. Sal was a hedge fund manager who loved mathematics (I am always relieved that someone does) and played the role of tutor to his cousins. He started playing around with the idea that learning maths should be fun and made a few short videos – his cousins absolutely loved them. So he started to make more and load them up on YouTube.

Two thousand four hundred videos and seventy million and counting viewings later, the not-for-profit Khan Academy is well on its way to fulfilling Sal's mission to democratise education, so that anyone, anywhere in the world, can have the same access to learning. Sal is now focused on partnering with schools so that teachers can use the videos in their lessons together with software that allows every student to progress at their own pace and use class time for interaction and projects. It's a great way for young people to go at their own pace and, with the diagnostic tools that Sal has built, you can see where the child might be struggling. If Sal's software and personal computers had been around when I was at Stowe who knows how different my life might have been? Maybe I could have learned how to read spreadsheets and find all kinds of financial reasons to say 'Screw this we won't do it', or there again maybe some things in life are just meant to be. But I digress ...

It's really interesting to see this new breed of entrepreneurs like Sal who are wired to focus on open source – trying to get information available as widely as possible and really decentralising power. In a couple of interviews Sal was asked two questions to which I thought he gave brilliant answers. The first, in the *San Francisco Chronicle*, was, why do you do this? Sal said: 'For so little effort on my own part, I can empower an unlimited amount of people for all time. I can't imagine a better use of my time.' The second question posted on his website was, what religion are you? His brilliant response was: 'If you believe in trying to make the best of the finite years we have on this planet (while not making it worse for anyone else), think that pride and self-righteousness are the cause of most conflict and negativity and are humbled by the vastness and mystery of the universe, then I'm the same religion as you.'

* * *

My old friend, Chris Moss, who worked for Virgin for many years, has recently set up a new organisation called Untap.it, which I've agreed to chair. It aims to inspire millions of people worldwide to discover the super 'U' inside them. Imagine if we could untap all that potential and put it to use in the real world, what a difference it would make. They are gathering inspiring videos from people all over the world that show how you can follow your dreams and shape your own path. These videos, combined with a powerful set of easy to use on-line profiling tools, will help millions of people make sure that they can reach their true potential. This is a perfect example of an inspired approach to education using social media. I'm incredibly excited to be a part of the genesis of this great idea.

One of the largest new frontiers is the organic and ethical food and drinks industry. There were some great early pioneers in this area, such as the wonderful Ben and Jerry. It amuses me how, decades after they started up, everyone is using loads of buzz words to describe what Ben and Jerry simply went out there and got done. Before they joined us on Necker in the summer of 2010, I thumbed through their book; it read like a textbook on how to build a good business and do well at the same time (and written, of course, in the inimitable Ben & Jerry style). They were well ahead of the pack and continue to this day to do good in the world. We've been lucky enough to convince them to join the Virgin Unite Board and I look forward to working with and learning from them as well as the occasional tub of 'Cherry Garcia' – my favourite.

It would be remiss of me if I failed to mention Paul Newman and Newman's Own. Started in 1982, their wonderful motto is 'Shameless exploitation for the common good'. They've grown from a single salad dressing to over one hundred product lines and continue to give 100 per cent of the not inconsiderable profits to charity. To date they've donated over $300 million and support over a hundred worthy causes including The Hole in the Wall Gang Camp for kids with cancer which Paul started back in 1988. Following in the footsteps of these pioneers are a new breed of entrepreneurs, one of whom has been a friend for many years.

I first met Adam Balon when he worked for Virgin Cola as the marketing manager a decade or so ago. We would meet at product launches and at the staff parties I held at my home near Oxford and had some interesting chats. When I heard that he and some fellow graduates from Cambridge were launching their own ethically sustainable soft drinks company, I kept an eye out with a great deal of interest in their activities. It was good to see that Adam had taken something with him when he left us.

After university Adam worked for a couple of consultancy firms but then wanted to learn a bit about marketing and

Virgin Cola fitted that bill. He joined as assistant brand manager in the UK, next he became brand manager then marketing manager for all the different Virgin drinks brands. He learned a lot with us, particularly that business is not all about having a corporate face, but you can be yourself as well and actually enjoy working. Another important lesson was that all Virgin people are encouraged to experience that sense that 'anything is possible'. At Virgin there really is no such thing as a silly idea – at least not until such time as we've poked it around and proved it be unworkable. I want all our people to be entrepreneurial, to work under their own initiative and to realise that if something isn't happening, then they have to make it happen. 'Screw it, let's do it' doesn't just apply to me; I want our people to feel the same way, too.

Despite loving it at Virgin, Adam, like his friends, Jon Wright and Richard Reed, were ambitious. They'd all gained good degrees at Cambridge – Adam in economics, Jon in manufacturing engineering and Richard in geography – and they'd got good jobs. But they wanted to do their own thing and constantly discussed setting up a business together. They all lived in the same part of west London – not far from my own first home on a houseboat in Little Venice – and they went on holiday together, usually snowboarding in the Alps. During the long drives across France, they'd come up with entrepreneurial ideas. Like a lot of bright ideas, nothing came of them. Eventually, during a trip in 1998, they had a kind of do or die moment. They decided that this time they would come up with the big idea and follow it through. They were all living in London, single, going out a lot, enjoying the good life, but feeling a bit guilty about it. They said, wouldn't it be wonderful if their business was something they could easily do and yet be cool, sustainable and healthy?

Adam – the marketing man – said, 'How about having all your fruit and goodness in a single little bottle?' The idea appealed to them. It would be very easy to do but could be easily assimilated into a lifestyle. One of them suggested smoothies. They all made smoothies in their own blenders on a regular basis – invaluable for life on the run, or as a hangover cure – so they already knew what they were and how simple the idea could be. It was kicked around a bit in the car, and other ideas surfaced, but next morning smoothies still looked like the best idea. During the rest of the holiday, their enthusiasm grew. On their return home, using the skills they'd learned in business, they decided to look into it seriously.

Dreams are great but a few wake-up calls were in store as the problems (sorry make that 'challenges') began to surface. There was the little matter of capital, or to be more precise the lack of it. There were also issues, such as what to put in the smoothies, what would appeal to people, how thick was too thick, how sweet to make them, where to source fruits, how to make them in bulk and how to keep the fruit fresh without loading up on preservatives. They agreed that their product had to be 100 per cent pure with no additives. A good name was crucial. The right bottle, the right pricing. Distribution.

Advertising. Market research. It was a fairly daunting list.

Luckily, they already knew many of the answers and Adam certainly knew a lot about the soft drinks trade. He was still working at Virgin, while the others also had their own well-paid day jobs during what was grandly termed the research and development stage – in reality more like the chatting-over-a-pint-in-the-pub stage. Many nights and weekends passed in 'R & D' until it got to the stage where they said, 'Look, let's do this. If we don't leave our jobs we'll never get going.'

It was the classic 'Screw it, do we have the guts to do it?' moment. Sink or swim; the launch into the unknown. I had done it when I left Stowe halfway through the school year. My insurance promise to pacify my parents, and even my old headmaster at Stowe, had been that if it didn't work out I'd go to a crammer and then take up articles to become a barrister, like my dad. I knew even then that I was hopelessly addicted to the idea of working for myself and would never go into further education. But, at whatever age you launch yourself into business, it can still be utterly gut-wrenching.

Rightly, however, Adam, Jon and Richard were still cautious. They decided their litmus test would be a market trial at a small open-air jazz festival in west London. If it worked there, *then* they'd give up their jobs and do it.

They made a load of smoothies, bottled them and stuck on a working title label – something quick and easy listing ingredients. They hired a stall and were almost ready for their market research. They were going to do a proper survey, by asking people to taste a smoothie and then tick some boxes on a questionnaire; but at the last moment it seemed unrealistic to grab people out of a crowd and shout their questions at them above the music.

As Adam put it, 'All these profiles and reports and jargon aren't needed. I'd learned that much at Virgin. Just simplicity is often best in the end. It's much more powerful than complicating things. There was only one question that needed answering: should we give up our jobs to make smoothies?'

They put two large waste bins in front of their stall for customers to deposit their empty cups, one labelled 'YES' the other 'NO'. The question on a sign above the bins read 'should we give up our jobs to make these smoothies?' By the end of the day, the 'yes' bin was overflowing. They had their answer.

Raising money was the next problem to be solved. They lived in one of the most expensive cities in the world and had never managed to save much. Adam sold his vintage Triumph classic sports car. By maxing out their credit cards, each of them chipped in £15,000, so their start-up capital was £45,000, not a great deal for a manufacturing business that needed a lot of equipment and stock (fruit, bottles) before they could expect to see a penny in return. And neither could their capital just be used for investment; they had to live on it too and pay their bills. They finally found themselves on the ropes whereby they were living on handouts from friends, family and girlfriends. When they went out to dinner, their girlfriends would pay. Something that is a great trick to pull if you can get away with it but as I recall has a limited shelf life.

'We were broke,' Adam said. It reminded me of how broke I'd been during the early days of *Student,* although in my case I hadn't given up a well-paying job to get there. My mother and sisters were bringing us Red Cross food parcels and Mum even gave us the proceeds from a diamond necklace she'd found. She'd handed it in to the police and when nobody claimed it she got it back, sold it and triumphantly rushed around waving £100 in an envelope. It was a lot of money at the time and kept us going for a few more weeks. That's the thing about being a true entrepreneur – there is no safety net. In retrospect, when an entrepreneur is successful it seems easy. The struggle is rarely mentioned. But in reality desperation often drives you to work harder and with more energy because you have to survive and get out of a hole.

During this period, they came up with the name Innocent for their company and got the branding and design for their logo: again, I saw parallels with our own name, Virgin. Innocent represented being new in business, and wholesome, simple ingredients. All three partners believed that what people put in their bodies in terms of food and drink is the single most important thing that determines their quality of life. That was what defined their branding and their purpose. However, lack of money was keeping them from demonstrating this purpose. When things hit rock bottom and every penny had been begged, borrowed and spent, in desperation they emailed everyone they knew to try to find investors. They even asked their friends to email their friends. In the nick of time, Maurice Pinto, an angel investor from the US came to the rescue with a very generous investment of £250,000. This enabled them to hire essential staff and lease premises– which, amusingly, they named 'Fruit Towers'. Walking to work along Ladbroke Grove on his first morning, Adam was alarmed to see a building with a discreet brass plaque that read 'Innocent'. It was just one hundred and fifty yards from Fruit Towers.

He stood on the pavement and said, 'Oh my God.' He could see trademark claims and lawsuits rearing their heads. To his bemusement however, this other Innocent turned out to be one of my own record company labels – the premises belonged to Virgin Records. The threat of any trademark action was removed since a drinks company and a record label have no similarities (actually, on second thoughts!). Innocent drinks quickly grew and they ran out of space before moving to larger premises a couple of miles away. Vegetable pots were introduced that contained a minimum of three portions of vegetables. Their branding was witty and fun, oriented to healthy living and families, with competitions, magazines and fun events at fairs and festivals like Fruitstock in London's Regents Park. Even Innocent vans look like dairy cows standing in a field of grass. After ten years, however, they were stymied in their plans for international expansion due to a lack of capital. This is where

Coca-Cola, and a great deal of controversy, came in.

They had known the people at Coca-Cola for some time, having met at industry events. They chatted, compared notes, shared a smoothie or a large Coke and moved on. So when they decided they were at the stage of development where a substantial cash investment was needed, they thought of Coca-Cola. Other companies had made them offers down the years, but they weren't ready. When they were, they looked at all the offers on the table and decided that Coca-Cola was the best match. Innocent's clear purpose was to make natural, delicious food and drink that benefited people throughout their lives. Getting a substantial investment from Coca-Cola – initially some £30 million for a 10 to 20 per cent stake – was simply a way of fulfilling that purpose in a bigger, better and faster way. Innocent felt that if they were able to sell more healthy food and drinks in more countries to more people with Coca-Cola's weight and resources behind them, they would do a great deal of good. While their staff, suppliers and even customers were happy with the partnership with Coca-Cola (and Adam, Jon and Richard even said they wouldn't have done it without the full endorsement of their entire team) there were some snide comments in the press about 'selling out'.

According to Adam, Coca-Cola invested in them because they saw the importance of the mission Innocent was on to help people eat and drink well. Importantly, if Coca-Cola wasn't already doing good things socially and environmentally, then Innocent wouldn't have sold shares to them.

'Coca-Cola is a big company and people don't believe they're doing these things. Probably in the past they didn't do great things, but it's eye-opening to see the amount of time, effort and money that go into vast sustainability projects that they do and the scale at which they operate.' Innocent operates on an entirely different, smaller scale, but they have many shared values. The founders of Innocent believe that Coca-Cola can gain much from them. In other words, they impact on each other. There has been no sell-out.

Ironically, when the lease of Fruit Towers expired again, Innocent asked an agent to help locate new premises for them. It wasn't until they had signed a lease and moved in that they realised that their new home was Virgin Records old home. Adam seems to have an ongoing affinity with Virgin, one way or another.

In terms of sustainability, climate change is having a dramatic impact on Innocent's fruit farmers around the world. Drought is a serious problem in Kenya and India, where they source their mangoes and in southern Spain, where they source their strawberries. In Spain, water resources are being put under considerable strain from a combination of increased agricultural production and property developments. Water supply in this area is particularly important given its proximity to the Doñana National Park – an area of vital wetland for six million migratory birds that fly every year from Northern Europe to Southern Africa.

In 2010 Innocent began a project in partnership with their supplier and a team from the University of Cordoba to map the water footprint of a number of their strawberry farms. The footprint shows exactly how much water each farm has used throughout an entire season (from planting to the end of harvest). Data will be shared with all farmers across the region and with the WWF to assist them with their input into current water management planning for the entire region – for example, using water pipes instead of open channels reduces evaporation.

In Kenya, a similar study is being undertaken by the Gates Foundation and Coca-Cola; and another one is being carried out in India, where they grow the aromatic and especially sweet Alphonso mangoes used in their smoothies, to identify how climate change will impact the growing of the fruit used. To save on transport costs and fuel, Innocent prepares mango purée in the countries of origin and ships it to the UK to be made into smoothies. The project highlighted a number of concerns, one of which was that these regions are already experiencing climatic change and that this is likely to intensify in coming years. There are warmer winters, changes to the annual monsoon, reduced pollination levels and even the occurrence of hail storms (apparently not that common). Farming practices are being developed that will help the mango trees adjust to the changing climate and still allow the production of quality fruit. The farms participating in the trial used 50 per cent fewer agrochemicals, achieved between 25 and 40 per cent greater fruit retention and also a slightly larger fruit size. Good for the farmers, good for the environment and a great result given the changing climate.

More often than not, businesses are born out of sudden, inspiring ideas. Someone sees a way of making money – perhaps of doing good at the same time – and a business is born. Amy's Kitchen had an accidental start that came at a perfect time when the world was starting to wake up to the idea that healthy food could make a huge difference to personal wellbeing. In 1987 Rachel Berliner was pregnant with her daughter, Amy, when she pulled a muscle. A vegetarian, she was unable to cook because of her injury so she asked her husband, Andy, to run to their local health food store and pick up some frozen meals. 'They all tasted like cardboard,' Rachel said.

Rachel and Andy were an enterprising couple looking for an idea. They knew it would probably be in the health food business because Rachel had been brought up by parents who had grown their own organic vegetables and Andy ran an organic tea business, Magic Mountain. But so far they had failed to come up with the perfect idea that would give them a good living and put their unborn child through college. There seemed to be plenty of competition and so they knew they had to come up with a really original idea. Oddly, when they did come up with the idea of producing delicious vegetarian frozen meals – as opposed to cardboard-flavoured ones – it was into a limited market. There weren't a lot of offerings and the freezers in the natural foods stores were quite small, and without a lot of inventory. But they were convinced that there were a lot of people out there like themselves who would purchase a great tasting, natural and organic convenience meal, if it was available.

It's hard to make vegetarian food tasty. Much of it is based on soya beans or tofu and that can be pretty tasteless. Andy, who grew up eating frozen pot pies, suggested that would be a good place to start because they were the single most popular food item at the time in the general frozen food market. But there weren't any organic or vegetarian ones available. In a way it was madness – if you're going to compete in an already crowded market, why compete with the most popular item in that market? 'We knew we could do it,' the Berliners said, 'and if we succeeded then we would be flying.'

Rachel's mother created a recipe for a tasty vegetable and tofu pot pie and they spent hours in the kitchen cooking and tasting until they had the perfect one. Then they quickly made and froze a hundred pies by hand to take from their home in northern California to the San Francisco health food show that was just days away. It was a frantic rush – but, to their amazement, they got orders. Obviously they had hoped for orders, but they just weren't ready. They didn't have a commercial kitchen, they had no capital – their resources were exhausted. Selling a watch and some gold coins and borrowing against Rachel's car raised $20,000. They found suppliers of organic vegetables, both fresh locally and frozen from Washington State, which they shipped in. They managed to find an organic bakery near their home that had spare capacity to bake their pies for them. With so much outlay and orders pouring in – orders that paid in arrears – they ran out of money. One bank after another turned them down, while orders were still pouring in and piling up. Eventually a local bank did agree to give them a line of credit, with the immortal words, 'Some day you will be our biggest customers.'

They were so successful that the little local bakery couldn't keep up and gave them notice. Undeterred, Rachel and Andy advertised for more staff. They found five bakers – three are still with them a quarter of a century later – and, employing Rachel's mother as well, they worked in a frenzy to catch up on the backlog of orders in a spare kitchen one of the bakeries let them use. An early problem was putting the same amount of filling in each pie. Rather cheekily, Andy telephoned a major manufacturer of pot pies, and asked them how to make pot pies. On another occasion, their freezer broke and 100,000 pies turned black with mould.

Rachel and Andy said these are the kinds of problems all new businesses have to deal with in order to survive. 'You have to have courage. Above all, you have to work all hours and then go that extra mile. Coming up with good ideas is a piece of cake. Putting in the hard work and making them work isn't. You just have to do it.' In the beginning it was pretty much on Andy's shoulders, with Rachel supplying the emotional support and creating a strong home environment. Rachel was more than a full-time mother but her involvement was gradual as Amy became more independent. For them, all their hard work paid off. Today, Amy's Kitchen is the leading company selling prepared organic food in the US. They employ 1,600 people and make 140 different kinds of healthy vegetarian products, and expect to turn over a billion dollars within three years. They're carbon-conscious, use sustainable packaging and have plans to open an east coast hub to save on fuel. As for Amy, she has graduated from college and is now working in Sales and Marketing for their new division in the UK.

There is a lot about Rachel and Andy that I can identify with. People who set up their own business do take a gigantic leap of faith. They work harder than they ever imagined possible, harder than any employee. They know what sleepless nights are and they struggle with cash flow. A good idea is a great beginning, but it's just the tip of the iceberg. As the Titanic discovered, it's the 90 per cent that lies beneath the surface that can be the troublesome part.

The Body Shop, led by the visionary Anita Roddick, was another early leader in the world of doing good to do well. She too had the foresight to see that agriculture was an important tool to help lift people out of poverty. She and her team created thousands of jobs around the world through their supply chains. One of the organisations the Body Shop invested in back in 1997 was a cooperative of cocoa farmers in Ghana who had decided to set up their own chocolate company in the UK to give them direct access to the lucrative UK chocolate industry. The Day Chocolate Company was established with a third of shares owned by the cooperative, Kuapa Kokoo, and the other shares owned by Body Shop and Twin Trading. Back then there were two thousand farmers from twenty-two villages involved; now they are improving the lives of over 45,000 farmer members from 1,200 villages.

In 1998 Divine, the first ever Fairtrade chocolate bar, was launched in the UK. Today it is growing globally and continues to be a huge success. Interestingly, it is the only Fairtrade chocolate bar that is 45 per cent owned by the farmers themselves. Fairtrade ensures they get a better deal on their cocoa, and ownership means they get a share of the profit and have a voice in the cocoa industry.

As I'm writing about these businesses, all of which depend on and support farmers, I'm reminded of a conversation I had with Strive Masiyiwa, founder and chairman of Econet, one of the largest telecommunications companies in the world, and a fellow founder of the Carbon War Room. Strive is passionate about Africa gaining full economic freedom. His businesses have already created thousands of jobs across the continent, but he wanted to make an even bigger difference and felt that agriculture was the way to do it. So he teamed up with Kofi Annan, Mo Ibrahim, the Gates Foundation, the Rockefeller Foundation and several African partners to create the Alliance for a Green Revolution in Africa (AGRA). Its mission is to provide food security and prosperity across Africa through the support of smallholding farmers. They are doing this through some smart business practices, getting farmers information, access to good seeds and healthy soils, access to markets, finance and storage and transport. They have some pretty ambitious goals (which is no surprise with Strive and Kofi being involved). They are planning to reduce food insecurity by 50 per cent in more than twenty countries, to double the income of twenty million smallholding farmers and get African countries leading a green revolution that will help protect them from the ravages of climate change.

AGRA is another great example of a marriage between government, business and the social sector. Watching the famine unfolding in Somalia and other parts of East Africa that is impacting over thirteen million people, I'm reminded that we need countless more efforts like AGRA to stop the incredible needless suffering still occurring in a world as wealthy as ours.

The frightening thing is that famine caused by drought and other environmental issues is set to get worse as we continue to rapidly deplete our natural resources. It has been very interesting watching countries from the Middle East and China purchase land in Africa and other parts of the world for food and water security. The scarcity of natural resources will be the cause of many of the burning issues in the coming decades, but it also creates lots of opportunities right now. Probably the greatest frontier of opportunity is the creation of businesses that protect and harness our natural resources – with the obvious added benefit of reducing our carbon output.

Web: virginunite.com/screwbusinessasusual
Twitter: @virginunite #sbau
Facebook: Facebook.com/VirginUnite

5 Gaia Rocks

'Along with Eric Ryan, I founded method on the idea that business, as the largest and most powerful institution on the planet, had the greatest opportunity to create solutions to our environmental and health crises. Since the dawn of the industrial age, business has traded off people's health and the state of the planet for growth and profit, but it doesn't need to be so. In fact, after having spent a number of years working on environmental issues at the Carnegie Institution, I was convinced that business is the most powerful agent for positive change on the planet. But it's not business as we know it today. It is fundamentally and profoundly different. It is business redesigned' – Adam Lowry, co-founder, method

The other day I had a pleasant surprise. I received an email from a man named Peter Carroll, whom I did not know, but I certainly knew the man he mentioned, wildlife artist David Shepherd. Attached to Peter's email was a scanned copy of a two-page letter I had written as a schoolboy at Stowe, when I was starting up *Student* magazine. It was dated 4 January 1967. I had written to David thanking him for granting me an interview. I'm not sure now why I had wanted to interview him, other than that he had been a scholar at Stowe twenty years earlier and at that stage was one of the world's leading wildlife artists – much admired by my artistic sister, Vanessa, who was bursting to meet him!

It brought so many memories rushing back: a dry, sunny and rather mild day for January during the Christmas holidays, driving with my parents and Vanessa to the Shepherds' home in Sussex, and an afternoon spent with my clunky old tape recorder and my novice attempts to interview one of my first subjects, while my parents were entertained to tea by his kind wife who seemed not at all put out by having so many people descend on them. The first thing I noticed when I looked at the letter after a gap of some thirty-five years was that, unfortunately, I had spelled his name wrong:

Dear David Sheperd [sic],

Having just gone through your interview for a third time I am setting out to buy some new batteries after this. Every word is so stimulating and interesting that I find it difficult to express my thanks to you. I sincerely feel that your words of advice could well do much for many of our readers – it was an interview so far from the deadly 'yes' 'no' answers of so many people of today – hell I don't know how to thank you.

I will certainly send you a copy of it as soon as possible – but I can't tell you when we are going to press, until we've cleared up the finances.

Do please thank your wife for being such a charming hostess – I'm so sorry that she found herself landed with the large proportion of the family.

Good luck with the pictures for America and the eye 'op'. I look forward to seeing you at Stowe next term. Thanks once again,

Yours, Richard.

The author of the email, Peter Carroll, was the man behind the successful Gurkha Justice campaign with Joanna Lumley. As a result of this success, David Shepherd had asked Peter to help him and his foundation at www.davidshepherd.org to succeed in his lifetime ambition to save the tiger in the wild through his campaign, TigerTime. Peter wrote: 'When David was born, there were 100,000 wild tigers in India alone. Now, in his eightieth year there are thought to be fewer than 3,500 wild tigers on the planet. The situation is desperate.'

I was aware of how desperate the situation was because Virgin Unite had already connected me with WildAid, run by Peter Knights, who, with a tiny staff, is working tirelessly to help save endangered species. One of his rescue targets is the tiger. Virgin Unite is now working with Peter and his team to support a tiger reserve in India. I'm also working with Peter on helping to save sharks around the world. I had already seen filmmaker, and a friend of Sam's, Rob Stewart's gripping documentary *Sharkwater*, exposing the voracious shark-hunting industry. The horrible reality is that the demand for shark's fin soup is very high, with up to 73 million being used for soup every year and thousands of sharks are brutally caught, their fins are cut off and they are left to drown. I recently spent one of the best days of my life swimming with three hundred whale sharks off the coast of Cancún. These gentle giants, many of them the size of a bus and weighing in at over 20 tons, are magnificent creatures. Sadly they too are on the threatened species list.

In September 2011 Virgin Unite and I joined basketball star Yao Ming, my friends at WildAid, and Chinese business leader Zhang Yue in Shanghai to call for a ban on shark fin soup in China (including Hong Kong) – a measure which could save tens of millions of sharks every year. Over breakfast with gentle giant Yao Ming he spoke of his guilt at once eating shark fin soup before realising the horrors behind its production: 'The shark fin soup doesn't even have any flavour, but more importantly if you take all the sharks out of the ocean you destroy the ecosystem and we lose the other fish that sustain us every day.' Now retired from basketball, it's wonderful that Yao says his number one priority in life is to use his high profile to make a difference and do good in the world. I also spoke with California Governor Jerry Brown, urging him to sign a bill which has received overwhelming support from the people of California and has passed the Assembly and Senate there to ban shark fin sales.

We've also been adding our weight to a wonderful organisation called Peace Parks Foundation. In the colonial era old tribal lands of Africa were split up into new countries, with no regard for the people who inhabited them, or for the natural migratory routes of the animals. Everybody is aware of the amazing migration of wildebeest across the Serengeti plains. People know of the strange, secret roads of elephants, which roam like ghosts across hundreds and thousands of miles. But few are aware that artificial borders curtailed and controlled these vast seasonal migrations. For example, the long-running civil wars in Mozambique had decimated almost all the animals there; they had suffered terribly, either being shot for food, blown up by land mines or driven by fear away from their natural habitats. But the Kruger National Park in neighbouring South Africa had too many animals, so many, in fact, that they were in danger of being culled. Then Peace Parks Foundation was founded in 1997 by Dr Anton Rupert, Prince Bernhard of the Netherlands and Nelson Mandela as a not-for-profit organisation to allow the free movement of wild game animals across national borders. The largest contributor was the Dutch Postcode Lottery.

Lemurs are another species close to my heart. Several years ago Rob Stewart visited Necker. At that time he was completing his shocking film *Sharkwater*, about the plight of the world's sharks. It turned out that Rob also had a passion for another species on the brink of extinction: lemurs. Lemurs are a species indigenous to Madagascar and their numbers have been declining very rapidly due to loss of habitat. Once lemurs disappear from Madagascar, they are likely to become extinct altogether as they've not been introduced into any other habitats. So Rob and I enlisted several lemur experts and started working on a plan to look at how we could trial a home for them on Moskito Island, another British Virgin Island I had recently purchased, near Necker. So, armed with the advice of a group of world-renowned lemur experts, we prepared to bring in a group of lemurs from their respective captivity in zoos. Fuelled by a few environmentalists in the Caribbean, controversy erupted over the lemurs and whether we were doing the right thing. It was a heartbreaking experience for me: I honestly believed that I was doing the right thing for these beautiful animals. As I watched the debate rage online among conservationists, I realised that valid points were being made, but also that some of the input was way off base. I decided that the best thing to do would be to embrace the range of views and have an open discussion about the best way to introduce the lemurs. I posted this message online:

I have been given sight to much of your email chain and am grateful for it. The debate about the plight of the lemurs and what should be done about them, and whether or not my idea was a good idea or bad idea, was certainly an eye-opener to me and I suspect to all of us. So first of all thank you for all your contributions.

I would like to begin by saying I became interested in lemur conservation because these truly unique and wonderful animals are in a very difficult situation in their home country of Madagascar, the only place in the world where they occur naturally. Madagascar has already lost most of its natural habitat, many of its lemur species are critically endangered and the situation there has been seriously exacerbated since the coup two years ago.

In terms of my contribution to lemur conservation, I am committed to the following: using the advice of the world's leading experts on lemurs, I would like to select a handful of endangered and critically endangered species for ex situ breeding – to provide assurance colonies should they disappear or become severely depleted in the wild. Possible candidate species include the ruffed lemurs, black and white ruffed lemurs and the blue-eye black lemur. These particular species have not bred well in most zoos because they are apt to become slightly obese from lack of exercise. I should also emphasise that I do not intend to import animals from the wild in Madagascar, but rather to acquire them from existing captive colonies.

Many of you have noted that I have already imported several ring-tailed lemurs to my island. Although these are not a priority species (being the most abundant primate species in captivity), I thought they would be a good species to learn and start off with.

Many of you are also concerned that I would release lemurs into the wild in the Caribbean and, having listened, I understand your concerns. I have also spoken at length with Simon Stuart, who Chairs the IUCN Species Survival Commission, and Russ Mittermeier, who Chairs the IUCN SSC Primate Specialist group. They have suggested that I keep the lemurs in large open-air fenced enclosures (which should enable them to breed) to avoid impacting native Caribbean species of fauna and flora in any way. I have agreed to do that and have told them that I will welcome their future advice in the years to come to make this programme a great success.

I also fully recognise that ex situ breeding can only make a small contribution to the plight of the 101 species and subspecies of lemurs, a large number of which do not survive well outside their natural habitat. Therefore, I am also committed to helping with targeted in situ conservation activities to ensure that representative populations of all threatened lemur species survive in the wild. I have already done this on a small scale (e.g. with the silky sifaka in north-eastern Madagascar), but intend to increase my commitment to lemur conservation in Madagascar more broadly in the very near future, and am exploring possible channels for doing this.

In terms of conservation of the endangered species of the Caribbean itself, I will obviously continue to help on this. I was delighted to help in a small way in helping to protect the rock iguana and reintroducing flamingos to the British Virgin Islands. I have also pledged to work with the Caribbean Nature Conservancy in furthering their wonderful work starting with a possible conference on Necker.

Anyway, I'm glad you've educated me to do the right thing and now look forward to working with many of you in saving our species.

All the best,

Richard Branson

So why worry about lemurs, sharks, tigers, elephants and parks when we have so many other issues in the world? How we treat our world is a reflection of our humanity, our intelligence, our conscience and, ultimately, our very survival. The rapid depletion of our natural resources since the start of the industrial age is the root cause of many of the impending environmental issues, such as climate change. This really hit home to me during my many conversations with James Lovelock. I've named this chapter in honour of James and his creation of the theory of Gaia, named after the Greek Goddess of the Earth. James proposes that the earth really is a living organism and that everything is closely integrated to form a single and self-regulating complex system which maintains the conditions for life on the planet. For decades he has been telling the world that we are destroying our own home. With every species and habitat we destroy we are upsetting the overall balance of Gaia. I'll never forget an article I read in the *Independent* newspaper in 2006 which was an emergency call from James showing how seriously he takes this threat to humanity:

'My Gaia theory sees the Earth behaving as if it were alive, and clearly anything alive can enjoy good health, or suffer disease. Gaia has made me a planetary physician and I take my profession seriously, and now I, too, have to bring bad news.

'The climate centres around the world, which are the equivalent of the pathology lab of a hospital, have reported the Earth's physical condition, and the climate specialists see it as seriously ill, and soon to pass into a morbid fever that may last as long as 100,000 years. I have to tell you, as members of the Earth's family and an intimate part of it, that you and especially civilisation are in grave danger.

'Our planet has kept itself healthy and fit for life, just like an animal does, for most of the more than three billion years of its existence. It was ill luck that we started polluting at a time when the sun is too hot for comfort. We have given Gaia a fever and soon her condition will worsen to a state like a coma. She has been there before and recovered, but it took more than 100,000 years. We are responsible and will suffer the consequences: as the century progresses, the temperature will rise 8 degrees centigrade in temperate regions and 5 degrees in the tropics.

'We should be the heart and mind of the Earth, not its malady. So let us be brave and cease thinking of human needs and rights alone, and see that we have harmed the living Earth and need to make our peace with Gaia. We must do it while we are still strong enough to negotiate, and not a broken rabble led by brutal war lords. Most of all, we should remember that we are a part of it, and it is indeed our home.'

Conversations with James, Al Gore and others were a big wake-up call for me and the Virgin Group to ensure we get our own house in order. As mentioned throughout this book, we are currently on that journey, but we also realise that we have a long way to go and are learning from many of the companies and organisations profiled here. The great news is that looking at how we protect and harness our natural resources is the largest 'great frontier' we will have in our lifetimes. If we get it right (which we can and must) this new frontier will create millions of new jobs, save money for existing businesses and propel us into a way of life that is far more harmonious with nature and prosperous for all.

I have come to realise that, while we must have a sense of urgency about this message, we can't be too zealous. People who are just trying to keep a roof over their heads and food on the table – or trying to keep their jobs – with the best will in the world really don't have much time or energy to think too much about climate change and the demise of biodiversity, tigers, whales or lemurs. The doomsday scenario just doesn't cut it for the average person who remains pretty sceptical when the sun still shines and the snow still falls. Also, they see it as costing a lot of money with new-fangled light bulbs and windmills springing up all over the place while their electricity and food bills keep going up. Many of those people who live in poverty, or on the verge of poverty, will be the ones who will be most impacted by climate change and some of the other environmental issues heading our way.

I think Mary Robinson, the former President of Ireland and

former UN High Commissioner for Human Rights, summed it up very neatly after a climate conference I attended at Copenhagen, when she said that the trouble with all these climate conferences is that too many experts present complicated and jargonistic data. 'They're all specialists,' she said as we chatted later. 'Copenhagen's keynote speeches should have been given by farmers who'd lost their living by drought or flood. They should have been given by fishermen who no longer have any fish to catch.'

Environmentalists. Space scientists. Geologists. These people are important. Without their brilliance, their precision, their intellectual honesty, their courage and their passion, we wouldn't have a clue about the crisis we're hurtling towards. But these are not the people to wake up a busy and self-involved world. The science behind global warming is solid – but it's the stories of ordinary people which engage your attention when you've half an ear to the radio and you're racing to pack your kids off to school. It's their stories that stick in your mind clearly enough that you can deliver them with confidence over a drink with a friend. It's their plight that makes you think, 'What if something like this happened to my family?'

It's true that the planet has had numerous and extreme climate changes in relatively short periods of time. Humans evolved and found new ways of surviving and thriving. The difference between *then* – historically speaking – and *now* is that there weren't some seven billion people around *then*. Earlier I mentioned the weight of the resources that went into producing a single laptop computer – a staggering 40,000 pounds. But people worldwide want more than laptops. Rightly, they want their share – their turn. They want cars and televisions. They want central heating and air conditioning, they want fast food and fancy modern kitchens with dishwashers and washing machines – the list is endless. Take a quick look around your home, your street, your office. Every single thing you can see is manufactured, using natural materials that had to be mined or extracted, and all of this pumps out carbon dioxide – *more* carbon dioxide than the planet would produce naturally without people around. If a single laptop takes 40,000 pounds of raw material, how much does a car take? I have no idea – but you get the picture. Now, extrapolate that by what eight or nine billion people want for themselves — every day, every week, every year – and the problem becomes instantly clear.

It is *people* who are affecting the natural cycles of the planet. This is why the issue is so immediate and so important. The world never had this sheer weight of people and consumption before. The difference between life continuing as we know it or breaking down past the point of no return starts at just one degree.

According to Nature Climate Change, 'Research predicts that a one degree centigrade rise in average temperature will reduce yields across two-thirds of the maize-growing region of Africa, even in the absence of drought. Add drought and that effect spreads over the entire area.' Each degree above that causes another breakdown in the environmental chain. Sadly, we could be starting to see these effects with the current devastating drought in East Africa. According to scientists I trust, like James Lovelock, *four degrees* is the point of no return. It doesn't really matter if you believe in climate change or not, if you say it's all a big con or not – little will be noticed by the average person until it is too late. The damage is being done incrementally so on the surface all still seems well. It's a bit like a hairline crack in a dam; nothing is seen until the dam breaks.

Coral reefs are just one example. Warmer, acidic seas kill them off. An underwater food chain is destroyed. With nothing to feed on, shoals of millions of brightly coloured little fish vanish. Bigger fish – the ones that feed people – go hungry and die. But they're not the only thing that goes. Tourists who come for the scuba diving stop coming. Hotels close and local people have no jobs and no income. Fishermen and their boats don't put to sea because, with no fish, there's no point. The domino effect is frightening.

Bees are yet another example. I love bees because I think that the beehive is a metaphor for the world. Every member of the community is of equal value although they have different tasks. The bees go out to work and return with pollen. They turn this into produce: honey and wax – all they need to survive. The eggs and larvae are the future of the hive; and at the heart is the queen. She is like Gaia, who lives at the heart of our planet. The queen bee – and Gaia – must be protected at all costs because without the queen we won't survive.

That might seem very airy-fairy, so let's look at it like

this, from a strictly business point of view. The produce of the hive goes way beyond the value of honey. The honey in a single hive earns around £130. But the value of the crops, the fruit and the vegetables that the hive pollinates is around £600. In the UK this is worth over £1 billion. In the United States alone, the service of bees as pollinators is worth $15–$20 billion a year – and worldwide it's estimated to be worth $200–$400 billion. Bees are suffering from many new diseases, such as foul brood and mites, but beekeepers who work hard to maintain a healthy colony can make a good living beyond the value of the honey they produce by hiring out their hives' services to a farmer to pollinate his crops. No matter how delicious honey is, we can live without it – but we can't do without the *work* of bees. Bees fertilise crops and those crops feed the world. Bees are just one of the many natural resources humanity has built our wealth upon that need to be valued in a radically different way going forward so that we make sure they are around for many generations to come. The good news is that there are some great pioneers leading the way to change what businesses value and measure.

One of those pioneers is Jochen Zeitz, the CEO of the Sport & Lifestyle Group and CSO of PPR and Chairman of the Board of PUMA after serving eighteen years as Chairman and CEO at PUMA. Our paths in business have followed different directions. I evolved as an entrepreneur and was self-made and largely self-taught and I think almost intuitively; while Jochen is as sharp as a rapier and highly intelligent. After deciding that medicine wasn't for him and dropping out of medical school – his parents were both in medicine – he switched to taking a degree at one of Europe's finest business schools in Germany. He became the youngest chairman and CEO of a listed public company in German history when he was appointed at PUMA at the age of thirty. His meteoric rise to the top saw a seven-year losing streak with mounting losses halted and PUMA becoming over the years the most profitable company in the industry, surging ahead, with sales expected to reach over 3 billion euros by the end of 2011, more than a fifteen-fold increase since Jochen took PUMA's helm, with the share price rising from 8.6 euros in his first year as CEO to an all time high of 350 euros, gaining around 4,000 per cent in thirteen years. There are many parallels between us. We both have a passion for Africa and, while I have a game reserve in South Africa, Jochen has had one in Kenya for the last six years.

We first met in 2009 at Ulusaba when Jochen joined us on a Virgin Unite Connection Trip to South Africa. Guests on the Unite Connection Trips usually spend a few days with me, looking at the tangible results of our projects in Johannesburg and in the villages around Ulusaba. I enjoy it because, hopefully, entrepreneurs 'wake up' or make the connection that they can create change and do good and, above all, it's fun!

I always watch new visitors to see if they're having a good time. I like to engage with each one in turn and have a heart-to-heart chat with them about their thoughts, their dreams and aspirations because I think we both learn a lot that way. I was much taken by the way in which Jochen became totally involved.

Jochen commented to Jean: 'You know, Richard has this way of being open to all and any and his spirit of generosity and mischievousness makes everyone feel relaxed. I felt mesmerised by him at first, not sure whether I was being charmed by a beast with the nature of a lion or a golden retriever. He has a particularly oversized comic book smile.'

Jean laughed, enjoying the frank description. 'And what did you conclude?' she asked him, later relaying the conversation to me. Jochen replied, 'In the end I would say he's both lion-hearted and doggedly loyal.' Jochen was particularly generous on that trip because, even though he has set up his own foundation – the Zeitz Foundation, in 2008 – to support creative and innovative sustainable projects and solutions that holistically balance conservation, community development, culture and commerce (or the '4cs' as he calls it), after more than a few shared drinks with us all around the long table he was sufficiently inspired to make a donation to Unite for the Branson Centre of Entrepreneurship.

A year or two after that initial meeting Jochen was climbing even higher up the corporate ladder and was appointed Chairman of the Board of PUMA SE as well as CEO of the newly created Sport & Leisure Group at PPR – the parent company of PUMA, with brands like Gucci, Stella McCartney, Yves Saint Laurent, Balenciaga, Alexander McQueen, and Bottega Veneta, among others, with complete freedom to take the Sport & Lifestyle Group in whatever direction he saw fit. I admired this in their board; you either trust someone or you don't. If you trust them, you should let them fly. It's how I work at Virgin. By delegating, I feel relaxed that I have chosen the right people and then just let them get on with it. Way too many companies specialise in delegating just one thing: blame!

I don't think I fully appreciated how fast Jochen was moving on truly turning PUMA into a force for good in the world. In June 2008 he introduced PUMAVision – a new paradigm of corporate social and environmental sustainability – and implemented it right across every part of the company, to contribute towards, as Jochen puts it, 'a better world for the generations to come'. As part of this vision, PUMA recently announced its focus on an 'honest balance sheet', or what they call their Environmental Profit & Loss (EP&L) Account. This was driven by Jochen's awareness that many of the problematic issues in the world can be traced back to businesses using the earth's resources to create wealth, without recognising any value for them since they have been traditionally used and viewed as 'free services'. PUMA are pioneers in this area, the first international company to put a monetary valuation on the environmental impact of its entire supply chain, with the belief that placing a price tag on nature is the best way of saving it. Under Jochen's leadership, PUMA has also committed to the even more challenging goal of integrating its social and economic impact, including safety and working conditions, fair wages as well as accounting for the many benefits a business brings, including job creation, tax contributions, philanthropic initiatives and other value-adding elements, into the next stages of development which will complete an Environmental, Social and Economic P&L statement. He is doing so because he believes that ethical business is necessary and because this is the Fair, Honest, Positive and Creative way of doing things – or the '4Keys' as he calls them, which is a guide to ensure best practices and doing good business is adhered to.

I was delighted when Jochen announced that PPR HOME – PPR's new sustainability initiative across the brands of the Group – which he also heads, was happy to partner with Unite in any shape or form in our new concept for a fresh way of looking at capitalism by doing good. He has already played a key role in an initiative we are working on together called the Business Leaders Group. He also had a great idea to expand PUMA's link to Virgin to include Galactic and Oceanic and perhaps designing apparel that would donate to Virgin Unite's work. For me, this is the way forward: a kind of symbiotic business approach where like-minded companies join forces under the same umbrella and do good together. It's brilliant when it works so smoothly.

After being in business for over twenty years, Ray Anderson's carpet tile company, Interface Inc issued its first Sustainability Report in 1998. Interface accounted for 10,500 tons of solid waste, over 600 million gallons of contaminated water, over 700 tons of toxic gases and 63,000 tons of carbon dioxide a year. Ray was making a very healthy profit selling carpet tiles to major customers such as corporate offices, malls and hotels and he felt confident of his place in the market and proud of his achievements. His was a good company. It charged fair prices for products that gave people a pleasant environment in which to work.

So when, somewhat bafflingly, some of Interface's customers began coming to the company with an unfamiliar question, Ray wasn't that worried. The question was: what is Interface doing for the environment?

What on earth? Interface made carpet tiles. It obeyed all the regulations and codes of practice set down for the production of carpet tiles. If it didn't actually *do* anything for the environment, it didn't do it any harm either. Ray did wonder, though, why the question? Something had to be going on at ground level if customers were starting to ask that kind of question. And there were more. 'What's in a carpet tile? Does it contain additives or E numbers? Is it organic? Will it exacerbate my allergies? Will it poison me or my kids?'

There was a palpable feeling in the air that people no longer blindly accepted everything they ate or even walked on in everyday life. What struck Ray especially was that Interface's customers were asking more questions that he did not have the answers to – he was concerned about losing projects to competitors. Around the same time one question kept coming back to Interface's salesforce. Architects and interior designers – people very important to Ray's business – kept asking his sales people what Interface was doing for the environment. Finally it dawned on Ray that, while he was ducking this issue, his sales people were being hung out to dry.

Others in the company were faster off the mark than Ray himself. They came to him with the proposal of creating a taskforce to provide detailed answers to the environment question. 'Great,' said Ray. 'Go for it.' There was one hitch: they wanted Ray to launch the project. 'Give it a kickoff speech with your environmental vision,' they said. But Ray didn't have an environmental vision. He'd done quite nicely without one for twenty years, and so, until recently, had his customers.

What could he say? 'Interface obeys the law!' 'Interface complies!' As the date for Ray's inaugural speech loomed – 31 August 1994 – by the middle of the month he still hadn't the faintest idea what he was going to say. Then a book landed on his desk, Paul Hawken's *The Ecology of Commerce*. 'I began to thumb through it,' he remembered, 'and on page nineteen I came to a chapter heading about species extinction.' The chapter was titled 'The Death of Birth'.

For Ray it was an epiphany. 'It was like the point of a spear, and as I read on and came to the central point of the book, the spear just went deeper and deeper.' The point Paul Hawken made was simple and unavoidable. The biosphere is in decline. Industry is the major culprit, because of the way it extracts resources, and uses them to make products that, sooner or later, end up in landfill. There is only one institution on earth that is large enough, powerful enough, pervasive enough and wealthy enough really to change that system

– and it's the same institution that's doing the damage.

Ray had his speech. 'And at that point you could say the spear touched my heart, and I was convicted, right there, as a plunderer of the earth.' He went from having no environmental vision at all to becoming – of all things – *an environmentally friendly industrialist.* He asked his team to audit his entire supply chain comprehensively and from the final report he learned that his factories and suppliers together extracted from the earth and processed over *1.2 billion pounds* of material so that they could sell $802 million worth of products. He was shocked. Ultimately, the costs of that level of waste would be borne by future generations – what Ray called generational tyranny, a kind of taxation without representation levied by us on future generations.

Ray set about transforming his company. In the three and a half years following the audit, Interface reduced its total worldwide waste by 40 per cent. This saved it $67 million – money which was set aside to pay for the rest of Interface's revolution. He then worked out a way to measure his company's ecological footprint, by *adding* costs to his balance sheet, items that convention and expedience preferred to ignore. 'Under our QUEST program, we define waste as any cost that goes into a product that does not produce value for our customers. Our definition of waste includes not just off-quality and scrap, the traditional notion of waste; it also means anything we don't do right the first time. A misdirected shipment. A mispriced invoice. A bad debt. We have declared that energy derived from fossil fuels is waste, waste to be eliminated systemati-cally, first through efficiency improvement and, eventually, by replacing it with renewable energy.'

Today Interface is a leaner manufacturer having divested many of its non-core business and continues to make signifi-cant progress on its sustainability initiatives. For example, as of 2010 Interface has reduced energy use per unit of produc-tion by 43 per cent, and 30 per cent of the energy that it uses in manufacturing facilities is from renewable sources. Water use per unit of production has decreased by 82 per cent, and 40 per cent of the materials that it uses to make carpet are from recycled or bio-based sources. Interface employees work in safer conditions than ever as the frequency rate of reportable accidents have been reduced by 70 per cent from 1999 levels.

This shows the brilliance of Ray's efforts to change the way he did business. He showed how he could use the balance sheet as an ally in becoming an ecological pioneer. Interface tries not to sell broadloom carpet and carpet tiles any more. It tries to rent them by offering customers a lease program for carpet, called Evergreen lease. It replaces damaged ones free of charge and, when the lease is up, it recalls them all and recycles them, saving even more basic materials. Remarkably – and to Ray's surprise – the company can make more money this way. Part of this saving comes because the company wastes less and saves on buying so many raw mate-rials – but it is also because customers preferred to lease. The company could now answer that original question – 'what is Interface doing for the environment?' – and tell customers how it is helping to do good for the environment – and, as is usually the case, they are building their customer-base and their profits as a consequence.

As I mentioned earlier, the world lost a wonderful visionary and human being when Ray Anderson died in August 2011. It is up to all of us to ensure we carry on the great work he started.

I've certainly been inspired by Ray, Jochen, James Lovelock, Al Gore and many others over the years who have committed their lives to looking at how we can do far better for the planet. I also learned a lot from Ted Turner, the America's Cup winner in 1977 and founder of the CNN news channel and the UN Foundation. From a commercial perspective, I had been thinking about all kinds of ways to reduce our airline fuel bill. Ted helped me get a broader perspective on things when he said to me: 'Why not build a refinery for clean rather than dirty fuel? Come and meet my people. They'll convince you that there is another way.' Ted's 'people' turned out to be a room full of experts from the Energy Future Coalition, convened by Tim Wirth, president of the United Nations Foundation. The world-changing idea on their agenda that day was biofuels. After this, we did start investing in biofuels and learned lots of lessons in the early years about the complexities of the right type of biofuels to ensure that we were not actually using more energy in its production than other types of fuels and were not eating into the food supply.

Quite soon after that meeting with the rocket scientists and my breakfast with Al Gore, I was set to make an announcement at the Clinton Global Initiative. We had looked at all sort of different ideas, but in the end I decided that the biggest difference I could make was to start to show people the great opportunity we have to invest in renewable fuels and energy efficiency. So I estimated how much Virgin Group's share of the profits would be from our transport companies over the next ten years, at the time we thought as much as $3 billion, and decided that we would publicly commit to ploughing those profits into investments in renewable energy and energy efficiency across the Virgin Group and beyond. The commitment coincided with the start of a fierce global recession which has decimated aviation profits. Luckily we do have a profitable train company and we have used the train dividends to make a number of investments.

At the time of the announcement, I recruited Shai Weiss to launch the Virgin Green Fund, a private equity growth fund making investments across a wide range of innovative new companies. These range from biofuels, solar, lighting efficiency, water desalination and a whole host of other companies that reduce our dependency on traditional energy by harnessing new types of clean and renewable energy and make consumption of energy and other resources including water far more efficient. It has been incredibly exciting to see some of these new companies emerge. It is this new generation of entrepreneurs who will truly redesign how we live in the world. There have been a few who have really inspired me, so I thought that I would share a couple of their stories.

Sam Wyly was born to Louisiana cotton farmers during the Great Depression, and went on to make billions in business. Wyly told the *Dallas Morning News* that when his daughter was in the fifth grade and believed her dad could accomplish anything he put his mind to, she asked him the question: 'Dad, what are you going to do about all this toxic waste being put into the air?' His daughter's question planted a seed that would eventually bring about the creation of Green Mountain Energy. The company was founded in 1997 when Wyly saw an opportunity to take advantage of the deregulation of electricity providers taking place around the country. He hoped that by offering customers a chance to buy their energy from clean sources, he could change the way electricity was produced. After false starts in California, Pennsylvania and Ohio, Green Mountain Energy finally found traction in Texas and today is a thriving company.

Through sheer persistence, Sam has managed to build a company that delivers a clean, reliable electricity service to more than 300,000 households. Since the company's founding, they've kept more than 11.3 billion pounds of CO_2 out of the atmosphere. The company have helped facilitate the creation of more than forty wind and solar plants and they're thriving as a business, increasing their customer-base by an average of 20 per cent every year. They've become one of the fastest growing and most profitable green electricity companies in the United States, turning over more than $500 million in annual revenue and $50 million in profit. In 2010, the company was acquired by NRG for $350 million in cash. Sam has not only done something great for the planet, he has shown that clean energy is serious business. He also proved that you should listen closely to questions asked by your kids, as the answers can lead to the most amazing things.

Born in India, Jigar Shah and his family moved to Sterling, Illinois, when he was one year old. Growing up there instilled in Jigar what he calls his 'Midwest sensibility'.

Jigar, who is a perpetual student and expert on energy and infrastructure is convinced that climate change is 'the largest wealth creation opportunity of our lifetime'. He believes clean energy will clean up in the marketplace, ushering in a sustainable low-carbon future. He stakes his fortune on it. In fact, he *made* his fortune on it.

'What you find with electricity bills is that about 50 per cent of your money pays for the wholesale generation, which is what most traditional energy officials use as the basis for costs comparison with other forms of energy. The other 50 per cent of your bill pays for the fixed expenses of the energy company, including management salaries. Some of your bill might even cover an energy company's mistakes. For example, imagine your utility company set about building a nuclear power plant, but it runs out of money and only builds half of it, so that it never gets turned on. This has actually happened, by the way. The half-built station still has to be paid for, and an energy company will pass those costs down to the consumer.

'The magic of solar energy is it sits on top of your building, and, well, *that's it*. Solar energy has the potential to offset everything but the wholesale figure. That's why I'm confident that solar will be the first mainstream source of power that will be cost-effective, without a single tax credit, subsidy, or incentive, for at least 20 per cent of the world's population.'

Jigar Shah launched SunEdison in 2003, basing his company on a business plan he developed in 1999 for a university class. That model smashed the decades-old assumption that if you wanted to use solar energy, you had to pay a huge up-front installation cost. And I mean huge: for a decent-sized commercial building, a rooftop array or a ground-based solar farm can cost anywhere from $10,000 to $10 million! This inspired Shah to find a solution: 'Do you want to be in the solar power-plant business? Or do you just want to buy electricity-on-demand generated by solar power?'

(Do you want the carpet? Or do you just want the *services* of the carpet? Do you want a Boeing Dreamliner, or just an air ticket? Once again, we're seeing the advantages of thinking about the value of services, rather than the price of products.)

SunEdison customers have no upfront costs for their solar system. SunEdison installs, owns and operates the plants. Customers sign a power-purchasing agreement, or PPA, with SunEdison and agree to buy the electricity the solar plant produces at a locked-in price for at least ten years. Businesses, of course, loved the idea of predictable fuel costs, year after year: at a single stroke it ended their exposure to the highest rates in the fuel market, instead of paying the daily fluctuation rates for power generated by utilities at central stations and transmitted over ageing and congested transmission lines.

Once Jigar had secured enough PPAs, he approached banks, investment companies and private backers and used those PPAs as collateral against which to borrow money to expand his company further. Revenue collected through PPAs repaid SunEdison's investors, who earned a tidy return. SunEdison now has more solar energy systems and megawatts under management than any other company – and Jigar Shah has helped turn solar services into a multi-billion dollar industry.

'Solar is a becoming a significant portion of the global energy portfolio already,' Jigar maintains. 'It'll be worth something like $100 billion next year. Where people go wrong is they fail to look at the incremental figures. There's no point comparing solar to the energy sector that's already in place, because the energy grid has been built over the past one hundred years. So, to maintain the grid, we will need some investment. But, to measure change you have to see how much new stuff gets installed each year, and work out what percentage of that new stuff is clean energy. Clean energy is about 10 per cent of new stuff today, heading towards 20 to 25 per cent within the next three years. By 2020, at current rates of growth, solar and other technologies that do not burn fossil fuels will represent 100 per cent of all new stuff in electricity generation! In the US it'll happen faster – by about 2013. And think what that means: in a few decades' time, everything that's going into the energy sector will be clean!' Jigar built SunEdison into North America's largest solar service provider, and then it was time to move on to a new challenge. Luckily we were there to grab him to help us set up and execute the vision of the Carbon War Room. More on this soon.

But it's not all about new energy and efficiency; the opportunities are endless when we think about how we can harness and protect the best of Mother Nature. Chris Kilham is a charismatic ethnobotanist who has been described by the *New York Times* as 'part David Attenborough, part Indiana Jones'. He has gone from being a hippy from Massachusetts with a passion for yoga and yoghurt to unlocking the health secrets that plants hold and turning promotion of them into good business. His fascination for keeping people healthy and the mysterious qualities of little-known flora has led him to spend years roaming the world looking for natural herbs and medicines that can benefit people – and he's found tons. His first such trip was to India thirty years ago to track down exotic plants that were mentioned in ancient manuscripts. He has learned from witch doctors, shamans and ordinary people who use these medicines and herbal remedies in their everyday life and he's written books, delivered lectures – he created a holistic health course called 'The Shaman's Pharmacy' at the University of Massachusetts at Amherst, where he is now on the faculty – and he made films about his travels and experiences often travelling with his wife Zoe Helene. All this travelling and research over many years costs a great deal of money and, very cleverly, Chris has found a way to fund his work and to do good. He has linked up with international pharmaceutical companies on lucrative retainers – to draw their attention to his new discoveries; but far more than that are the opportunities he is bringing to remote peoples to earn a decent living for the plants and medicines they grow and which they have been using for thousands of years. Chris says, 'You know the expression, "It's not personal; it's business"? We sneer at such rot. All business is personal, all the time.'

At the moment the market for medicinal plants is worth some $100 billion, but with the growing interest in what's out there, and with people like Chris who are eager to share the possibilities with the world, the market is actually boundless. Many people like Chris believe that we blindly accept the chemically based medicines that drugs companies offer us at inflated prices when pure plant medicines can do the job more safely and with great effectiveness. As Chris points out, 'Around 62 per cent of all cancer drugs alone come from the discoveries of bio-prospectors like me – and, yes, they're approved of by the Food and Drug Administration.'

I am enthusiastic about the opportunities that are there for the picking, so to speak, mostly because we need to save our rainforests. If developing a commercial market can pay impoverished indigenous people for their ancient secrets and helps save forests and wild places from the encroachment of 'civilisation' looking for oil and cutting down millions of acres to grow cattle and palm oil, then we should do it.

Chris is developing a TV series entitled *The Medicine Hunter* with our film/TVproduction company, Virgin Produced. I'm planning to go with him into the Amazon on at least one trip and am looking at how we can market his natural remedies through the Virgin Group of companies.

Many of the medicines that Chris has found live in these wonderful forests. Forests, especially rainforests, play a vital role in keeping us all alive by absorbing significant amounts of carbon and recycling it as oxygen. Some 20 per cent of the world's oxygen is produced by the Amazon rainforest. These beautiful forests used to cover 14 per cent of the planet but today, thanks to deforestation, they cover less than 6 per cent. Many scientists fear the rainforests could disappear within the next forty years, which would make it almost impossible to stop the current rate of global warming. Today deforestation already accounts for 25 per cent of global emissions of heat-trapping gases that contribute to climate change. Large scale timber cutting and GMC soybean farming are leading causes of tropical deforestation. This must be discouraged if we are to fight the one per cent war, let alone the four per cent one. One way forward is to give indigenous people the opportunity to protect the natural environment by working with them to create fair markets for the products and services that are coming from the rainforests.

Tyler Gage was a student at Rhode Island's Brown University when he went on a trip to South America and stumbled upon a little known plant, guayusa (pronounced 'gwhy-you-sa').

In the time-honoured way of so many students, he found himself in a remote village studying indigenous cultures and participating in some of their rituals. He noticed that first thing each day men and women brewed a big cauldron of something that consisted of hot water and leaves, and they drank it from gourds they cradled in their hands for warmth against the chill morning air. Guayusa seemed both to revive and stimulate them. In fact, they positively bloomed under the effects of a few gourds of the stuff. They said that this ancient tradition made them 'Runa' – whole human beings.

Tyler was curious and when he came back to Brown after his travels, shared his experiences with his friends, including co-Founder Dan MacCombie. They and a team of students began investigating the properties of guayusa and the potential to build a sustainable development and commercial model around it. Research revealed the guayusa to be a fifty-foot Amazonian tree that lives for a hundred years and only grows in the rainforest. Conveniently for such a tall tree, it sends out myriad little side shoots that are useful when picking the hard, glossy leaves. Its caffeine content is what drew people to drink it. It had more than twice the caffeine of regular tea and more than coffee. It also contained anti-oxidants, vitamins and amino acids. It was what could be termed a balanced stimulant to awaken the mind and fortify the body.

Tyler, Dan and their team believed they could help create markets for this remarkable tea and decided to work with the farmers to grow large tracts of it without using the slash and burn technique.

They joined forces with the farmers and together they set up a company to grow and market guayusa through their company they fittingly named Runa. Moving quickly, in less than a year, Runa, the company, planted over 75,000 trees in more than 120 hectares of forest plots – but as part of the forest, not in clearings. In addition, while this was going on they paid 150 farmers for guayusa leaves harvested from existing trees. Runa then helped these farmers receive USDA Organic certification in 2010 and the farmers' incomes have been boosted by over 25 per cent to date. Their five-year plan is to plant over two million trees under the forest canopy on 2,000 hectares – which will generate a million dollars a year and increase the income of 2,500 families by 200 per cent. Runa's guayusa is now sold in their own and other companies' products in hundreds of stores across the US in loose leaf, bagged, and, soon, bottled form. They continue working day and night to develop this market and create a strong and direct connection between Kichwa farmers and the millions of consumers with whom they are sharing guayusa. A great outcome for the forests, for the local farmers, and for 'whole' human beings everywhere. Runa – as is marketed – boasts 25 per cent less caffeine than coffee and a startling 60 per cent more antioxidants than green tea. Put that in you cup and drink it!

Sam, Jigar, Chris and Tyler have succeeded by doing what's right for the planet – wonderful examples from all of them of Capitalism 24902 at work. There are thousands of great success stories of entrepreneurs who are looking at issues through a slightly different lens and working out how we can solve some of our environmental challenges through innovative business ideas. But what about some of the larger global brands? What kind of change could they drive if they truly transformed themselves?

Let's start with Walmart, unquestionably the five thousand pound gorilla in the room. Sam Walton's life's work now has 100,000 suppliers, 2.1 million employees, 200 million customer visits per week and annual sales of over $419 billion (greater than the GDP of more than 166 countries).With all those zeros there also have to be a million opportunities for Walmart to improve the way it does business. And they are the first to admit that they are on a long journey to turn themselves into a company that always does what is right for people and the planet. Just their sheer size means that when they do get something right it has incredible ripple effects. They can shift a whole industry by applying pressure in the right places. For example, Walmart has made a public pledge to cut 20 million metric tonnes of greenhouse gas emissions from its supply chain by the end of 2015 – the equivalent of removing 3.8 million cars from the road for one year. They can also create millions of opportunities when they shift their buying strategy. They just committed that by 2015 they would sell over $1 billion worth of food products from over one million small and medium-size farmers. This will not only generate significant efficiencies, but also create millions of jobs in the next five years. They've already had some pretty big wins, like the reduction of 50 million pounds' worth of bag wastage in 2010. Walmart is not only doing this out of the goodness of their hearts; they realise that they need to do it to survive and that ultimately it will be good for their business. As Walmart's CEO, Mike Duke, said in the company's 2009 Sustainability Report, 'The fact is sustainability at Wal-Mart isn't a stand-alone issue that's separate from or unrelated to our business. It's not an abstract or philanthropic program. We don't even see it as corporate social responsibility. Sustainability is built into our business. It's completely aligned with our model, our mission and our culture. Simply put, sustainability is built into our business because it's so good for our business.'

Another giant, General Electric (GE), had expanded spectacularly under the leadership of the legendary Jack Welch, and had consumed and contaminated vast areas of the US in doing so. It had earned global notoriety for the way it had poisoned the Hudson River with its chemicals. When Jeffrey Immelt succeeded Jack Welch as CEO in 2001 things didn't look good. Industry insiders were forecasting that a dirty giant like GE that burned coal and poisoned rivers couldn't possibly survive in a low-carbon economy.

Immelt felt he had few choices; and, besides, he wanted to do the right thing. He agreed that GE should clean up the chemicals in the Hudson. Work was slow at first, because the technology needed to clean up the river was still being developed. But while the Hudson crept slowly back to health, Immelt was busy setting his house in order right across the company. He told senior executives that every part of GE's business would have to meet strict carbon dioxide and greenhouse gas targets.

From the outside these targets looked anything but strict. In fact, they looked strictly laughable. How was a mere *one per cent* reduction in emissions, between 2004 and 2012, ever going to do anything for the company, let alone the planet? I don't run a power company, but I observed GE with some interest because I have interests in several airlines as well as a train service which by their very nature burn fuel and, inescapably, fuel pollutes. We were doing our best to cut down on those emissions by making our planes and trains as light and as fuel efficient as possible, even though it costs more. I was intrigued to see how Jeffrey Immelt's GE would set about it.

Immelt's targets were actually very radical because he had a plan. This was to reduce GE's emissions while still maintaining the colossal growth the company had enjoyed under Jack Welch. Immelt's vision was to turn GE into the first great green tech industrial powerhouse of the twenty-first century. On that scale its projected growth would generate a 40 per cent *increase* in its emissions: Immelt, on the contrary, believed GE could achieve a one per cent *reduction*, which, for a company like GE, was a big reduction overall.

Such a reduction didn't seem possible. It's not easy to maintain perpetual growth on a finite planet. If we all said, 'Let's keep expanding, while pumping out carbon at our current rate', that still wouldn't do anything to address global warming, the depletion of the earth's resources, the acidification of the seas and all the rest. Immelt's plan included exerting pressure on its suppliers to go green and reduce their own emissions. It was like dominoes – he would push and they would fall into line. Their compliance would become part of GE's compliance. Overall, the savings in CO_2 emissions would be considerable.

Immelt and the team decided that they were going to view the world's environmental problems as an enormous business opportunity. In 2005, with this philosophy at its core, they launched Ecomagination and committed to spend $1.5 billion annually by 2010 on research and development for clean technology. These initiatives did so well that they crashed through their target and spent that much in 2009. For the first five years of the programme they spent $5 billion on R&D and generated $70 billion in Ecomagination revenue – not a bad return!

What about the planet, though? Here's the biggest and best surprise of all: through technology and ideas born out of Ecomagination, GE has reduced its own greenhouse gas emissions, not by one per cent, but by 21 per cent compared with 2004. And it has improved its energy intensity by 34 per cent compared with that same year. The new clean tech products created by Ecomagination are also having significant positive impact on the planet: a new locomotive that reduces fuel burn by 6 per cent, a new aircraft engine which has 15 per cent lower fuel burn than the one it replaced – and a whole host of other products in healthcare, water, lighting and many more areas. GE has unleashed a storm of entrepreneurial energy that redesigned products to make them better for the planet, proving that they could do good and make money. It's a remarkable turnaround and, frankly, one that should set the bar for all companies.

Indeed, Virgin America has been working hard to make air travel better for the planet and so they've partnered with GE to become the launch partner for their new engine. In January 2011, Virgin America announced one of the year's single largest aircraft orders with an order for sixty new Airbus A320 family aircraft, thirty of which were the first commercial order for the new eco-efficient Airbus A320neo engine option. And then, on 15 June 2011, Virgin America became the launch customer for GE/CFM International's advanced LEAP engine, which will power thirty new Airbus A320neo aircraft scheduled to begin delivery in 2016. The neo/LEAP will be an additional 15 per cent more fuel efficient than its current fleet, which already burns up to 25 per cent less fuel than some other domestic fleets; double-digit reductions in NOx (nitrogen oxide) emissions; reduced engine noise; and an annual fuel saving of $1.9 million per aircraft. Each aircraft will emit 3,600 fewer tons of CO_2 per aircraft annually – equivalent to the CO_2 absorbed by 240,000 mature trees in a year! The day they made the milestone new engine announcement, GE and CFM also purchased carbon offsets for all flyers who purchased a ticket that day (5,000 flights). Virgin America and GE are showing that responsible investments like these can be good for both economic and environmental bottom lines.

In mid-2007, over dinner with my lovely wife Joan, we were chatting about my obsession with reducing carbon emissions in the world. With her usual Scottish pragmatism, Joan simply said 'If carbon is a problem then there must be somebody out there with half a brain who can come up with a way to remove it from the atmosphere. There are millions of scientists and technology experts and you only need one to crack it.' The problem was that there was no financial incentive to crack it, so everyone was busy doing other things. At breakfast the next morning we came up with the idea of the Earth Challenge, a $25 million prize to encourage inventors to come up with ideas for removing carbon. I had read Dava Sobel's book *Longitude*, about the successful prize launched by the British government in 1714 to reward anyone who could come up with a way of measuring a ship's longitude. Using this as inspiration we pulled together the prize and launched it with an esteemed panel of judges, including James Lovelock, Tim Flannery, Al Gore, James Hansen and Sir Crispin Tickell.

To date we have had more than 2,500 entries but as yet have not found one grand prizewinner with a proven and commercially viable technology. Instead, we have managed to whittle down the entries to a select handful that we are going to support with events, grants to help them develop their technologies and in some cases partnerships with Virgin companies. Some of the most promising concepts have come from ideas that recycle carbon into food and fuel related products. These range from biochar, which makes charcoal from biomass and can be added to degraded soil to improve its quality through to ideas for growing algae to produce biofuel.

Our work with Virgin Unite also got me thinking about a wider issue for Gaia: who is in charge globally of protecting her? As she knows no geographic boundaries, or any other for that matter, how could our outdated geographically constrained political systems ever resolve the issues we are facing?

Web: virginunite.com/screwbusinessasusual
Twitter: @virginunite #sbau
Facebook: Facebook.com/VirginUnite

The Global Village

'We are not going to be able to operate our Spaceship Earth successfully nor for much longer unless we see it as a whole spaceship and our fate as common. It has to be everybody or nobody' – R Buckminster Fuller

'The world's most dangerous idea is that we are not all the same' – Zinny Thabethe, co-founder iTeach and South African AIDS activist

The global village is here. And as Peter Gabriel has reminded me constantly over the last couple of decades, it is our future. Peter never ceases to amaze me. Often I'll watch him talk about ideas in meetings and his thinking is so visionary that I'll see people's eyes glaze over as they try to grasp the concept. Needless to say, years later the penny finally drops and the rest of the world catches up. When Peter started talking about the power of our interconnected world and the global village, he also warned of a dark side if we didn't get it right by taking better care of one another in our newly wired world. I can't help but think of this as I've watched two world-changing events unfold in the last several months of 2011.

First was the so-called Arab Spring, the people- and technology-led revolutions in Tunisia, Egypt and other parts of the Middle East. We were fortunate to have the Al Jazeera journalist Ayman Mohyeldin join us for one of Virgin Unite's leadership gatherings a couple of months after the start of the Egyptian revolution. Ayman is a good example of the newly emerging generation of truly global citizens. His mother was Palestinian and his father Egyptian. He was educated in the US and has spent much of his adult life travelling the world and reporting from places like Gaza. After he left us he was off to Syria.

He very bravely spent hours on the rooftop of a house on Tahrir Square, Cairo, to bring the revolution into all our homes. Or at least into some of our homes. At the time I was very surprised to learn that many US cable stations enforced a blackout on Al Jazeera, mainly due to misinformed views about the content and journalism. So, Al Jazeera was not available in the majority of the fifty US states to the general public. As one of my favourite stations, one that enables the viewer to get a true understanding about what is happening in the world, I find this astonishing. How are we ever going to come together as a true global village unless we have access to and understand each other's perspectives?

Ayman had all of us on the edges of our seats as he talked about what had happened in Egypt and across the region and how social media, notably Twitter and Facebook, had brought true democracy of information – no hierarchy, everyone was equal. Ayman also had a good sense of the dark side of the global village where one nation's involvement with another can have unintended consequences. I recently saw a piece from him in *New York* magazine that summed up how the Egyptian people might have felt about the American government during the revolution:

'The reality is that the US government has armed, financed, and essentially bankrolled this authoritarian regime. The result has been a regime that felt very much in control and by many people's assessment, usurped his power, curbed civil and human rights, and in exchange the US was given a partner that promoted stability and was a close ally in the so-called War on Terror and was involved in the US rendition program through the CIA. So you can understand why there's a great deal of skepticism toward the US's reluctance to come out and promote values of human rights and democracy. The Egyptian people don't understand why they don't support that wholeheartedly as much as they supported this regime for 30 years. That disconnect is very, very apparent to every ordinary Egyptian citizen – not just the elite or the intellectuals.'

What will be critical for Egyptians and the world in general is how all of us support the rise of Egypt as a strong new nation, as well as the other countries in the Middle East which have experienced transformation in the past few months. We are hoping to do something through Virgin Unite to support the growth of entrepreneurship in Egypt in the near future.

The beauty of the Arab Spring was that it showed how technology can truly put power into the hands of the people to help them drive positive change. Ayman is right: social media and other tools give people an equal voice. First, though, as with all new things, what the Arab Spring actually means in terms of revolution and people power has to be defined. The citizens who have rebelled have demanded citizenship that unites, not divides. They no longer want an 'us and them' society but one in which everyone has equal rights and is easy in his own skin. The world has watched and listened; the early stages of the revolution proved so inspirational because they offered a strong sense of national identity built on the idea of citizenship.

On the other hand, the second event, the recent riots in London in summer 2011, showed the darker side of connectivity. Twenty years ago, the looters would have struggled to mobilise so quickly in such overwhelming numbers. Social media has now given them the tools to do this. Sadly, as Camila Batmanghelidjh (quoted earlier) made clear, this probably would not have happened if the young people involved had felt part of the community. There is never an excuse for violence, but these riots were certainly a wake-up call for all of us to look at how we can ensure that young people do not feel excluded. The great news was that after the riots people showed the positive side of social media by using the same tools to rally communities to help with the clean up effort.

The 'global village' and its time have finally come, with all the wonderful opportunities and challenges it brings with it. It is now a lot more difficult for any individual, government or organisation to build its power and wealth off the back of people, no matter where they are in the world. The fall of the Berlin wall in 1989 was probably one of the first manifestations of technology quite literally tearing down barriers between peoples and regimes. While the wall had stopped the passage of people for over forty years it met its match when faced with satellite broadcasting. Suddenly everyone on the eastern side had access to an uncensored view of everything that was happening on the western side.

Eric Schmidt and Jared Cohen of Google also had the foresight to forecast some of the implications of our newly wired world. They call this level of connectivity and the universal diffusion of power the Digital Disruption. They distilled their ideas in an article published in *Foreign Affairs*, the highly influential journal of the US Council on Foreign Relations:

'The advent and power of connection technologies – tools that connect people to vast amounts of information and to one another – will make the twenty-first century all about surprises. Governments will be caught off-guard when large numbers of their citizens, armed with virtually nothing but cell phones, take part in mini-rebellions that challenge their authority. For the media, reporting will increasingly become a collaborative enterprise between traditional news organizations and the quickly growing number of citizen journalists. And technology companies will find themselves outsmarted by their competition and surprised by consumers who have little loyalty and no patience. Today, more than fifty percent of the world's population has access to some combination of cell phones (five billion users) and the Internet (two billion). These people communicate within and across borders, forming virtual communities that empower citizens at the expense of governments ... Faced with these opportunities, democratic governments have an obligation to join together while also respecting the power of the private and non-profit sectors to bring about change. They must listen to those on the front lines and recognize that their citizens' use of technology can be an effective vehicle to promote the values of freedom, equality, and human rights globally. In a new age of shared power, no one can make progress alone.'

So what does this mean for businesses and entrepreneurs? Just as revolutions have bubbled up against governments who are abusing their people, so too business leaders have started to and will continue to face the same challenges. We've finally moved out of the 'Industrial Age' and into the 'Age of People'. Which is really at the core of Capitalism 24902. While the industrial age was all about wealth, unsustainable growth through depletion of natural resources and delivering profit to your shareholders, this new era, the 'Age of People', is all about shifting the focus to how businesses can and must deliver benefits to people and the planet – as well as shareholders.

Businesses which say *screw business as usual* and embrace Capitalism 24902 will thrive – those that don't will struggle for a bit to hold their power, but will ultimately fail as they will no longer be in control of how they are perceived in the marketplace. People all over the world now have the power to shape others' perceptions of brands, including promoting those that are doing good things.

Before I launch into some of the roles that business can play in the global village by screwing business as usual, I want to reflect on the fact that the global village would not be here if it weren't for business. Technology and mobile phone companies all over the world have successfully given us the tools to connect. One of the people responsible for this communications revolution is one of my co-founders in the Carbon War Room, Strive Masiyiwa.

In 1965, when Strive was seven years old, Rhodesia's leader Ian Smith authored a unilateral declaration of independence from Britain. Strive's parents left the country, sending their son to a boarding school in Edinburgh. Strive longed to return home and he planned eventually to go to Zambia and join the guerrillas, just across the border, to fight in the armed struggle against Smith's ruling white minority. But then he talked to his cousin – who ran a training camp for the guerrilla army that would one day become Robert Mugabe's Zanu-PF party – who told him he was too late: the war was all but won. What the new country needed now, more than soldiers, was educated people. Strive listened to his cousin's wise words and stayed in Britain to study, earned his degree, and, returning to what was now Zimbabwe, he went to work for the national telephone company.

Growing emerging markets and mobile phone networks have become a marriage made in heaven. Mobile networks are quicker and cheaper to build than landlines. In 1993, Strive had no trouble acquiring the finance needed to launch his first mobile phone company. The trouble was that Mugabe did not want to grant any licenses for new mobile phone companies. Strive's legal battles with Mugabe came to a head in 1996 when a presidential decree banned private cell phone operations. But Strive did not give up and decided to take the government to court. In December 1997 he won his case and proceeded to set up Econet as a successful mobile phone company in Zimbabwe.

By then, however, Strive's vision had grown. His ambitions had extended beyond his troubled country's frontiers, and from his headquarters in Johannesburg he decided to create a truly multinational African business, one that today spans seven countries, boasts more than twenty-five million customers and generates an estimated $3 billion (£1.8 billion) in annual revenues. Econet is a celebrated example of African entrepreneurship and is changing people's lives for the better every day.

Strive also has a deep sense of responsibility about giving something back to the community. Through the Capernaum Trust, which he set up with his wife, profits have so far provided education for 26,000 orphans. Strive sits on the Board of Trustees of the Rockefeller Foundation and works with Kofi Annan's Alliance for a Green Revolution in Africa – as well as being a co-founder with me and seven other entrepreneurs in the Carbon War Room.

Just as important as what he is doing individually are the values Strive has instilled in his company. The firm provides counselling and antiretroviral drugs for its employees and their families who are living with HIV/AIDS. It spreads entrepreneurial opportunity, investing heavily in community phone shops and payphones throughout its local markets to bring connectivity to people who would normally not be able to afford it. In bringing telecommunications to those communities, Econet is empowering local populations, giving them the chance to be entrepreneurs by running these businesses. Econet's phones, like millions of others around the world, are also becoming doctors, insurance companies, banks and much more.

The opportunity to use the mobile phone to drive change in the world is enormous, with over 5.3 billion mobile phone users in the world and 90 per cent of the world's population able to get access to a mobile service. Take health: by 2015, five hundred million people will be using mobile health applications around the world. This simple device is transforming our response to health issues, from prevention of disease such as HIV with education through mobile games, to diagnostic and treatment support, to outbreak tracking. The list goes on.

What about carrying your bank in your pocket? M-PESA customers in Kenya can deposit and withdraw money from a network of agents that includes airtime resellers and retail outlets acting as banking agents; they can transfer funds and also pay bills. Launched in 2007, they already have 6.5 million subscribers with two million daily transactions.

Phones are even being used as matchmakers. I am talking about this in the business sense but I am sure there are some dating services too! Souktel, a company that works mainly in the Middle East, matches people looking for jobs with companies looking for people. They create SMS-based 'mini CVs' and 'mini job ads' and then start connecting potential employees with employers. They've also just set up a vehicle to link communities that need help with aid agencies.

Platforms such as Ushahidi (meaning 'testimony' in Swahili) have also sprung up to support citizens' journalism, helping to get people's stories out in times of crisis. There is a company called txteagle that gives global brands the chance to connect with one billion emerging market customers via text messaging and in return gives free talk time to the customer. A whole new world of activism and advertising!

But it's not just mobile phones that are connecting this new global village; it's also online groups like Avaaz and Wikipedia that are redefining how we think of the community. Businesses have a great opportunity in this new connected world to use technology and our increased level of connectivity to come up with wonderful new ideas that are not only good business, but also make a difference to the global village. Capitalism 24902 is all about how we take better care of our communities and the planet, no matter where those communities are. Now we finally have the tools to do this.

So the great news is that mobile phones, the internet, media and travel are all bringing us closer together and changing the way the world works. The bad news is that our leadership models have simply been unable to keep pace with these innovations. Most of the existing leadership models have been built in silos, that is, we've created isolated areas of responsibility for different sectors. There is little or no encouragement for them to work together, and they are limited in their geographical scope. The problem is that the issues we are facing don't care about boundaries. Many of these issues are also set to get worse as our natural resources continue to be depleted and climate change continues apace.

The Copenhagen climate change conference in 2009 and the world's slow response to the worsening environmental crisis is one of the best examples of the silo effect, leaving no one in charge of what's best for people and the planet. Sadly, because of the way we've built our political systems, driven as they are by the power of the vote, politicians' hands are tied as they attempt to do what's right in the short term for their constituencies rather than for the planet. Similarly, corporate hands are often tied because of the shareholder focus on profits, with the wider stakeholders not having a voice. Charities are struggling as they compete with the recession and other organisations for funding, with little to no incentive to collaborate in order to make a greater impact. Large multilateral organisations like the United Nations are often held hostage by the less than united interests of their own members. So what ends up happening is what we got at Copenhagen – not much. But the issues are not going away and we all need to work together – businesses, governments and not-for-profit organisations – must align to tackle these challenges together.

As I watched the scores of committed people in Copenhagen who were all desperate to figure out how we could build an agreement in time to stop continuing on the disastrous path the world is currently heading down, it became clearer than ever that one of the missing pieces was someone to steer the ship. Basically, the planet needed someone rooting for it, someone who didn't have any other agenda and who was powerful enough to get people to listen. Everywhere I turned, I saw good intentioned people, almost blinkered by one specific part of the issue or by their own national agenda. This made me even more committed to figuring out how we could encourage business leaders to play a role in bringing together partners and using business practices to establish new approaches to global leadership. I realised the unique role we could play in bringing together unlikely marriages between business, governments and social sectors to create business-based approaches to new leadership models. Many others were also starting to take on this challenge, such as Ray Chambers, whom I admire greatly.

Ray is a man of many talents. When he was studying accountancy, he went on the road in his free time as a singer and piano player in a rock and roll band. Perhaps it was our musical roots that led us both to click immediately! After giving up his music career, Ray became chairman of a very successful private equity company called Wesray Capital Corporation. Once he had made his fortune he decided to retire and devote all his time to driving positive change in the world.

Ray is one of the calmest and most articulate people I have ever met (although I must admit that, after working with the likes of the Sex Pistols for so many years, I struggle to visualise him in a rock band – Johnny Rotten he ain't). He did however have a non-musical instrumental role in helping Virgin Unite get The Elders initiative off the ground – Ray was one of the first to join the Advisory Board. When he and his wife joined us for the initial Elders meeting at Ulusaba, I remember thinking, Wow, this man really knows his stuff. Every question he asked was spot-on. The best thing about Ray is that he brings his sharp business mind to the table to guide anything he does in the not-for-profit sector. When he decided to take on malaria, he had a very clear and audacious goal in mind: by 2015 there will be no more deaths from malaria in Africa. Malaria is a perfect example of one of those global issues that knows no boundaries. More than two thousand people (most of them children) die from malaria every single day in Africa, even though it is a preventable and treatable disease.

To achieve his goal, Ray decided he needed to set up an organisation that broke through the silos and attacked malaria globally. So, along with Peter Chernin, one of the world's most influential media executives, he founded Malaria No More. The organisation brings together partners from all sectors to leverage high-impact global advocacy, awareness campaigns and targeted social investments. In 2008, Ray was invited by the Secretary General of the United Nations, Ban Ki-moon, to be the first Special Envoy of the Secretary General for Malaria. He accepted this invitation and has worked tirelessly over the last several years to end malaria.

Ray is all about partnerships, so he brought in governments, businesses and not-for-profit organisations. He somehow cajoled and browbeat them into committing $4 billion dollars – an unprecedented level of funding. Just as importantly, they also leveraged their other assets, from people to distribution channels to using their voices in the media. All to fight together for a common goal that will save over 4.2 million lives by 2015. In Ray's words:

'Working together, the World Bank, the Global Fund to Fight AIDS, Tuberculosis and Malaria, led by the United Nations and the World Health Organisation, the Rollback Malaria partnership and the Gates Foundation and UNICEF – we are at the point where over $4 billion has been raised in the last several years and we are responding to the Secretary General's call to cover all 700 million people at risk of malaria with mosquito nets by the end 2010. I believe very strongly and with heartfelt passion that if we keep working all together as hard and as cooperatively as we've been working, we will have taken a disease that had become a genocide and virtually eliminate deaths from it until a vaccine comes along. This is really unprecedented in our lifetimes and it should encourage us with regard to maternal health, child mortality, HIV/AIDS, TB [tuberculosis] and other diseases. I think malaria can stand up as an example of just what progress we can make by all working together.'

Ray set a wonderful example by using his business and personal skills to bring together a new approach to global leadership in the quest to eradicate malaria. As part of *screwing business as usual*, business leaders must take on more responsibility not just for their direct shareholders, but for the wider group of stakeholders in the global village. The *Harvard Business Review* blog from 2010 on the future of leadership summed up his ingredients for success:

'1. A simple solution/technology that everyone could understand and rally around. Long lasting insecticide treated bed-nets stop 90% of malaria infections.

2. An honest broker. Ray, who was trusted by many, rallied the interested parties.

3. A half-dozen key groups who lock hands and commit to working together. Hundreds of organizations fell in line once the coalition had five or six credible participants.

4. An enabler to ensure the collaboration continues and progress toward its goals are measured and coordinated. Ray was made the Special Envoy for Malaria to the Secretary General of the United Nations and set up a small office to track the collaboration's goals, ensure bed-net coverage was measured by country, flagging problems, and focusing senior level attention on problems as they arose. In four years, Ray put together a collaboration that will save a million lives a year.'

I want to relate one more story about Ray that was told to me by my good friend Lewis Katz, that clearly demonstrates why he is a leader in *screwing business as usual*. In the 1980s, Ray and former US Treasury Secretary William E Simon went into business together. Later that decade they had a bit of a falling out, decided to break up the business and went their separate ways. At the time of the split there was a transaction in progress. They had bought a company called Avis. Ray asked William how he wanted to deal with the Avis business since he was still entitled to a share but William indicated that he wanted no part of Avis and no part of Ray or their business, and it was excluded from the closing documents.

They spoke little over the course of the next eighteen months. But in that time, by Ray's good fortune, luck and brilliance and that of his colleagues, they sold Avis for $700 million profit. Ray immediately convened a meeting of his junior partners. In typical Ray Chambers' fashion he said to his partners, 'I don't feel right splitting up this incredible win without including William'. Needless to say the younger partners weren't as enthusiastic to include him, but what Ray did next was extraordinary. He wrote a letter to William in which he said he knew that William didn't want part of the transaction, he remembered the conversation, he remembered the split, he remembered that it was excluded in the documents, but it just didn't sit right with him, that it would be a fair way of ending a relationship. So he enclosed in his letter a cheque for $140 million. This extraordinary act of generosity saw their friendship revived and Ray was even a pallbearer at William's funeral in 2000.

Through my work with The Elders I've had the great pleasure of spending time with a remarkable leader, President Fernando Henrique Cardoso, the former President of Brazil (or, as he humbly calls himself, the accidental President of Brazil). When speaking with Cardoso at one of The Elders meetings he mentioned to me that for several years he has been working on drug reform to end the 'war on drugs'. He had established a Global Commission on Drug Policy and I was honoured when he asked me to join as one of the Commissioners. The Commission is another great example of a global approach to tackling a very tough issue. It has representation from the business community, including George Soros, several former presidents of Latin American countries, well-known authors and activists, former US government officials such as George Schultz, the Prime Minister of Greece, George Papandreou, Kofi Annan and a host of other impressive individuals.

The Commission had been working tirelessly at pulling together data from all over the world to create a fact-based report to promote an open discussion among governments and the public. Virgin Unite has worked closely with them on the communications front, as have other organisations such as Avaaz and Google. The Commission held a press conference in New York in June 2011 to launch their report and start the debate. My son, Sam, joined me at the conference so that he could interview some of the Commissioners. As mentioned, he is working with his company, Current Sponge, on creating a film that exposes the myths about drugs and generates debate on what we need to do to solve the problem. It was great fun being there with Sam and sharing this historic moment with him. I was incredibly proud of him as I watched him swing into action, ensuring that his team got all the right footage.

I was fortunate enough to have the chance to say the following few words at the start of the very packed press conference:

'I'm honoured to be a part of the Global Commission on Drug Policy. Great credit goes to President Cardoso and the other Commissioners who started this initiative to say enough is enough. The war on drugs has increased drug usage, filled our jails, cost millions of taxpayer dollars and fuelled organised crime – it is definitely time for an alternative approach. The good news is that new approaches focused on regulation and decriminalisation have proven to work. We need more leaders to start looking at alternative, fact-based approaches. We need more humane and effective ways to reduce the harm caused by drugs. The one thing we cannot afford to do is to go on pretending the "war on drugs" is working.

'The aims of the UN and policy makers were laudable fifty years ago. It was 1961 and the goal was to create a drug-free world. Their aim was to keep us safe from harm. But fifty long years later we see no reduction in harm – in fact we have a global drugs trade fuelling organised crime by over US$300 billion each year. A trade which kills millions through murder and corruption and, far from eradicating harm, we have labelled millions of otherwise law-abiding citizens as criminals and stigmatised many more.

'And let us be clear, this isn't just a problem for countries that produce drugs – it is an issue that affects us all. Whether you take drugs or not, we all pay taxes that fight this unwinnable war and are impacted by the decimation that our current "war" has caused in our own backyards.

'It's estimated that over US$1 trillion has been spent on fighting this battle. The irony is that a regulated market, one that is tightly controlled, one that would offer healthcare – not prison, to those with drug problems, would cost a fraction of the price.

'It is time to rewrite the rules and to ensure that the voices of people around the world are heard.

'This is one of the most pressing issues in the world today, so I'd like to thank you for being here and taking part in a special day in history – a day when we start to end the war on drugs and start to get the UN and leaders all over the world to open up the debate and move towards policies that end prohibition and put in place humane policies that help lead us towards a healthier and more peaceful world.'

There was great press pick-up from the launch and most journalists agreed with the approach of opening up an honest debate. Martin Wolf wrote a very good article in the *Financial Times* calling the war on drugs a 'disaster'. 'While failing to reduce the ills of drug use at which it is addressed, it has created massive "collateral damage": the spread of avoidable diseases; use of drugs in dangerous forms; mass criminalisation and incarceration; a gigantic waste of public resources; corruption; creation of a cross-border network of organised crime; and the subversion of states ... It is a war with myriad innocent victims.' I also particularly liked the summary at the end of an article published in the *Independent*:

'Here in Britain our political leaders are just as resistant to new approaches. The previous Labour government downgraded cannabis to class C status, but then promptly returned it to class B in order to curry favour with the right-wing press. In 2009 when the government's own drugs adviser, David Nutt, tried to launch a debate about the relative harm of various substances, he was promptly sacked. This commission is to be commended for telling the truth about drugs prohibition and for making an admirably clear argument for a different strategy. The tragedy is that world leaders still show no inclination to listen.'

The author was right: we have a long way to go to ensure that world leaders truly listen and start to work together to stop the war on drugs. This is an issue that I'm personally incredibly passionate about as the mindless focus on fighting drugs has led to so much suffering in the world. Drugs also know no boundaries, so this issue, like so many others, has become lost without the right global leadership. Thanks to Cardoso and the other Commissioners for helping to step into this leadership gap for the global village. The work is just beginning and, with Virgin Unite and Sam, I look forward to continuing to support them in whatever way I can.

So why did I put this story in a book about screwing business as usual? The war on drugs impacts all of us, whether it's in the countries where the drugs are produced or where they are used. The current focus on criminalisation is costing our prison systems millions and keeping the drug trade underground while lining the pockets of organised crime and petty criminals. Solving this is the responsibility of all of us and each of us can do something, whether it be using our voices, helping come up with entrepreneurial solutions, giving ex-offenders jobs. In the new world of Capitalism 24902, business leaders must take on a wider responsibility on issues like this that impact on every corner of our global village.

*   *   *

Nelson Mandela was not convinced. He and Peter and I were sitting around the lunch table in my Holland Park house and we were talking about establishing a group of retired statesmen to stand up as the conscience of the world. 'You would lead them, Madiba!'

He could see what we were getting at. But we had not sold him on the idea – yet. As I mentioned at the start of this chapter, Peter Gabriel was excited about the potential of the 'global village' that was being shaped by the internet, travel, the media and the vast array of new technologies emerging in the world. He was also very aware of the leadership gap in this village. There were very few leaders who were focused solely on what was best for humanity. Most were limited by some type of boundary, geographical, military, religious, tribal or economic, so Peter was thinking about trying to bring together this group of Elders who could help lead and listen to the global village.

My passion for the idea came from a slightly different direction. In 2003, just before the start of the Iraq War, I called Nelson Mandela to see if he would lead a group of global leaders to Iraq to persuade Saddam Hussein to step down in the interests of his people and go into exile in Libya. Mandela agreed to go so long as he wasn't stepping on the toes of the UN. I also contacted Kofi Annan and he agreed to come along.

The very week they were due to travel, and before Mandela could board a private plane to fly from Johannesburg to Baghdad, the United States and its allies, including the United Kingdom, began their military assault and we were launched into a war that has radically shaken the foundations of peace in the world. I remember, when I heard the news my first thought was of Madiba and Peter. Having come so close to averting a war, we could at least try to avoid other conflicts in the future.

On 29 November 2004, musicians, politicians, celebrities, business leaders and philanthropists all came together with a sea of hopeful people in a Cape Town stadium to join Nelson Mandela in launching an initiative that bore his prison number, 46664, to help stop the spread of AIDS in South Africa. The next day, Peter and I, Bob Geldof, Dave Stewart, Jackie McQuillan and Jean had brunch in a beautiful setting in Stellenbosch, and discussed the value of elders in our society. We argued about how we could leverage their assets to make the world a better place. This conversation got Peter and I excited about engaging Madiba once again. On the plane home we scribbled him a note and sent it off.

Maybe the idea had stuck in Madiba's head after all, because he wrote back asking for more information. We quickly mobilised the team at Virgin Unite to start building a full 'business case' for The Elders. It might seem strange to use the word business linked to The Elders, but for us it was important to look at the establishment of this new initiative the same way we would look at any business. We wanted to ensure we went out and listened and learned from as many relevant people as possible, mapped out who was already working in similar areas to identify partners and avoid duplication, defined clearly what the 'brand' values and principles would be, identified what would make them different, clearly outlined their areas of focus and expected impact, created a five year budget and very importantly looked at bringing in the best possible management structure and leadership team. Madiba was very disappointed that the Iraq trip had had to be cancelled and was furious with President Bush and Prime Minister Tony Blair for launching the war. I think it was this that convinced him of the need for The Elders. Mandela and his wife Graça Machel agreed to be the founding Elders, Archbishop Tutu agreed to chair the group and we knew that we had the core of something very special.

Late one evening in early 2006 I flew into Davos with Peter and Jean on a magical helicopter ride through the Swiss Alps. The next three days were filled with meetings to start to build support for the Elders concept. While most people looked at us as if we were crazy, a few understood the vision and agreed to give their support in helping to get it off the ground. Peter Schwartz, the co-founder and chairman of Global Business Network, and his wife were two of those early supporters. Immediately after Davos, they hosted a gathering at their home, with a fantastic cast of characters including Jimmy Wales from Wikipedia, Pam Omidyar from Humanity United and Larry Brilliant from Google.org.

On the flight over to the meeting, I fortuitously bumped into Ajaz Ahmed, founder of the web company AKQA, and kidnapped him and brought him to the meeting. Ajaz ended up being a wonderful resource for The Elders and generously gave of his and his team's time to build the initial website. While this session at Peter's house was still firmly in brain-storming mode, the idea started to crystallise. What was most helpful from this session was not what we should be doing, but further clarity on what The Elders should not be doing.

The team, mostly volunteers, that came together to shape the idea included Jean, Jane Tewson, the historian and documentary maker Andrea Barron, Jane Wales and Scilla Elworthy, the founder of Peace Direct, a grassroots organi-sation devoted to developing conflict resolution skills. One of the most rewarding parts of creating The Elders was being with this stimulating group of committed people who gath-ered together over the years as the project took shape. I'll never forget phoning Andrea and saying, 'I have someone you should meet, I think you will be good friends.' Never did she realise that she was going to end up volunteering the next two years of her life to getting The Elders off the ground. She

and Jean met in New York and, as I expected, hit it off immediately. In the early days when they were shaping the idea,
Peter and I would meet Jean and Andrea for discussions over
lunch at The Roof Gardens in London. Little did we know
that they nicknamed these 'the Roof Gardens moments' as,
every time they thought they had the idea down pat, Peter
and I would send them off in another direction.

As the idea began to take shape we had lots of discussions about what characteristics best described an Elder. We
agreed, first of all, that they should not be currently involved
in politics; they should have no personal agenda, or represent
any vested interest. They should have earned international
trust, demonstrated outstanding integrity and built a reputa-
tion for non-coercive leadership.

'It was important to find people who had displayed moral
courage,' Scilla always reiterated. 'In other words, they had
been in some situation that had demanded them to stand
up against oppressive forces, dictatorship or whatever.' For
Scilla, Aung San Suu Kyi was an outstanding example – and,
throughout her imprisonment, a chair was left empty for her
at every Elders meeting.

They also had to have courage at their core. Each of the
Elders has moved beyond his or her own fear in a significant way. Nelson Mandela put up with twenty-seven years
of incarceration and faced fear daily, especially in the early
years. Then there was the ability to listen, which everybody
involved in this considers extremely important. 'And the last
thing,' Scilla recalls, 'was the realisation that all the truly

great people have a sense of humour. Archbishop Tutu absolutely epitomises that.'

We wanted this initiative to be a true demonstration of breaking down the silos to bring together business leaders, philanthropists, scientists, artists and front-line leaders to support the shaping and the future work of The Elders. So, in the summer of 2006, we held three gatherings back-to-back at Necker Island, and invited a wonderful mix of people. We were also lucky to have two potential Elders with us for most of the fortnight: former US President Jimmy Carter and Archbishop Desmond Tutu.

Jimmy Carter was not sold on the idea at the start of the meeting and let us (and the rest of the guests) know it. This was just about the most depressing moment Peter, Jean and I have ever shared. I remember us going off into a small room, feeling very small and downtrodden. A couple of days in, however, and Jimmy Carter was captivated and got very involved in shaping the idea. It was a lesson to us that we should allow for a range of opinions and disagreements and thus help make the idea a far better one than if we had just created it ourselves. It was the unlikely partnerships that formed during those two weeks on Necker that helped to shape the philosophy of The Elders and form a strong foundation from which the idea could grow. One of the most beautiful moments for me was when Peter Gabriel and I taught Archbishop Tutu how to swim: a world famous rock musician, a businessman and a celebrated archbishop bobbing about in the pool together – brilliant!

Peter had a slightly different magical moment. 'One of the most exciting moments for me was when The Elders were asked what they should be doing,' Peter recalls. 'Almost everyone said, straightaway, "Listening". Listening was job number one.'

After these meetings on Necker we completed the plan and Scilla produced a large file filled with the backgrounds of potential Elders. Jean and I had the privilege of spending an afternoon with Graça and Madiba as they considered who to invite to join this remarkable group. Every time Madiba heard Desmond Tutu's name his face broke out in a wide grin with a wonderful twinkle in his eye, almost undoubtedly remembering some mischievous moment they had shared.

Central to the idea was the creation of 'an engine' that would not only provide The Elders with financial support, but would also help the group to leverage their work further and bring to the table a range of experiences and resources. We wanted to form this engine from a select group of ten to twelve partners who would join forces with The Elders and allow them to have the independence they needed in order to make this a success.

As the Virgin Unite team hit the road to find partners, the initial meetings tended to be slightly uncomfortable as people looked at us in disbelief when we talked through the scale of the vision for The Elders. We kept fighting, and then slowly started to build a small group of 'believers'. Kathy Calvin and Mike Madnick from the UN Foundation were two of these early adopters and, with Ray, they were instrumental in helping us build The Elders. Pam Omidyar and Randy Newcomb from Humanity United and Shannon Sedgwick Davis from Bridgeway Foundation also came on board at an early stage. With these people on board, and Elders starting to join, our potential partners meetings became a great deal easier.

On 24 May 2007 the first meeting of The Elders was held at Ulusaba. The three days were filled with magical moments. We were fortunate to have Madiba with us at this first gathering. When he walked towards the lodge all the staff burst into song and danced with him into the main house. He then sat with The Elders and gave a beautiful opening speech that set the scene perfectly for the next couple of days. Another unforgettable moment was when Kofi Annan, who could not be there in person, appeared on the video conferencing screen and said the simple words 'I'm in'. At one point during the meetings Pam and Randy passed a note to Jean and I pledging that they wanted to triple their commitment. Listening to the vision of Mary Robinson, Graça Machel, Archbishop Tutu, President Carter, Madiba and the others, there was an incredible sense of potential building. Everyone was truly inspired by the level of commitment from The Elders. Their sense of humour, humility and wisdom shone through at every stage of the gathering.

By the end of the three days, The Elders had decided that they wanted to launch on Madiba's eighty-ninth birthday, 18 July 2007. As this was only about six weeks away and, with no management team yet in place, a frantic scramble began. We recruited Jackie and Alexia Hargrave and many others from across the Virgin Group to help with the launch.

We also needed to find the final group of partners to secure funds for three years of costs for The Elders. Jean and I set ourselves a challenge to come up with all the funds in the five weeks we had left before the launch. Ray Chambers stepped up and brought his son Michael in as a founder and also connected us to Jeff Skoll, who came on board as well. We met Amy Robbins from the Nduna Foundation at a rather dry UN meeting and were so impressed by her in the meeting that we kidnapped her afterwards and she became an early partner. Others came on board over the next few weeks – and miraculously we reached our goal of raising $18 million before the launch.

On 28 July 2007, The Elders was launched to the waiting world. Madiba opened the day and was joined by the beautiful singing of a choir from CIDA City Campus. Archbishop Tutu made an incredibly moving speech and each of the Elders said a few words. Peter was put on the spot to sing his hauntingly beautiful song 'Biko'; many tears were shed.

Behind the scenes, there was the usual chaos, but we will forever be indebted to Miles from Watermark who had the foresight to have not one but three back-up generators – so when the first two went, we were still able to celebrate the beginning of a much longer story!

Today The Elders is a fully independent organisation managed by a wonderful leader, Mabel van Oranje. In essence, The Elders are a group of respected global leaders who use their moral courage, wisdom and leadership to help tackle some of the tougher issues facing the world. They are completely independent and have no other agenda than that of humanity. But they have the ears of the world, and this in itself can be a powerful tool. Most of their work is discreet, conducted away from the public gaze. It was in that spirit that, in November 2008, three members of The Elders, Jimmy Carter, Graça Machel and Kofi Annan, planned to visit Zimbabwe to see for themselves the country's escalating humanitarian and economic problems. The day before they were due to travel, the Zimbabwe government sent a message via Thabo Mbeki that they would not be welcome – and they had to cancel their trip. Zimbabwe's state-controlled newspaper *The Herald* said: 'The visit has been deemed a partisan mission by a group of people with partisan interests.'

Undeterred, Carter, Machel and Annan set up shop in Johannesburg and invited the people they had been due to meet in Zimbabwe to come and see them in South Africa. Political leaders, businessmen, aid workers, donors, UN agencies and civil society groups flocked to tell their stories. The Elders reached this conclusion: 'The state is no longer able to offer basic services. It can no longer feed, educate or care for its citizens. It is failing its people.' They also raised awareness of the escalating cholera crisis that was spreading across the country and posing a serious threat to the entire region. Zimbabwe's humanitarian crisis was thrust into the world's headlines and President Mugabe's acute mismanagement of his country could no longer be ignored.

In the late summer of 2009 I was able to join a trip to the Middle East with some of the Elders. On our second day there we took a short bus ride from Jerusalem, where we were based, to the West Bank. At the Qalandia checkpoint, with its heavily fortified walls and armed security towers, former US President Jimmy Carter decided he wanted to chat to some of the people crossing from the Palestinian to the Israeli side. Instantly, there was a scramble by security and photographers jockeying for position, some even trampling other Elders in their efforts to stay close to President Carter. Jeff Skoll and I are pretty solid, but we were almost knocked over in the scrum, while Archbishop Tutu was sent tottering to one side and I thought I saw Mary Robinson shoved in the back. The Secret Service guys were all but panicking behind their suits and dark glasses.

Jimmy was used to the attention, laid back and relaxed as always. He and the other Elders (who had managed to join him by then) listened as young Palestinians expressed their frustration about standing in long queues just to get work, school, medical treatment or to visit family. Sadly one old woman also reflected the volatility that exists in this place – she told us that were she to be evicted from her home she would have no qualms about becoming a suicide bomber.

After getting through the crossing we arrived at Ramallah, the administrative capital of the West Bank. While the Elders

– led by Jimmy Carter and Archbishop Tutu – were having some serious talks with Palestinian Prime Minister Salam Fayyad, Jeff Skoll – my business buddy on the trip – and I went to talk to a group of six fairly aggrieved Palestinian business leaders.

I had never been to the Palestinian Territories before, but Jeff had visited with his parents and on his own many times over the years, his last trip being some five years earlier. Before moving to the United States he'd grown up in the suburbs of Montreal in Canada. As an eight-year-old with a strong social conscience – much like myself at the same age – he went around his neighbourhood collecting money for Israel after the Yom Kippur War. He was welcomed by his Jewish neighbours but baffled when some of the doors he knocked on were slammed in his face. Only later did he learn that not all his neighbours were Jewish; some were Muslims, from Jordan, or from Egypt – or from Palestine.

During a heated conversation when the group from Ramallah was telling us about the many issues they had with their Israeli neighbours, Jeff sat quietly, taking it all in. He's a thoughtful man, quietly spoken, a good listener, but when things started to get noisy and the Palestinians remarked that Jews didn't understand or care about their problems, I drew Jeff into the conversation. 'Oh, but Jeff is Jewish,' I said.

I meant that he was a regular guy, just like them, and they could all get on if they communicated and knew each other better. It never occurred to me that this might create a slightly awkward situation. I looked at Jeff. For a brief moment, his face was a picture. A somewhat startled expression of 'oh boy, am I in the soup!' seemed to flit across his features, but he rallied quickly and through his courtesy and willingness to listen to their points of view won the group's respect.

Once again I saw that unfiltered, face to face communication is the key to many of the world's problems. It's the key to conflict resolution and leads to hope for the future. Words can change ideas, bring peace or war – or foment a revolution. Revolution can be many things, including turning old ideas on their heads and doing things another way – a better way.

In many ways, while the mission to the Middle East was very serious it had its humorous moments. Because Jeff and I were there to support the Elders – who undertook all the crucial meetings – we were invariably together. I noticed that we were constantly going in and out of doors, especially at hotels or restaurants, and becoming increasingly courteous with each other each time, almost to a ludicrous degree. I would step back and say, 'you first' to Jeff and he would say, 'no please, after you'. I would insist and he would look rather embarrassed: 'No, no, you first.' At times it seemed we were stuck in a doorway for an eternity. I suddenly realised that Jeff was fourteen years younger than me and he was probably giving me due deference for my great age. In the end we resolved our conflict by communication.

'Let's take turns,' I suggested. 'You go first through this door – and I'll go first through the next one.'

I hadn't been to Jerusalem before, so on our first afternoon there Jeff offered to show me around the Old City. He knew it well, he assured me. I said I'd like to see the Damascus Gate, about which I had read a great deal over the years. 'No problem,' Jeff said, 'I know the way like the back of my hand and I can point out one or two landmarks on our way.'

The first thing I did as soon as we got into the Old City proper was to slip on a slick marble pavement in the old market, the Suq Khan ez-Zeit. I went flying, in a classic banana-skin moment. Luckily, Jeff was on hand and with his help I managed to gain my balance before I did the splits and ruined my life. But I don't think Jeff was prepared for what I can only describe as being mobbed. In the cause of publicising the various Virgin businesses I had made my face very visible and it seemed that everyone we passed not only considered me their best friend – a strange phenomenon that actors say they experience regularly – but they all wanted their photos taken with me, and to chat or discuss their lives or amazing business schemes. The one thing they all had in common was their good nature and enthusiasm. I'd draw Jeff into the fun: 'This is Jeff Skoll. He'd love to talk to you.'

Blank stares would greet my announcement. 'Ah yes, Mr Sir Richard Branson, as I was saying, let me tell you about –'

'And, ehm, Jeff here, was the first employee and president of eBay –'

Incomprehension, coupled with nods and polite smiles.

'He's a film producer too. You might have seen his movies like *An Inconvenient Truth* or *Syriana* or *The Kite Runner* or *Charlie Wilson's War*,' I'd say, sounding like Jeff's PR as I rattled off a few of the films made by Jeff's company, Participant.

More nods and smiles

'Oh, and Jeff also dubbed Richard Attenborough's film *Gandhi* into Arabic so Palestinians could view it. Have you seen *Gandhi*?' I babbled, unsure if I was speaking to Israelis or Palestinians.

'Ah yes! We have seen your movies, Mr Hollywood Producer.'

Several thousand Palestinians had watched *Gandhi* and been moved by it and, luckily, some of them were the people we met on our progress through the market. Movies were indeed a universal Open Sesame. Almost immediately, I was elbowed to one side and they all wanted to pose for their photographs with the great Hollywood producer. Jeff looked alarmed. He muttered, 'You know I prefer to keep a low profile.'

'This is no time to be shy,' I assured him.

We ducked into a café and quickly struck up a conversation with two young Palestinians. They spoke fluent English and were articulate in their conviction that peace was impossible because Israel didn't want peace. According to them, Israel wanted to foment war in order to keep Palestinians down and out, while they – Israel – grabbed all the best land. 'Israel will soon be at war with all her neighbours,' they stated, 'Gaza, Hezbollah, then Iran. All they want to do is fight. And when they lose it will be a real mess. The whole region will go up like a bomb.'

'We believe in peace. We have to give peace a chance,' I said. Jeff chimed in with, 'President Obama is working really hard to change things. We have to help him by believing that peace is possible.'

By the time we had drunk a few cups of coffee with them, the Palestinians were agreeing with us. John Lennon would have been proud of us. 'Give peace a chance!' they said, making the peace sign.

'That was pretty good,' Jeff said as we left the café. 'Changing hearts and minds one latte at a time.' While we walked, Jeff admitted that the Elders had far more stamina than he had. They wore him out. 'They do all the work, take all the high-powered meetings and they're not young, you know. I have come to realise that they didn't become world figures by lolling about and reading briefs at the hotel. Can you imagine what it must have been like when they were in office?'

Some nights we sat up until 1 a.m. with The Elders and people from the United Nations and the World Bank who were there to join in the talks. It was incredible hearing some of the intimate and unique anecdotes about the terms in office from Presidents Carter, Cardoso (former President of Brazil), Robinson (former President of Ireland) and Gro Brundtland (former Prime Minister of Norway), not to mention Ela Bhatt, and Archbishop Tutu. Such an awe-inspiring team, all gathered together around a dining table in Jerusalem – I would never have dreamed it possible all those years ago when Peter Gabriel and I first discussed setting up such an organisation. No wonder nobody went to bed – nobody wanted to be the first to leave the magic circle around the table.

When I first met Jeff Skoll at the Clinton Global Initiative, I described The Elders and what we hoped they would achieve. I was incredibly enthusiastic and thought my enthusiasm might be catching, but Jeff was laid back about it. 'Yeah, great idea', he might say, but that was it. Six months later, Jeff was having breakfast with Ray Chambers. Ray had just returned from the initial Elders meeting at Ulusaba, presided over by Madiba.

When Jeff heard that, he sat up. He told me, 'When you first chatted about it, I thought it was just another idea – one of the many we all have all the time. I didn't realise how serious you were. Hearing about it from Ray was like a light bulb going on. I instantly knew I wanted to be involved.'

Which brought us full circle, to getting lost in Jerusalem that day. As we stood there discussing the best way out of the market, a gust of wind caught a large and very heavy parasol and it was inches away from crashing down on Jeff's head. I managed to grab it in time, and pulled him out of the way. Remarking on the way in which he had grabbed me before I did the splits earlier, and our doorway etiquette, I said, 'We're a good team.'

The Elders themselves have become a very strong team. We have been amazed at the level of commitment the individual Elders have given to the initiative. They have truly embraced the opportunity to work collectively, much of the time behind the scenes, to tackle some of the tougher issues in the world. They've joined forces to support government transitions in Kenya, the Ivory Coast and Zimbabwe, been asked to support the peace process in North and South Korea, listened and amplified the voices of people in Sudan and the Middle East, brought together a strong alliance to help stop child marriages, and the list goes on. We could not have dreamt of a better, more inspirational group of committed people as have formed through The Elders and we feel lucky every day to be there to support them.

Here's a complete list of The Elders:

Current

- Martti Ahtisaari
- Kofi Annan
- Ela Bhatt
- Lakhdar Brahimi
- Gro Brundtland
- Fernando H Cardoso
- Jimmy Carter
- Graça Machel
- Mary Robinson
- Desmond Tutu

Honorary

- Aung San Suu Kyi
- Nelson Mandela

Former

- Muhammad Yunus

It's that combination of The Elders themselves, the 'engine' that we now call the Advisory Council and the Elders' support team, all from very diverse backgrounds, that has helped ensure that The Elders organisation serves the global village by leading through wisdom and focusing on what's right for humanity. This is a perfect example of Capitalism 24902, where business leaders partner with leaders from other sectors to tackle global issues. *Screwing business as usual* isn't only about doing well by doing good for your business, it's also about doing well by taking care of the global village of which we are all members. Once The Elders was up and running, we turned our attention to another leadership gap in the global village, the protection of the planet.

Some people believe that the threat to the planet is as serious as the First and Second World Wars combined. If that is the case, I thought, where is the coordinating body to fight the war against this new enemy – carbon? We set up the Carbon War Room precisely for this reason; to coordinate our attack on carbon. As I mentioned earlier in this chapter, the lack of a comprehensive agreement at the Copenhagen summit in December 2009 on ways to reduce the impact of climate change was a disappointment. However, it reminded me of the need for businesses and industries to take on more responsibility and to set their own targets to reduce carbon emissions and protect our natural assets. Too much has been left to governments, and I fear we could be waiting a long time for clear direction. Rather, we need better collaboration between business, governments and not-for-profits to make sure we can move at the pace we need to.

So a few years ago Virgin Unite set about looking at how we could bring together a group of entrepreneurs to turn the issues we faced with our rapidly depleting natural assets into the biggest opportunity of our lifetime.

As we did with The Elders, we wanted to approach the start of the Carbon War Room with the same rigorous business approach. So we spent a good year better understanding the landscape, finding the gaps, mapping out potential areas of focus, road testing them with the right people and finding the right partners and management team to ensure the success of this new venture. This was one of the most interesting 'screw business as usual' moments in my career as I watched how antagonistic many of the environmental groups were towards getting businesses involved. Rightly so, they were very cynical. They had watched businesses ruthlessly destroy our natural resources and were somewhat perplexed about why a business would want to get involved in trying to create a business movement towards protecting and harnessing our natural assets. All of the initial awkward moments were worth it as I saw the great unlikely partnerships that were formed across the business and environmental sectors, basically reinventing how business and the world worked. The only way we are going to win this war on increasing levels of carbon is if all of us bring everything we've got to the table to try and use business (which has created many of the problems) as a vehicle for change in the world.

The Carbon War Room today is a great example of how we can use business not only to help solve problems, but how we can turn problems upside down into opportunities to create thousands of new jobs and better ways of living for people all over the world. As with many ideas, there were any number of twists and turns as the team from Virgin Unite brought together all kinds of people to help shape the idea. Necker once again became the centre of many discussions that helped to crystallise the concept and bring in a strong group of supporters. One of the early volunteers who gave hours of his time to help us shape the idea was George Polk who is a Board member of the Carbon War Room and continues to remain incredibly committed.

We were also able to bring in a very strong management team. Jigar Shah became the CEO and José María Figueres, the Chairman. Peter Boyd, who had worked for Virgin for many years, worked with Virgin Unite on the early stages and then went across to become COO. As a team, they have done a brilliant job focusing the Carbon War Room on business-based approaches to the reduction of carbon in our atmosphere.

We've also managed to attract a great group of founders, such as Strive Masiyiwa and Mark Shuttleworth from South Africa, Idan Ofer from Israel, Vladas Lašas from Lithuania, Boudewijn Poelmann and Marieke van Schaik from the Dutch Postcode Lottery and Michael Haas and Shelley Meyers from the US. The experience of the founders combined with the strength of the management team have allowed the Carbon War Room to gain traction rapidly. Tackling the problem industry by industry, the Carbon War Room has already gained inroads with partners in shipping and in buildings.

Each year, the shipping industry transports over 90 per cent of the world's goods but produces over one billion tons of carbon dioxide while doing so. Only five countries in the world emit more CO_2. Shipping is more efficient than other modes of transport for moving most types of goods around the world, but the industry could be saving over 30 per cent without new technology or relying on new policy. That's a saving of $70 billion a year just in fuel costs! Add the associated large CO_2 reduction opportunities and you have a great first project for the Carbon War Room. The Carbon War Room's shipping operation, led by Peter and industry expert Alisdair Pettigrew, is working with shipping companies, shipping customers, technology entrepreneurs, ports, banks and governments to help accelerate the use of existing technologies to reduce carbon output and save money.

So the team went about looking at how they could make a difference. 'The key was getting into the middle of the industry, which remains in many ways traditional and conservative. It's really a process of listening, learning and applying the expertise we have from outside the industry into identifying the barriers locked in the sector, and providing solutions to breaking down those barriers,' Peter explains. 'The shipping industry's leaders, including the largest shipping company in the world AP Moeller-Maersk, agreed with many of our ideas and we have gathered a tremendous amount of support for our vision of a low carbon shipping industry.'

The Carbon War Room also spent a lot of its time listening to entrepreneurs who had come up with great ideas on how to make ships more efficient. It quickly emerged that all these entrepreneurs faced the same difficulty: there was no demand for their product! They would say things like, 'My hull coating paint pays for itself in two years, but nobody is buying from me.'

This made no sense. As Jigar said to me, 'Large firms pay hundreds of millions of dollars a year on shipping fuel. They'd save millions if the ships they used were painted with the latest hull coatings or air lubrication technologies. Companies like Walmart, Rio Tinto, BP and Cargill aren't dumb – how have they not got on to this trick?'

The shipping operation team soon discovered that companies were, of course, painfully familiar with the size of their own bills. But they had no convenient way of finding out which of the ships they leased were fuel efficient, and which were belching unnecessary carbon into the atmosphere, along with a chunk of their profits. They simply didn't have the right data. It's astounding to think that the simple inability to choose the most efficient ships is causing customers to miss out on cost savings of between 15 and 30 per cent.

The problem with shipping is, at its core, really very simple. It's the same problem a tenant has when faced with a big fuel bill. The house they rent is cold and draughty and could be easily and cheaply insulated. But since they're the one paying the heating bills, nothing gets done to fix the problem. The landlord doesn't care that the house is cold, draughty and wasteful. It doesn't cost him anything.

What if there were a way of knowing, before you rented a house, just how expensive it was to heat? What if you could avoid big, draughty houses? What if you could point to a figure and say, 'I will rent your house, but only after you've lagged the attic'? This, essentially, is what the Carbon War Room is doing for the shipping industry. 'And, naturally enough, the best and most responsible shipbuilders and shipowners are very keen to work with us,' Jigar points out. 'This way they might finally get some recognition for being far-sighted players.'

The Carbon War Room recently launched a new shipping efficiency website, www.shippingefficiency.org, which is starting to help transform the industry. This was a perfect example of where this new independent approach to leadership could make a huge difference to the planet.

It is a strange sight: José María Figueres, former President of Costa Rica, and Jigar Shah, solar pioneer, waxing lyrical about smart air conditioners and double glazing.

One of the projects that has been both exciting and tricky for the team at the Carbon War Room is their attempt to make our cities more energy efficient. To put it bluntly, nobody wants to spend money in order to save money.Encouraging new capital to support 'greening' buildings has been another of the Carbon War Room's early battles against climate change – and one of the biggest opportunities. More than 70 per cent of all carbon emissions come from buildings.

That's why, besides planning new buildings that make environmental sense, we must refurbish outdated structures. Another perfect challenge for the Carbon War Room that requires accessible financing from national and local governments, possibly new legislation and a raft of new entrepreneurs to design and refit the buildings.

During the Winter Olympics in Vancouver, the Carbon War Room convened a meeting of thirty mayors from some of the largest cities around the world (which I chaired with the Mayor of Vancouver) to find out what was stopping them from turning their cities green. Over 50 per cent of all carbon worldwide comes from inefficient buildings.

The answer they gave us was simple: lack of finance.

So our team at the Carbon War Room set out to develop a scheme for cities that would be a massive win-win for everyone and in particular the environment. Jigar, Peter, and operation head Murati Armoruster catalysed an innovative financing system that, simply put, gave lenders almost watertight security by having the loans for double-glazing, solar panels, etc. repaid out of slightly increased property taxes. They tested this idea in Miami and Sacramento and quickly had $650 million committed from private enterprise to retrofit buildings there which will slash energy consumption and create thousands of jobs. As a result, local governments worldwide can now tap private capital to finance renewable energy and efficiency improvements for residential and commercial properties. The owners of these buildings will dramatically reduce their energy bills.

Now that this first scheme has been put to bed, there is no reason why every city in the world shouldn't replicate it, creating literally millions of jobs and reducing as much as five gigatons of carbon a year (out of the 25 gigatons a year the world needs to save to avoid disaster). The Carbon War Room is ready to help roll it out. Brilliant!

In my mind, this is a perfect example of Virgin Unite's ability to create real change by incubating new initiatives such as the Carbon War Room and then to leverage huge change in the world using business as a force for good.

The last forty years have seen great progress in information technology, software and computing, and many fortunes have been made. I believe that as part of Capitalism 24902 the next forty years will see similar levels of progress in the clean, green sector, a host of new fortunes made and the creation of a more equitable, cleaner and safer world. I am confident that the Carbon War Room will play a role in a new approach to global leadership in helping speed up this process to protect the beautiful world the global village calls home.

Similar to the Carbon War Room and The Elders, we are continuing to work with the South African government to establish the Disease Control Hub for South Africa and eventually beyond to support Sub-Saharan Africa. This initiative has needed a bit of a longer lead time than any business venture I've ever been part of, but when it happens, the impact on human lives will make every minute we've spent on this worthwhile. Watch this space!

As an important part of the global village and Capitalism

24902, business leaders have a role to play, not just with their individual businesses, but also with the wider group of stakeholders with whom they share the village. Many global brands cross borders far more easily than governments and so have an opportunity to *screw business as usual* and use this power to help encourage new approaches to leadership in the world. One of the things we've learned as we've created The Elders and the Carbon War Room is the importance of independence for these new leadership approaches. This new army of leaders like Mabel van Oranje and Jigar Shah must be allowed to lead purely on behalf of humanity and the planet – with no other agenda. At times it is tough to step back and do this, but it has been well worth it as it allows them to bring together the right unlikely marriages and make the correct decisions for people everywhere.

Web: virginunite.com/screwbusinessasusual
Twitter: @virginunite #sbau
Facebook: Facebook.com/VirginUnite

7 The Power of Communities

'There is a rise of a movement that is a shift between a world created by and for privilege to a world created by community ... the rise of over one million organisations in the world who address civil liberties, social justice and the environment. And even though they're atomized and there's many of them and they don't seem connected, due to modern technology – cell, texting, internet – they're starting to intertwine, morph and come together in ways that is making it much more powerful than it has been before' – Paul Hawken in his book *Blessed Unrest* (2007)

'The world of business will either be socially responsible or there won't be a world for business to be in' – Paul Hawken, quoted in an interview with *Inc* magazine (2001)

I began this book by explaining that the core of Capitalism 24902 is people. Throughout the book we've celebrated many individuals who have effected change in the world, but change does not happen through any one individual. Change happens through the power of communities. And never has there been a better and more exciting time for communities to drive change than now in our connected global village. Capitalism 24902 is ultimately all about communities.

In his groundbreaking book *Blessed Unrest*, Paul Hawken talks about how the power of this new world created by community 'resides in its ideas, not in force'. Although it certainly has teeth: 'It has been capable of bringing down governments, companies, and leaders through witnessing, informing, and massing.' Certainly we've seen that play out for the better and in some cases for the worse in the last few months.

Margaret Mead was one of the first great cultural anthropologists whose work on the people of Samoa is still a textbook study. David Shepherd says her words inspired him: 'Never doubt that a small group of thoughtful, citizens can change the world. Indeed, it is the only thing that ever has'. He wrote to me, 'Changing the world is no mean feat; but this quote reveals two of the great truths of the world. First, the world can be changed. Second, every great movement in the world starts with a tiny group of people who simply refuse to accept a situation. They gather their ideas and their passion and drive forward. If there is a problem they solve it or simply overcome it. They are not intimidated by the odds.'

As part of Capitalism 24902 and our quest to *screw business as usual*, I've been thinking a lot about the role that business has in building communities that will drive change in the world. Global brands have built powerful communities in their own right linked to their products and services; imagine if all those companies focused on supporting those communities to mobilise change in the world. Coca-Cola alone serves 1.7 billion drinks every single day. The exact same bottles of Coke are consumed in expensive Paris cafés as in the slums of Mumbai. Imagine now if a fraction of those consumers were inspired to do something good each time they drank a Coke. That really would be teaching the world to sing.

The beauty of business is that it does not just have one single community; as organisations we're made up of our people, our suppliers and our customers. The businesses that are most successful connect with everyone as an individual, not just as an order number or a transaction. There have been many pioneers in this area who have successfully built communities and mobilised them to act. Among them are Ben and Jerry who made people feel part of their family right from the start; hell, they even got their customers to churn their ice cream for them! What Ben and Jerry did brilliantly is that they used their products to create a movement around things that were not acceptable in the world. I'll never forget their 'Peace Pops', a product they launched to raise awareness and build support for their campaign to get the US military to shift one per cent of its budget to life-improving rather than life-taking goals. Later, in 2006, this evolved into an American Pie campaign (and a new ice-cream flavour) to get consumers to demand a shift in spending priorities. There were many more campaigns that they got behind, from encouraging people to vote to raising awareness about the rainforest. The wonderful thing was that it was not all about them; it was about getting their community mobilised behind issues.

I remember listening to Ben Cohen when he was on Necker for a Virgin Unite leadership gathering. 'I think that business is the most powerful force in the country,' he said. 'When business starts using its voice for the benefit of the country as a whole, not just in its narrow self-interest, it can really be the force that can make the changes that need to be made.'

Anita Roddick had a similarly magical touch whereby customers at the Body Shop felt more like a family doing good for the world when they bought something, rather than making a meaningless transaction. The tricky thing is how you keep that community going strong, especially when your business is sold and does not have a visionary leader at the helm. I asked Ben this question. 'It certainly has not been smooth sailing 100 per cent of the time since Unilever took over. We've had our ups and downs, and I think finally after several years we've now landed in a place where we feel comfortable that Ben & Jerry's can maintain its mission to do good in the world. Jerry and I now play an ongoing consultant role with the team from Ben & Jerry's. The great opportunity we have is to act like a virus for good within a huge company like Unilever to influence their core decision-making across all their brands.'

Many companies are following in the footsteps of these pioneers and putting a community focus on everything they do. One such company is Cafédirect, which started in 1991. Their purpose is to 'change lives and build communities'. In 1989, when an international coffee agreement that had fixed global prices according to the cost of production collapsed, a community of growers from Peru, Costa Rica and Mexico came together to stop middlemen from buying up the coffee at rock-bottom prices and destroying the lives of millions of smallholding farmers. Growers shipped their coffee beans to the UK and they were sold through charity shops and at local events. It was the start of an inspiring community across many borders.

Today, twenty years later, Cafédirect is the largest Fair Trade hot drinks company in the world. They've built a community with over 260,000 coffee, tea, and cocoa growers across fourteen countries. These growers are not just partners; over 75 per cent of them are also owners in the company. They have also reinvested over half of their profits into supporting the growers with things like market information, climate change impact reports and a host of other activities to ensure the growers thrive. They've not only done well in business over the last twenty years, they've also improved the lives of over 1.8 million people. A perfect example of Capitalism 24902 and the power of a company's community.

Many other companies are springing up that use the internet and social media to build powerful communities that are radically reinventing how we live in the world. Twitter already has more than two hundred million community members and Facebook has 750 million. These communities are changing the way we interact every day and can be used as powerful forces for good, and sometimes sadly the not so good. As Camila Batmanghelidjh pointed out so eloquently, it's all about community inclusion in the wider society and getting people to want to do the right thing because they feel part of something positive.

There is also an interesting new generation of social enterprises that is using the internet to drive change and provide free and fair access to information, such as Avaaz and Wikipedia.

As we prepared for our briefing before the press conference for the Global Commission on Drug Policy I looked around the room and realised that I was one of the youngest Commissioners at the table. Sadly being the youngest in any group is a rarity for me these days! As I was musing on my elder status, a young man walked into the room and sat down confidently at the end of the table. I wasn't quite sure who he was until he cheerfully proclaimed, 'We've reached over a half-million signatures.' The room broke into applause. It was Ricken Patel, the CEO of Avaaz. Ricken and his team had worked with President Cardoso's team to rapidly set up a petition to get people to sign up in support of ending the war on drugs. The petition's objective was to show the world that people really do want an open debate on alternatives to the present approach to drugs.

Avaaz – the word means 'voice' in several European, Middle Eastern and Asian languages – was launched in 2007 with a simple democratic mission: organise citizens of all nations to close the gap between the world we have and the world most people everywhere want. Avaaz empowers millions of people from all walks of life to take action on pressing global, regional and national issues, from corruption and poverty to conflict and climate change. It is a brilliant example of a community of over 9.7 million members that has taken over forty-nine million actions. Most importantly, that community feels it is playing a part in how we transform our future. One member, Ibrahim Ceesay from Gambia, explained it from his point of view: 'Avaaz to me means power to the people to shape the future the way they want it to be. It is a world parliament stronger and more pro-active than the UN and all other international organizations combined.'

The day after the press conference I had the chance to spend some more time with Ricken as we joined the Commissioners in delivering the petition and the 500,000 signatures to the UN Secretary General. Here is what Ricken wrote in his report back to members about that visit: 'We did it! Last week Avaaz Executive Director Ricken Patel hand-delivered our over half a million signatures to the UN Secretary General Ban Ki-moon, world leaders and the global media in New York. At the meeting Ban Ki-moon heard our call to action and agreed to create a new UN task force to develop a comprehensive approach to drugs and organized crime. This is a major step forward towards ending the war on drugs as the approach will include a public health, education and prevention focus. We will continue to push to make sure this senseless and brutal war is ended. Stay tuned for how together we can keep up the pressure.'

This experience got me even more excited about the power of communities and the role that Virgin could have in bringing together some pretty powerful groups. As a company, we've always built our businesses as if they were families, putting our people first. I'm really proud that many people in the Virgin Group stay not just for a few years, but for their entire careers. Across the Group they've also always had the tendency to want to give back. So when we started Virgin Unite there was heaps of enthusiasm across the Group to be part of a community that was going to make a real difference in the world.

But it has certainly not been plain sailing along the way. I remember, when we first started Virgin Unite some seven years ago, we wanted to ensure we focused on how we gave staff the opportunity to give their time. So we came up with a really fun campaign based around the Seven Deadly Sins, called 'spend some time with your better side', and thought that people from across the Virgin Group would fall over each other to get involved. They didn't. We went back to the drawing board and spent more time with our staff and partners and found that what they all wanted was quality versus quantity. They told us that they didn't want hundreds of volunteer opportunities such as painting walls that take time for the charity to organise and don't use people's skills. Rather, they wanted some tailored opportunities that would have far more impact. They also wanted to join together with others from across the Virgin family. So we created what we called 'Hit Squads' and 'Connection Trips' and we still have a host of individual opportunities for those who are independently minded.

The Hit Squads are a great way for staff members to get involved for a few days of very focused time to support a not-for-profit organisation with their professional skills, some of them bringing together marketing experts across the group and others with a mixed sets of skills. Often we will also throw into the mix some external resources to add another dimension. For every Hit Squad, even though they are doing it for nothing, we treat it as if they were being paid for consultancy projects to ensure that the not-for-profit organisation and the team take it seriously and have clear deliverable tasks. I've seen entire annual strategies come out of these sessions in five days.

They are not only great for staff morale; they are also a great training and development tool. We've done them for some very small grassroots organisations, as well as for some large ones such as Archbishop Tutu's Peace Centre and Kate Winslet's Golden Hat Foundation. The power of this really hit home when a team member from Virgin Holidays wrote to me: 'The ActionAid Hit Squad provided us with a great opportunity to use our sales skills and experience in a different way, allowing us to really give something back. Knowing that the information we shared will indirectly help vulnerable children across the world made for a hugely satisfying experience. It made me proud to be part of Virgin.'

We also started Connection Trips where we take groups of people from across the Virgin Group to see projects first hand. There is nothing better than listening directly to and learning from the people who are impacted by the issues. These trips have radically changed the lives of many people who have experienced them. As one Virgin Atlantic crew member put it, 'Seeing this stuff on the news is very different to seeing it first hand. Thank you for getting me off the couch and into the front line.'

As Unite started to grow, we began to see wonderful communities developing across the businesses. We have a group of people who formed a Steering Committee and another group who became ambassadors within their businesses, called Business Champions. Nick Fox and his team have done a brilliant job at pulling together a bunch of people across all the businesses to ensure they get their core basics in order. Nick has also worked with Debbie Dar at Virgin USA and others to raise millions each year for Virgin Unite through the speeches that I've been giving around the world. A more recent group that has just come together is the Insiders, people from across the Group who want to help build a wider global community for Virgin Unite. Virgin Atlantic staff never cease to amaze me by their generosity and kindness. Over the last three years they have raised almost £500,000 and volunteered in many overseas projects with Free the Children. Although raising money is important, the best part is seeing everyone's adventurous spirit; climbing Mount Kenya, running marathons, cycling hundreds of miles in rural India, unicycling over the Golden Gate Bridge, the list goes on and on! Part of this is down to one of our adventurous Captains, Chris Hall, who organises many of these incredible events for all departments to get involved in. These communities are what make Virgin and Virgin Unite special. These communities are what drive us towards Capitalism 24902.

Communities all over the world have driven large-scale change such as the civil rights movement or the end of apartheid. Andrea Barron connected us to a very special person, Auret van Heerden, who made an incredibly moving speech at one of our Virgin Unite leadership gatherings. His story really resonated with me as it was all about helping to end apartheid from the inside out of a business by mobilising a community of workers.

Auret is a revolutionary who has spent his entire life fighting for the rights of workers – men, women and children. His work is a shining example of *screw business as usual*. He is the CEO of the Fair Labour Association (FLA), a coalition of twenty brand-name companies, as well as universities and NGOs, that seeks improvements in global labour practices and helps companies source their raw materials ethically and sustainably. He deals with details, processes and policies but Auret is much, much more than a 'details person'. His own extraordinary story reveals a vital human dimension in his work – one that explains, far better than I ever could, why we need to screw up and throw away our old ideas of how businesses should treat people.

Auret was a white student radical in South Africa, mobilising communities of black workers to stand up against apartheid. He says: 'At least, that was the theory. It turned out, though, that some of the black workers we approached were more worried about funerals than the big political issues of the day.'

It's a tradition in South Africa that funerals are lavish affairs, and it's a matter of honour that all family members attend. These funerals are enormously expensive. Families travel back to their homelands, and pay for everyone to go. They provide tents, blankets and food for several weeks' mourning for the extended families they bring together. Limousines are hired to drive the coffin and cortege hundreds of miles. Even a simple funeral often costs the equivalent of an entire family's food bill for a year and moneylenders thrive. Many companies employing black workers, however, were not contributing money to their workers' funeral expenses; worse, they were not even giving their workers time off to attend them. People had to go and, when they did, they were dismissed. With no income, their debts spiralled.

Auret and his fellow student activists quickly saw that it it was essential to win the hearts of the workers by doing something about the high cost of funerals. He and his friends helped set up mutual funeral savings societies, so that workers could afford to pay for and attend their family funerals. These funeral societies became powerful communities and were amongst the foundations for a new black trade union movement in South Africa – a movement that was crucial to the overthrow of apartheid. Auret and his radical friends achieved more by listening to people's real needs, and by working with people to address them, than they ever did when they just talked politics.

Real needs have this magical property: you can't argue with them. If you ignore them they don't just go away. Auret tells a neat story to demonstrate the point. One of the more stupid regulations shoring up apartheid was an ordinance requiring the segregation of toilets. Inevitably, this meant black workers were left with no bathroom facilities – they had no alternative but to use gutters in public which was incredibly demeaning. It kept the worker at an inhuman level. Unexpectedly, Auret found himself talking toilets with multinational companies with factories in South Africa. The managers of the factories agreed that the rule was stupid, but what could they do? The law was the law.

Auret responded simply and practically. He insisted, 'Never mind the law. It's your factory. Desegregate the toilets. The government will do nothing. If they took you to court it would generate headlines and cartoons and general mockery in every newspaper from London to LA, and the government knows it.'

His strong, pragmatic approach worked. Businesses approached to make changes incrementally and logically gave South Africa desegregated workplaces before such reforms were even on the table politically.

His reform strategies drew the attention of the apartheid government. They didn't appreciate a book he had co-authored on trade union rights, or the fact that he served two terms as president of the National Union of South African Students. Inevitably, there were repercussions as Auret became more and more active in the fight against apartheid. He and some of his friends were arrested, and Auret found himself incarcerated and repeatedly tortured in the same prison block that housed Steve Biko. When Auret sued the government for mistreatment, no one understood how he and his torturers could hang around together outside the courtroom, chatting. The fact was, throughout his ordeal, Auret had treated his jailers with respect. 'All I had, the only thing they couldn't take away from me – it wasn't anger, because anger tires you out. I think it was respect and love for my fellow human beings.'

His civility had, in several cases, clearly disarmed them and undermined their purpose. It had probably saved his life, too. And even in the court convened to examine this terrible wrong, it allowed torturer and victim to acknowledge each other's humanity face to face in the court room.

Eventually the tables were turned in South Africa. Nelson Mandela was freed and apartheid was ended. Most surprising of all, the respect for people that Auret embodied saved South Africa from the bloody recriminations everyone had expected would tear the young country apart. It's a quality South Africans call Ubuntu: the sense that what makes us human is our connection with other human beings.

One of The Elders has also been humbly working on bringing together communities to drive change. Ela Bhatt has quietly built one of the largest grassroots communities in the world through the belief that people must have the chance to work. She started the Self-Employed Women's Association of India (SEWA – much as I hate acronyms I think I had better use this one: I'll never remember that name in full) back in 1972 and today it has over 1.25 million members. SEWA members are India's poorest and most marginalized women who earn a living through their own labour or small businesses – the unprotected and uncounted workers who make up about 94 per cent of the female labour force.

I love watching Ela in The Elders' meetings. She normally sits and listens to everyone's opinions and when she joins the discussion it's clearly with a voice that comes directly from the people who are living with the issues every day on the front lines. Her entire life has been built around the power of poor people and communities. She has also been showing us all how to *screw business as usual* to create job opportunities at the grassroots level and to create communities to support this effort. She gave a beautiful speech at the UNDP in June 2011 that I want to share with you:

'My appeal is that before we rush ahead to modernize and urbanize our world, armed with technology and capital, we must pause and look more closely at the economic and social structures that are collapsing, or are being dismantled in the name of development. Urbanization is not development.

Technology, if it creates imbalances, is not a solution.

'If profit is our only measure of success, we will turn a blind eye to the exploitation of people and nature. So long as the goal is maximizing production and consumption, and progress and wealth are measured by a country's capital-intensive industries, exports, and GDP, we are embracing both imbalance and inequality. But if our goal is to build a society where everyone's basic needs for food, clothing and housing are fully met, and where the full potential of every human being is realized, we will need a radically different approach.

'We will need to get in partnership with our conscience; we will need to get in partnership with our fellow human beings and we will need a long-term partnership with Mother Nature.

'Along those lines, my own vision is of a society where six of our primary needs – our daily staple food, shelter, clothing, primary education, health services and banking services can be found within, say, a hundred-mile radius. With this approach, we address the fundamental issue of creating livelihoods, building the local economy and feeding the world. The demand for local products generates local employment. It brings to full potential the multiple skills of villagers, and there is work for everyone, for all levels of ability, and for all types of rewards.

'Let us not dismiss this as a utopian dream. At SEWA, we have already made a beginning. Let us, in all humility, look into how lightly we can live on this earth.

'What we need is a shared vision, and a partnership with the poor. We need the active engagement of each community, and its organizations.'

When I originally bought Necker Island I saw it as a place where the rock stars on the Virgin Records label could record and relax in private, tranquil surroundings. Only later did I begin to develop it more as a resort, albeit a very exclusive one, where no more than twenty-eight people could stay at any one time. Back then, I didn't see it as a place where astonishing ideas could be incubated and grow. I didn't envisage that the most brilliant minds and people with the noblest aspirations would gather together there to share ideas and make things happen. I didn't even imagine that the sharpest, brightest young entrepreneurs would congregate to network and have fun. I certainly didn't see Necker itself as becoming a force for good and a force for change ... and yet it did. The dream was perhaps always there, somewhere at the back of my mind.

I think the biggest change came about when we held The Elders' first development meetings on Necker in July 2006. In the end, Necker helped bring out the magic, but the power really lay within the wonderful people we gathered together and was multiplied by the communities we formed with these eclectic individuals. Those two weeks on Necker taught me a lot about the genesis of an idea and how to make it truly great. It was very painful at times watching a newly hatched idea get torn to shreds by many different people. As

I mentioned, this came from a number of individuals: from Jimmy Carter standing up on the first day and essentially saying he didn't believe in the idea, to Zacky Achmat from the front lines in South Africa's war on AIDS reminding us each day that it had to be practical and support those in the villages – or it was not worth shit!

It was this broad based thinking and true testing of the idea that made The Elders the success it is. This got us thinking about how Virgin Unite could play a role, not just on Necker, but in all kinds of places all over the world by bringing people on connection trips to South Africa, to housing projects in the US, to Aboriginal communities in Australia – basically anywhere they could see issues first hand and work with people on the front lines to help solve them.

So we gradually built an incredible global community of people, all of whom have entrepreneurial thinking at their core and want to work together to make change happen. This community of people is at the core of Capitalism 24902 and they are all about never accepting the unacceptable.

I'll never forget one very special group of people who braved Hurricane Earl with me in September 2010. Julie Hill was one of these people. She grew up in the United States and, after obtaining a master's degree in marketing and management, she went into the land and housing development field and eventually became CEO of a major division of a huge international corporation based in Britain – Costain, the people who built the Channel Tunnel. She says she did this by working her butt off. Her achievements in a world that was heavily biased in favour of men won her the Elizabeth Dole 'Glass Ceiling' Award of the American Red Cross and the 'Amelia Earhart' Award from the University of California, at Irvine. One thing made her fight harder to break through the glass ceiling for all women: being fed up with the male-dominated status quo of the business club. 'I've always found myself wound up by the anomaly of being the only woman in the room.' Today she is on numerous corporate and philanthropic boards, but still often finds she is the only woman in a boardroom full of men.

Through the time-honoured tradition of networking, one of Julie's friends in California, Kelly Smith, who runs the Center for Living Peace Foundation, based in Orange County at UCI, invited Julie and her husband, Peter Hill (Chief Executive of Laird, an electronics and technology conglomerate based in London), to come on one of our Virgin Unite programmes on Necker that was looking at new approaches to world issues. They joined a group of about twenty people that included Virgin Unite Trustees, Ben Cohen and Jerry Greenfield, and President Mary Robinson of Ireland.

Julie and her husband arrived late. They unpacked, had dinner and socialised briefly before retiring for the night. There was a tropical storm warning, but I said that even if it was a big storm there was little to worry about. I described how I had sat out the last hurricane in one of our swimming pools, watching as the storm blew over my head. It had been amazing to look up into the storm and then into its eye, and see the dark, velvety sky and sparkling stars – before the other wall of the spiralling storm hit. But I stressed that I had felt perfectly safe. I'm known for my practical jokes, and a few people looked doubtfully at me, including Nicola, Priya and Jean from the Virgin Unite team who were getting a bit worried about what I might do with their guests.

The next day the hurricane hit and the staff swiftly woke everyone up and speedily ushered them into the great house. People scrambled into their clothes and tumbled out into the rain and a fierce wind. The great house was built into the top of the highest hill on Necker, but the building itself, because it was built of stone and from massive timbers, was extremely solid. Everyone crowded in and the staff handed out blankets and pillows. That night and over the next few days as the storm raged everybody camped out in the great house. People didn't have to worry about getting their nice clothes soaked; most of them wore flip-flops, shorts and T-shirts, which became a kind of levelling uniform. As someone commented, 'These outfits are almost like a summer camp uniform – community bonding at its best.' There were terrific conversations and the air became charged with a kind of buzz from so many great ideas flying around.

Julie said: 'Well, I've been to other corporate events where they create a challenge as an artificial way of bonding but only you, Richard, could arrange for a Category 3 hurricane to hit the island!'

The storm lasted three days but we still tried to keep to some sort of schedule, but to say we were all piled in a heap

– and a soggy heap at that – describes it pretty well. The wind howled and the rain lashed down so hard that it ran along the floors. All of our sessions were highly charged, and we had a sense of isolation, as if we were the only people left on the planet. It was certainly very conducive to the quality of the conversation. During the odd lull, the ocean took on one of the most dramatically beautiful shades I've ever seen: pale grey, yet with a blue, almost luminescent light.

In the middle of the first morning I stood up and said, 'Let's go for a walk.'

People stared doubtfully at me, and then up at the rattling rafters and the heaving roof. I said, 'Some fresh air will do us good.'

We split the group in two and eleven out of twenty stood up and said, 'Fine, we'll troop around the island with you, Richard. Lead on!'

Julie was still wearing flip-flops and she kept sliding off into cactus patches. 'This is turning into the adventure of the nine cactus thistles,' she announced, hopping around and holding up her big toe for inspection. (On our return from the walk she even emailed a photo of her big toe to friends.)

At one point I looked back and saw Auret carrying Priya from the Unite team on his back as her flip-flops had blown away. Many of them found the experience challenging, but when we got back I took out the rest of the hardy souls – the semi-crazies as someone described them – to the shore to sit in the jacuzzi down by the ocean. The winds were fiercer and sand was being blown sideways, but I thought it would be a wild experience for us to share; it wasn't going to be a warm bath, more a sand-blast experience.

On our return I remember Julie saying, 'You know, Richard, this has been quite a vignette. It's a metaphor of your character.' She was right. I thrive on challenges. She shook her head. 'But it was great fun. I am so glad we're doing this. It's an amazing bonding experience.'

I was touched. Julie's words made me look at her in a different way. She seemed to have the same spark in her that I recognised in many of the people who had gathered around Virgin Unite over the last few years. Jean and her team seemed to have a way of collecting Unite family members – from team members like Priya and Nicola to wonderful volunteers such as Andrea Barron and Jane Tewson who had given lifetimes of their support for Unite's initiatives. Julie was strongly motivated and wanted to drive change. I thought it would be interesting to see where this would lead.

It didn't take long to find out. The group divided up into four sections as our talks continued. Julie was asked to moderate the business section. I sat in and listened. They got into a discussion: how can we change business as a force for good?

Julie said, 'You know, one of the things I've been thinking about for a long time is that the CEO of a business has to have their own personal epiphany about why business has to have a wider stakeholder base than just the direction of the business itself. It must be a community – as Unite is. They have to be citizens of the world and have to understand it, to have a broader mission and become more powerful, almost like government. But,' she stressed, 'unless the CEOs themselves have this depth of world view of the humanist perspective, then the company will not be able to do anything. They may tick the boxes but won't actually move. People are starting to understand that we can't go on conducting business as usual. It's not a long-term strategy.' She looked directly at me. 'Richard, you've created this fabulous Elders group for human rights issues. What if we had business Elders?'

I felt electrified, pleased that my intuition had proved to be correct. I said, 'You're on. Do you want to work with us?' Little did she know what she was getting into as for the last year we had been developing a similar idea called 'Business Leaders', an idea that was sparked off when we decided to write this book a few years ago. We were ready for someone like Julie to work with the Unite team and, with a cast of committed volunteers to help get it off the ground, the timing could not have been better.

She said simply, 'Yes.'

I love it when that kind of thing happens because it's perfect – but it also shows how I work: the quick conviction and the quick decision. If someone is right, they're right – why dither around with dozens of meetings before deciding? Paralysis by analysis is a cancer that kills all sorts of companies. It's a slow painful death, one missed opportunity at a time as they re-revalidate the numbers that prove why procrastination is the safest course. There has to be that magic moment, that thunderbolt, when the spark catches and the fire begins to burn. Julie was that great thunderbolt and now she was well and truly part of the Virgin Unite family.

I read a powerful quote the other day by a man named Wafic Saïd, the founder of the Saïd Business School in Oxford. It struck me as making really good sense: 'The companies that focus most on profit are not necessarily the most profitable companies.'

Most politicians tend to care more about short-term votes and not future good or future value. Our society seems to encourage our elected representatives to offer the very antithesis of vision and leadership, which is why it is so difficult to get great young people to aspire to political roles. We need to work out how to change this and how to inspire people to look beyond their limited political boundaries and think of new leadership models that address the many pressing global issues we are facing.

Virgin Unite had been working on the idea of a 'Business Leaders' group for some time with some committed volunteers in the area of business as a force for good. Straight from Necker, Jean and the team went into a two-day scoping meeting in New York with people like John Fullerton from the Capital Institute and Heerad Sabeti from the Fourth Sector Network, both of whom are dedicating their lives to looking at how we truly *screw business as usual* and put people and the planet first. There were some incredibly lively debates about the objectives and how this could become a 'do-tank', rather than a 'think-tank' – making sure it supported rather than duplicated the great work that was already taking place around the world. The great news was that everyone felt there was a need for this group of leaders. This led to a series of meetings in London and Geneva which Julie joined to discuss a whole range of topics with some inspiring people. How would such a group be organised and staffed? What would its first mission be? The group would be provocative and would already have delivered significant change through their business. We wanted people who had strong ideas and were engines for change; but they also had to share some basic values. They would have common perceptions of where the world was going, but would almost certainly have a diversity of ideas about how to take it there.

I was excited that the hurricane meeting had done exactly what these gatherings are supposed to do – bring people together around brilliant ideas.

The Temple on Necker is a large circular room with solid teak pillars from sustainable forests in Indonesia. It was built specifically to be a meeting place for The Elders and it's also where we hold many of our Virgin Unite discussions. It's a beautiful, peaceful place with wonderful views out to sea. I love it there. Peace plays a big part in my life and has done so for many years. In a way it's one of the reasons The Elders came to be founded. When one of our guests to Necker, Kelly Smith, told me she was setting up a peace foundation, I was curious, interested, and slightly wary. She was a delightful woman with an air of innocence about her, and I wondered if she knew what she was getting herself into.

Kelly is a philanthropist from Orange County, California. She had been thinking about doing something for peace for a long time, inspired by Gandhi's famous advice to 'be the change you want to see in the world'. She aimed to help people connect to themselves, their spirit, to others, and to the world; and she was very surprised at how quickly it came together. It was as if people were thirsting for something like this to happen and ready to get involved.

Kelly had been to Necker before and was rapidly becoming a good friend and great fun. She was always so humble and yet filled with a very positive energy. We were lucky to have her along as part of the hurricane crew on Necker. One day I invited everyone to go hiking. Kelly was part of that group (as was Julie Hill) and as we walked we talked about her plans for the Center for Living Peace. She was very willing to share with me her plans about the centre. I was interested because of my work with the Elders and peacemaking in the world, but I told Kelly that it was so easy to get stuck with the label of being very hippy-trippy. I explained that I had seen so much of it in the sixties and seventies, and it wasn't taken that seriously. And, coming from Orange County as she did, she should know that people might take it even less seriously. I wasn't trying to put her off. I was grilling her to see how solid she was and if she really did know what she was doing.

We spent the rest of the week discussing it at every opportunity. I made her plans my mission for that week; and I found that under her gentle exterior was a very keen mind and someone who was 100 per cent sincere and driven. I told her that I didn't like the name. 'Are you sure you want that name? Are you sure that people won't think it's a cult.'

She told me that she wanted people to be challenged by the name. She wanted to help redefine what peace was in the world and bring it to a different level because the hippy thing had passed. Today, peace means what it says. It's not an excuse to get stoned and dream and wander off to an ashram in India. She was always waiting to find what her real passion was. She did some work with a woman who taught spirituality in business and who asked her, 'Kelly, if you had a magic wand and could change the world, how would you do it?'

Immediately Kelly said she would start with children and help them remember how special they are – how loving. She described how she had just seen a three-year-old run to greet his friend. He had bounded over and hugged his little friend joyfully. She wanted to know how we could help people keep that passion and love and unbounded freedom in their lives.

'I visualised what *love* looked like and started talking to people about it. Everyone said, "I want to be a part of it. I want to bring my kids there." My friend Charlize Theron and a couple of other successful people said, "We'll help you" – well, I said, wow, I can do this. Already, it's a living, breathing organism.'

'I'll help you,' I suddenly said, making up my mind. Sometimes you get a gut feeling that something is right – and this seemed right.

A few months later, I went to Orange County to help launch the Center for Living Peace. Kelly had started small, in a mall where there was a great deal of foot passage, across from a dancing school, a yoga centre and a fast food outlet. Students from the University of California, Irvine, and families with children are always passing by. The centre is free and welcomes everyone up to the age of eighteen – as well as their mums and dads.

I went to see them shortly after I had badly damaged a tendon in my leg in a skiing accident, so was hobbling on a stick. I sent Kelly a text message: 'I have a gammy leg and a cane, so I'm going to come as a pirate.' She loved the idea. I had a nice brocade coat, a ruffled shirt and cut-off britches. I was the first speaker. The Dalai Lama was to be there the following month. To my genuine surprise, Kelly handed me a cheque for $250,000 for Virgin Unite. The centre had collected it almost in a matter of days. This was serious stuff. It was remarkable how quickly things had taken off. I felt rather sheepish about my 'hippy-trippy' comments and my almost fierce quizzing on Necker. But Kelly graciously said she really appreciated my questioning. It made her feel that I was taking her work seriously.

Just telling these stories brings back a flood of memories from the many wonderful gatherings we've had on Necker and the many equally wonderful people who have become part of our family. I'll never forget this lanky Australian named Creel Price; he was a successful entrepreneur at the age of twelve and had his whole family working for him in a strawberry business. His success continued and by the time he was forty he had retired and was focused on how he could change the world, which is how he ended up on Necker.

Jean was presenting about the work we were doing in Zimbabwe, and immediately afterwards Creel ran up to her and said he wanted to help. A couple of weeks later he was on a plane to Zimbabwe and starting to invest jointly with us in a small-scale farming project. Creel later went on to give months of his time to support the Branson Centre in South Africa. He is one of those people who never, ever accepts that there is not a way to solve something. He is the living, breathing definition of an entrepreneur. He posted the following note on his blog after his trip to Necker: 'The aim was to start a movement of ideas and individuals committed to making the world a better place, with win-win collaboration at its core. It made me realise how I had been working in a void trying to scratch the surface of a similar vision by myself on the other side of the world. If we can replicate Virgin Unite's vibe and optimism in other forums, the world would be much better for it.'

Our Virgin Unite Connection Trips to South Africa have also brought some extraordinary people into our lives. One of them, Nina Quiros (another of the hurricane gang!), decided that she was going to devote three months of her life to doing something on the ground in South Africa. Nina was in the fashion industry and had her own business in

Colorado. At the same time, we had an entrepreneur named Lesego Malatsi in the Branson Centre in South Africa who had a fashion design business that he wanted to expand. They turned out to be a match made in heaven, so Nina set about moving to South Africa to help Lesego get his business, Mzansi Designers, take the world by storm. At the end of her visit I went out to see what was happening and was blown away by a fashion show that Nina had pulled together with Lesego. It was a magical moment watching the models on the catwalk parade past us all with his stunning clothes. Since then, Lesego has had shows in Britain and the US and is going great guns. This type of community, where successful entrepreneurs are supporting up and coming entrepreneurs, is yet another thing that Capitalism 24902 is all about.

I could tell countless more stories about the inspiring people we've met over the last seven years, but perhaps I will finish with a quote from one of the entrepreneurs who joined us on a Connection Trip, Iain MacGregor. He summed up beautifully the community we are building with Virgin Unite with like-minded entrepreneurs and individuals from all over the world: 'Through its wide-ranging projects spanning social and environmental issues, I was taken aback by the sense of responsibility within Virgin Unite. Whether it's solving world conflicts, reducing carbon in the environment, mitigating the spread of AIDS in Africa, to saving 3,200 tigers in the wild, there is a relentless force for good within Virgin Unite. The trip was about multiplying those efforts and making them sustainable. The opportunity to spend quality time with excellent people was both a learning experience and fun. Virgin Unite is now connected to a few extra soldiers, who are all inspired to do something incredible as a community.'

So, put simply, Capitalism 24902 is about people and the communities they are forming to change the world. Each and every business person, no matter how small or large his or her business is, has the opportunity to *screw business as usual* and help create powerful world-changing communities with their staff, customers, suppliers and the general public.

As I write these final few words I'm more inspired than ever that we are on the brink of a significant transformation in the world. One that will truly *screw business as usual* and herald a brand new way of doing business that will lead to more fulfilling lives for all of us and a much more fair, more equitable and healthy global village. Capitalism 24902's time has truly come. I look forward to partnering with you in this new adventure, filled with great opportunities that we can't even fully imagine yet.

The next hurricane to hit Necker was not so much fun and sadly burnt down the great house where The Elders and the Carbon War Room were formed. This experience reminded me about what is most important in life – not buildings or things – but my family and friends and the wonderful ideas that were inspired on Necker. My daughter Holly will get married on the ruins later this year. I would like to dedicate this book to all our grandchildren with the commitment that I will do everything I can so that they can experience to the fullest this incredible world we are all so lucky to live in.

Web: virginunite.com/screwbusinessasusual
Twitter: @virginunite #sbau
Facebook: Facebook.com/VirginUnite

Into the Future

The band REM has a great song titled 'It's the end of the world as we know it' with the payoff line being '... and I feel fine'. I have often wondered if we should officially adopt it as the anthem of Capitalism 24902.

Over the last several months, as I've been writing this book, that REM lyric has played over and over in my head because it's true – the world as we knew it has indeed changed: the revolutions in the Middle East, the earthquake and tsunami in Japan, the famine in East Africa, the US government almost defaulting on its debt, the near financial collapse of Greece, the riots in London. The list goes on.

All these events have an impact not only on a local but also on a global scale. The more I've thought about it since I finished this book and watched these events unfold, the more I've come to realise how urgent it is that we embrace a whole new way of doing business. Businesses have built global brands and managed to have an impact well beyond any geographic boundaries (some good and some bad!).

That experience, combined with new business models that value and reward doing the right thing, and unlikely marriages with governments and organisations on the front lines, can create a powerful force for good in the world.

I'm excited about the role that the Virgin Group and Virgin Unite can play in helping to make this happen as we continue our journey. Over the next few months we will be bringing together the initial group of business leaders that we discussed; The Elders will be meeting in Brazil as they do twice a year to continue their inspirational work; we are launching a major initiative with Virgin Media in the UK to truly listen to and amplify the voices of young people; we'll be taking a journey to India with WildAid to help save the last remaining tigers; we'll be launching a Branson Centre in the Caribbean with Virgin Holidays to support young entrepreneurs; and this list also goes on.

I realise we have a long way to go as a group of businesses, but I really believe we've got the right people and spirit in place to do our very best to try to *screw business as usual*. I was very heartened the other day when I was catching up with the Chair of the Virgin Group, Peter Norris, when he said, 'The future of the Virgin Group is all about how we become a "shared enterprise" where people and the planet are at the very heart of everything we do.' What a very exciting journey we have ahead of us.

Capitalism 24902's time has come. Now we just need to get on with it and make it happen – quickly! Can you imagine what a different world we will live in when businesses do what's right for communities and the environment in everything they do?

As many of the examples cited in the pages of this book serve to illustrate, those businesses that do well while doing good are the ones that will thrive in the coming decades. Those that continue with 'business as usual', focused solely on profit maximisation, will not be around for long (and don't deserve to be).

As I've been meeting people to gather stories for this book, I've been incredibly inspired and energised by some of the success stories of the new generation of entrepreneurs who have put this philosophy at their core and the leaders who are transforming their existing businesses. And, of course, I've enjoyed learning from some of the pioneers in this area who constantly remind me that amidst all of today's new jargon it's actually pretty simple: just do what's right for people and the planet in everything you do.

But it goes beyond business. We also need to look at how we as individuals can reinvent how we live in the world and turn compassion and empathy into something new, vibrant and sexy!

Over the last several decades people have been absorbed in a movement to 'find ourselves', which is certainly important, but I want to challenge all of us to start a new movement – 'finding each other'. I can guarantee that once we all start to look not only inward, but outward at the things that are not acceptable in the world, we will find ourselves (and much more) in the good that we do for each other.

So, let's get started. We've pulled together a few ways you can get involved in screwing business as usual right now ...

1. Join the Unite 24902 community
2. Share your story – tell me about your business, or one that you admire so that everyone can hear about the great changes happening in the world
3. Get inspired – we've pulled together some interesting case studies on businesses that have transformed themselves, and good start-ups – check them out
     Web: virginunite.com/screwbusinessasusual
     Twitter: @virginunite #sbau
     Facebook: Facebook.com/VirginUnite
4. Don't forget: never accept the unacceptable – and have fun along the way!

Happy screwing ... with business as usual that is!

Postscript

I wrote in the Preface about the horrendous fire that burned the great house at Necker Island to the ground shortly after I finished writing this book, and I thought it only proper to finish with another thought on the subject.

Having (I hope) read this book, you will realize the huge part Necker has played in my life. At the same time I have found myself wondering if the Necker fire and its aftermath could perhaps be a metaphor for some of the kinds of change we've just been talking about?

We built the house over thirty years ago, it was beautiful and served us well, but perhaps, as in business, there comes a stage when a complete restructuring is called for. As painful as the process of transitioning from the comfort zone of an established structure may seem up front (cactus thorns and all) the end results will invariably make it all seem worthwhile.

Acknowledgements

Thanks to all the wonderful people and organisations mentioned in this book for the inspirational work they are doing to *screw business as usual* and make the world a bit of a better place.

A special thank you to Jean Oelwang at Virgin Unite for helping me to pull this book together and for being the heart and soul behind our foundation and therefore much of this book.

Thanks also to the Virgin Unite community of people who have been a joy to work with over the last several years and whose commitment made many of the stories in this book possible; from our Trustees, to the Steering Committee and Business Champions, to the Virgin Unite team and the rest of the cast of entrepreneurial characters across the Virgin Group. A big thanks also to the many front-line partners, entrepreneurs and philanthropists who have joined our community to come together to create entrepreneurial approaches to changing the world (and of course have a bit of fun at the same time).

Lastly, and most importantly, thanks to Joan, Holly and Sam, my mother Eve and the rest of my wonderful family who have consistently been there by my side every step of the way (no matter how crazy my adventures).

Looking forward to the next chapter with all of you as we continue to screw business as usual!

Copyright Acknowledgements

I Rest My Case Studies

Over the last several years I've been lucky enough to have met lots of great people and businesses who are already delivering Capitalism 24902. This book has given me the chance to share a few of their stories – but not enough! So thanks for letting me cheekily fit in a few more. Hopefully they will inspire you to 'rest your case'.

ARAVIND EYE CARE SYSTEMS – sight for sore eyes

Aravind is sort of the Robin Hood of eye care and a great example of Capitalism 24902, as it charges wealthier patients more and poorer patients less. Founded by Dr Govindappa Venkataswamy, it is the world's largest eye care system. Forty-five million of the world's population is blind; twelve million of them live in India. Many lose their sight and livelihood by their early fifties, yet 80 per cent of this blindness could be prevented or cured.

Following the example of the American chain store model, Aravind trains individuals in world-class eye care, creating a franchise model capable of delivering the same quality of eye care anywhere in the world. In the year ending March 2010, over 2.5 million outpatients were treated and over 300,000 surgeries were performed.

The revenue from paying clients fuels growth and expansion and covers the subsidies to treat the poor. Aravind is able to treat over two-thirds of its patients at low to no cost based on their stream-lined service model. Well done to Dr Venkataswamy.

www.aravind.org

JOHN LEWIS – where the owners do all the work

Imagine a business with 76,500 owners, then think John Lewis, the UK department store chain. They've put their people firmly at the centre of their business by making them Partners who have a say in how the company is run, and receive a share of the profits. They are not focused on short-term profit to placate shareholders; they are focused on 'the happiness of our members, through their worthwhile and satisfying employment in a successful business' (as per their Partnership constitution). They even have five holiday centres that the partnership owns and runs for the benefit of its employees. These include a sixteenth-century castle with private beach on Brownsea Island in Poole Harbour, Dorset, an imposing Victorian pile on the shores of Lake Windermere, a twenty-four-room outdoor and watersports club on Lake Bala in North Wales, and a country house hotel in four thousand rolling acres of

Hampshire. Not too bad to help make 76,500 holidaymakers happy.

The John Lewis Partnership is the largest employee-owned company in the UK and their focus on people is working — their employees stay twice as long as the average in the retail industry.

Employee ownership is not right for everyone, but certainly in the case of John Lewis it has worked.

www.johnlewispartnership.co.uk

DUTCH POSTCODE LOTTERY –
improving the odds and upping the ante

Boudewijn Poelmann is an entrepreneur with a big heart who believed that he could change the world through business. When he started the Postcode Lottery in 1989, he wanted to turn the Dutch lottery upside down. He came from a background of business and development (and like me was a bit of an idealistic hippy) and was passionate about combining the two to drive significant change in the world. He wanted the business to be all about communities and he wanted to raise significant funds to support organisations working for a fairer, freer and greener world. So, 50 per cent of income goes to charity and, since its foundation, the lottery has contributed more than 3.5 billion euros to its beneficiaries and it has become one of the largest donors in the world.

The postcode lottery model is a unique one. You don't win as an individual — you win as a community. It is all based around post-codes. So if your postcode comes up as a winner, everyone in that community who has bought a ticket shares in the winnings. They have great block parties to bring everyone together to celebrate. They now have over 2.5 million participants who buy more than 4.5 million tickets, which allows them to distribute hundreds of millions of euros a year.

The lottery has now expanded beyond the Netherlands and is operating in Sweden, England and Scotland. They now have over 4 million families who buy more than 6.5 million tickets every month, which allows them to distribute hundreds of millions of euros a year to good causes and have a lot of great street parties.

www.postcodelottery.com

TOMS SHOES – walking the talk

When I met Blake Mycoskie for the first time, we played a bit of a practical joke on a journalist and I had him go into an interview pretending he was me, whilst the rest of us watched the scene unfold from a small window. The journalist seemed a bit taken back at my youthful appearance at first, but then launched into the interview. After painfully watching Blake try on his best British accent, with lots of 'brilliants' peppered in the conversation, we all finally burst into the interview room and had a wonderful laugh with the journalist who luckily had a good sense of humour. Blake is a 'brilliant' entrepreneur who witnessed poverty on a scale previously unknown to him whilst travelling in Argentina. In a small village outside Buenos Aires, he noticed a shoe drive and saw that most of the shoes being distributed were of poor quality and didn't fit well. That inspired him to take the traditional Argentinian 'alpargatas' a canvas slip-on shoe, worn by Argentine farmers for centuries, and start a shoe company with this distinctive shoe as its model. He called it the 'Shoes for Tomorrow' project, which was shortened to 'TOMS' so that the name would fit on the back of each shoe. Within the first few months, they had sold 10,000 pairs of the shoes. The exciting thing about TOMS is that they weren't just selling a pair of shoes — they invested in a one-for-one model where for every pair of shoes they sold, they gave a pair away to a child in need.

So why are shoes important? This isn't as silly a question as it may sound. Many millions of children in the developing world grow up going barefoot. Often they have to walk miles to school, gain access to clean water and medical help. They are at risk from soil-transmitted diseases, such as hookworm and tetanus. Dangerous and rocky terrain can cause cuts, which may become infected. Amazingly in some places children are barred from attending school without proper clothes and shoes. TOMS saw that, with a simple pair of shoes, children are set on a different path for a better future. With an expansion into eyewear, with the same one-for-one model they are now targeting the 285 million people worldwide who are visually impaired.

TOMS is a unique for-profit model, structured as such to ensure sustainability. They are creating 'customer benefactors', rather than fundraising for support. They look for communities that will benefit most from TOMS based on their economic, health and education needs while taking into account local business so as not to create a correlating negative effect. They produce shoes in three countries and give them away in twenty-three countries. Certainly not a company that can be accused of having feet of clay! **www.toms.com**

UNILEVER – taking it to the street

One of the most powerful tools for positive change that any business has is the opportunity to mobilise its extended community of their suppliers and their distributors. Unilever wanted to see how they could reach millions of potential customers in rural India and at the same time help create thousands of new jobs. So they set up Project Shakti, an initiative to empower female micro-entrepreneurs to set up small businesses, creating a direct-to-customer sales distribution network that allows Unilever to reach millions of new customers in rural Asia ever year.

Unilever partnered with not for profits, banks and governments and invited women across India to become direct-to-customer retail distributors for Unilever products. Working with community organisations, Project Shakti provides free training on the basics of business management and selling techniques. With a loan each entrepreneur buys a small stock of items (such as shampoo or soap) which is then sold directly to consumers in their homes.

Project Shakti entrepreneurs make a 10 per cent margin on products they sell, usually between 700 and 1,000 rupees per month, which is enough to double a typical household's income. By the end of 2009, 45,000 Shakti entrepreneurs were selling products to three million people — reaching new markets in 135,000 villages in fifteen states. Unilever's success in India has led the company to expand taking similar initiatives in Sri Lanka and Bangladesh; combined, the three make one of the largest sustained rural home-to-home sales operations in the world.

By leveraging its distribution network, Project Shakti has resulted in substantial new business for Unilever as well, contributing to 40 per cent of the company's growth in rural markets and to 15 per cent of rural business in India. Capitalism 24902 at its best — good business that has helped to transform the lives of thousands of people. www.unilever.co.uk

SALESFORCE.COM – hey, you, get on to my cloud

Salesforce.com is a company that makes software to help businesses manage more effectively, such as customer relationship management (CRM) systems. Founded in 1999 by Marc Benioff, a former Oracle executive, and expert software developers Parker Harris, Dave Moellenhoff and Frank Dominguez, Salesforce has become one of the top five fastest growing companies in the world. They also use everything they've got to make a difference.

The San Francisco-based company is incredibly creative about drawing on resources across all its operations to make a difference. For example, with its 100,000 customers, Salesforce is building a global alliance of businesses that are implementing solutions to protect natural resources and reduce carbon consumption through cloud computing. The company has developed the industry's most energy-efficient model for carbon savings with a system that uses 95 per cent less carbon than traditional computing systems. By sharing IT resources over a vast number of computers, Salesforce's model generates enormous economies of scale in fundamental shared resources — particularly carbon consumption. In 2010, Salesforce's customers saved 170,900 tonnes of CO_2 emissions — which is equivalent to taking 37,000 cars off the road.

With the 1-1-1 model, philanthropy is integrated throughout Salesforce's entire business through a simple idea: donate one per cent of the company's time, product and equity to organisations working to drive positive social and environmental change. Salesforce is also donating technology to more than nine thousand non-profits in seventy countries. Its five thousand employees have donated more than 200,000 hours to volunteering with non-profits, and every staff member has a desktop application that gives a window into their personal and their team's environmental performance. Truly a force to be reckoned with.

www.salesforce.com

ECOTACT – flush with success

You don't automatically think of sanitation as a potential business, but luckily David Kuria, founder of Ecotact, did. From 1950, Nairobi's population grew at an alarming rate, rising from six million to over 40 million in 2010. Yet the government had not invested in public sanitation facilities for over thirty years. In 2007, there were only 138 public facilities available in the whole of Kenya. During the night slum-dwellers would throw plastic bags, known as 'flying toilets', on to rooftops and wasteland to dispose of human waste. David Kuria saw an obvious problem that this was also causing disease to take hold in the slums. An architect by training, with an eye for infrastructure and a background in upgrading slum dwellings, Kuria felt frustrated by the experience of trying to effect change through a role with the government. He left to work directly with a not for profit, but even there became disillusioned with 'donor handout syndrome' that encouraged communities to become dependent on a donor-funding system that would ultimately prove unsustainable. He chose instead to take a private sector approach to fill the glaringly obvious need for public toilets. He built a franchise model for low-cost public toilet and sanitation stations that could give dignity to those living in under-served communities.

Ecotact has succeeded in changing attitudes around public toilets and sanitation through maintaining clean and attractive facilities, well-trained employees and public education on hygiene. The organisation now employs over one hundred people and municipalities in Kenya are serving an average of 300,000 people daily with safe water and sanitation. Facilities are giving urban residents dignity, a guarantee of safe drinking water and are saving the community huge costs in healthcare. For example, the typical cost of typhoid treatment is ksh1,000 per month as against ksh100 per month for an Ikotoilet. Despite the low cost to entry, the organisation is achieving sustainability through its entrepreneurial model of 'toilet malls' and innovative partnership with the municipalities. The Ikotoilet facilities run a build-operate-transfer (BOT) model, whereby the organisation enters into an agreement with municipal councils through which it bears the cost of constructing the Ikotoilet on municipal land, and is further granted the right to run the facilities on a commercial basis for a period of five years to ensure recovery of the investment. The facilities will eventually be turned over at no cost to the municipal councils, either to run them on their own account or to lease them out. The model ensures it can be repeated and scaled. Ecotact then rents out space to vendors in the toilet malls to generate additional revenue. Who would have thought the unlikely marriage of waste and entrepreneurship could be a successful business and impact the lives of thousands of people?

www.ecotact.org

PAVEGEN SLABS – walking on sunshine

Laurence Kemball-Cook is a young man with a mission in life – to create low-cost green power in an environmentally friendly way. Aged just twenty-five, he is a green paving slab pioneer with his own company, employing eight people. He invented Pavegen while studying industrial design and technology at Loughborough University.

Pavegen is a really simple idea: electricity-generating paving slabs made from recycled rubber, such as old car tyres. Cheap, non-polluting, low-energy electricity is generated, collected and stored by the simple action of people walking over these paving slabs in public places such as streets, shopping centres, airports, railway stations and schools – anywhere that people walk en masse every day. The more the slabs are walked on, the more power they generate. As a foot falls on the slab the slab moves under five millimetres and it is this imperceptible movement that is gathered and stored. Batteries store the power for three days, although the power is constantly being topped up. It's not part of the National Grid system but is useful as an additional source of power where it is installed – for example, as street-lighting. As each slab is stepped upon, 5 per cent of the energy generated makes it light up – the rest is stored.

Laurence admits that he was driven. He was entirely self-funding, using money he won in awards as well as loans from friends and family. He used old materials and appliances. He says as an engineer he always looks to fix things when they break, rather than throwing them away and adding to the world's pollution. It's really important to him that all the components used to make Pavegen are recycled. He likes the idea that he is taking something from the road — used car tyres — and putting them back into useful life in the form of pavement slabs. As his business develops he will insist that everything is manufactured locally, because, as he says, 'There is no point in having an eco product that then has to be shipped all over the world.'

www.pavegen.com

LIVING GOODS – the Avon of health

When Chuck Slaughter (president of Living Goods, founder of TravelSmith) enrolled as an Avon lady, make-up wasn't on his mind: he was after a business model that could reinvent retailing for the poor. His vision of Living Goods' impact moves further than empowering entrepreneurs — it makes Ugandans healthier and wealthier.

Every day, Living Goods supports networks of 'Avon-like' Health Entrepreneurs who go door-to-door teaching families how to improve their health and wealth, and selling low-cost, life-saving and life-changing products like mosquito nets, fortified weaning foods, simple treatments for malaria and diaorrhea, water filters, clean cook stoves, and solar lights.

Living Goods franchises its powerful brand and business model to poor women who work as independent self-employed agents. They receive free training, a below-market inventory loan, and a free 'Business in a Bag', including branded uniforms, signage, a locker, and basic health and business tools. The company harnesses the volume of thousands of franchisees and cuts out multiple middlemen, thus delivering better margins for sellers and lower prices for customers. Beautiful.

www.livinggoods.org

METHOD – a best smeller

'method', the San Francisco company that produces biodegradable, non-toxic cleaning supplies, has turned conventional thinking and behaviour in the consumer packaged-goods industry on its head.

Eric Ryan, a marketing guru who had worked at Gap and Saturn, knew that people were looking for stylish, effective household supplies that smell as good as they look. Adam Lowry, a climate scientist at the Carnegie Institution, knew how to make them without any toxic ingredients. The former roommates teamed up to start method in 2001 with a pretty simple philosophy: 'It's OK to use high-tech materials, products, and gadgets that make our lives better, we just need to design products so those materials can be infinitely reused.'

Adam and Eric built method around serial innovation and the company has broken barriers by creating solutions like the first compostable wipe, the first 8X laundry detergent and the first bottle made from 100 per cent old plastic. They've come up with lots of creative ways to protect our natural resources and reduce the company's (and its products') carbon footprint, like coming up with formulas that can be manufactured without heating, recycling all the water they use and building a supply chain around using rail and biodiesel to save fuel and carbon in shipping and green, local sourcing.

method hasn't just made a name for itself through its environmental and social achievements. Since making its first sale of four cleaning sprays in 2001, method has become a brilliant success story of the new economy. By 2006 it was one of the top ten fastest growing companies in the US and by 2008 it was turning over more than $100 million in annual sales. Its products are sold nationwide by giant retailers like Target and Costco in the US, as well as in Canada, the UK, Australia, France and Japan. The title on Adam Lowry's business card says a lot about their 'funtastic' new approach to business. He is the company's Chief Greens Keeper! **www.methodproducts.com**

VEEV – a spirited approach to doing good

Chicagoans Courtney and Carter Reum always knew that they wanted to do their own thing, but after graduating from Columbia University, the pair of brothers went to work as investment bankers at Goldman Sachs. After about five years of working on deals and growing tired of drinking Red Bull vodka cocktails to keep them awake, the pair set out to create 'a better way to drink'.

In 2003, they discovered açaí on a surfing trip, did some research and, deciding that the market 'was about to explode', made it the keystone ingredient of their new innovative beverage. Their company, VeeV, makes the world's first açaí spirit. A staple in the diets of over one hundred million people in Brazil, açaí is known for its super-food health attributes, and only one per cent of available açaí is harvested and consumed.

VeeV isn't just some new innovative cocktail ingredient, it's one of the fastest-growing spirit brands and private companies in the US, with three-year growth of an astounding 1,316 per cent. Courtney and Carter, now thirty-two and thirty respectively, brought the exotic-tasting spirit to market while simultaneously raising awareness and resources for the Brazilian rainforest and running a sustainable, carbon-neutral company. VeeV donates $1 for each bottle sold off the top-line average price of about $35 — to ensure açaí and surrounding flora and fauna are preserved and protected and directly benefit the farming communities that harvest the berries.

VeeV's creative approach to sustainability — like choosing raw ingedients (Rocky Mountain water and local neutral grains) based on its proximity to the distillery, choosing that distillery because it is powered by wind turbines and printing on its partially recycled glass bottles with organic soy ink — stands out because it was woven into the initial business plan rather than an afterthought. Through every step of their behind-the-scenes decision-making and their consumer-facing marketing campaigns, VeeV tries to raise awareness that every decision made every day has an impact, and it doesn't have to be a negative one.

www.veevlife.com

WORKING ASSETS – 1.5 million and counting

Working Assets is not your typical communications company. It is a perfect example of a Capitalism 24902 company, because, while they sell credit card, mobile and long-distance services, their mission is to support peace, equality, human rights and the environment. They have created a community of customers, staff, suppliers and activists that by 2010 was 1.5 million-strong.

The collective power of this community is powerful. So far, members have generated over thirty-two million calls, letters and emails advocating political change, and in 2010 members helped to raise nearly $3 billion for organisations working to change the world. So in addition to providing great mobile services, Working Assets is one of the strongest citizen-action communities in the USA.

Working Assets makes it easy for people to make a difference in the world — just by going about their daily lives. Each time a customer uses their mobile, credit card or long-distance service, Working Assets donates one per cent of charges to organisations tackling issues such as civil rights, the environment, economic and social justice and peace. Since it was founded in 1985, members have come together to generate more than $67 million to non-profits. Employees and customers also use the company's networks and technology to facilitate the formation of voluntary coalitions and putting strength of numbers behind lobbying pitches. Now, just imagine if every company mobilised their communities to make a difference.

www.workingassets.com

THE *BIG ISSUE* – 'a hand-up, not a hand-out'

The *Big Issue* – written by professional journalists and sold by homeless individuals – is the world's most widely circulated street newspaper. John Bird and Gordon Roddick started the paper in 1991 with a pretty simple idea: to give homeless people a chance to earn a legitimate income, and thereby also helping them to integrate into society.

Street vendors buy the magazine from the *Big Issue* for £1 and sell to the public for £2, keeping the difference. The magazine is read by over 670,000 people every week throughout the UK, and the *Big Issue* currently supports a community of over 2,900 homeless and vulnerably housed people across the country. Since 1995 The Big Issue Foundation has built a community by working with 10,000 people and supporting them to address issues such as health, employment and personal goals. By doing this, the *Big Issue* has become one of the world's foremost social enterprises, creating a model which has been imitated time and time again in Africa, Australia and Asia.

www.bigissue.com

KIMBERLY CLARK – loo's change

There are probably few things that equal the good old fashioned toilet roll as a staple item in every home in the western world. They have been the same for ever and who would ever think of changing them?

Well Kimberly Clark, one of the world's leading paper goods manufacturers did and has just announced the 'tubeless toilet roll'. Their Scott brand will shortly begin marketing toilet rolls without the little cardboard tube in the middle. No big deal you say? Think again. In the US alone 17 billion tubes go into landfills every year – that's about 160 million pounds of cardboard waste. Put another way placed end to end they'd stretch more than a million miles. Well done KC, may you be flushed with success!.

Only one problem here, what are little kids going to make binoculars and telescopes out of for school art projects now? **www.kimberly-clark.com**

BAREFOOT POWER – you light me up

Millions of children around the world do their homework by dim kerosene lighting every night, which is not just expensive, but also not so good for people's health and the environment.

Stewart Craine and Harry Andrews wanted to bring safe, affordable, high-quality lighting to one million people who don't have access to electricity.

After setting up Barefoot Power, based in Sydney, in 2005, they reached their goal this year with sales of solar products to communities across Africa, Asia-Pacific, and Latin America. Barefoot brings electricity to people who have none, and replaces the inefficient kerosene products still used by millions of people with solar lighting – a much cleaner, safer, and cheaper alternative. Marking this million-person milestone and reaching over twenty-five countries, Barefoot are well on their way to achieving their next targets of reaching five million people by next year, and 10 million by 2015.

What impresses me most about Barefoot is that the company has built a sustainable business model out of a product that reduces carbon emissions while helping to eliminate energy poverty.

Stewart and Harry started the company as a for-profit social enterprise to focus on communities' fundamental need for affordable, clean lighting. With more than 1.5 billion people lacking access to electricity, there is massive potential to develop this rich billion-dollar industry that can generate profits for companies like Barefoot and its partners, while helping communities to break free from their reliance on out-dated, dirty, and dangerous energy sources. Seems like a pretty bright idea to me.

www.barefootpower.com

Index

Avis 264, 265
Avis, Peter 44–51

B&M Football5's 53
Babylon restaurant, Roof
  Gardens, Kensington 44–51
Balon, Adam 190–8
Bangladesh 100–1, 102, 105,
  107, 345
Barber, Sarah 76
Barber, Victoria 76
Barbosa, Fabio 2–3
Barchester Healthcare 61
Barclays Bank 57
Barefoot Power 356–7
Barnett, Jo 135
Barron, Andrea 273, 274, 307,
  318
Barry, Mike 41
Batmanghelidjh, Camila 141–8,
  252, 302
BBC 17, 146
Beatrice, Princess 136
bees 220–1
Ben & Jerry 126–7, 189–90,
  299–300
Benioff, Marc 345
Berliner, Andy 200–3
Berliner, Rachel 200–3
Bernhard of the Netherlands,
  Prince 211
Bery, Priya 169–70
Bhatt, Ela 285, 287, 311–12
Bhubezi Community Health
  Centre 168, 173
Biafra 28
Biba 45

Big Issue, The 355
Bihar, India 98, 177
Biko, Steve 25–6, 278, 310
'Biko' (Gabriel) 25–6, 278
Bill & Melinda Gates
  Foundation 127, 174, 175,
  177, 199, 204, 262
Bird, John 355
Black Consciousness Movement
  (BCM) 25
black fever 177
Blackwell, Chris 68
Blair, Cherie 169
Blair, Tony 272
Blecher, Taddy 62–5, 86, 91
Blessed Unrest (Hawken) 297,
  298
Body Shop, The 203, 300
Botswana 174, 175
bottom of the pyramid market
  112–14
Boyce, Chris 182
Boyd, Peter 148, 149, 150, 290
Brady, Jill 139
Brahimi, Lakhdar 110, 287
Branson Centre: South Africa
  53–4, 61, 62, 65, 66–7, 70–1,
  80–7, 129, 140, 182, 223,
  325, 325; Caribbean 67–8,
  330
Branson Scholars 60–1, 75–6
Branson, Eve (mother) ix, 26,
  27, 55, 56, 72, 114, 115, 195
Branson, Holly (daughter) ix,
  x, xi, 14, 50, 60, 136, 138–9,
  184, 327
Branson, Ivo (nephew) 14
Branson, Joan (wife) ix, x–xi,